COOKBOOK COMMITTEE

Peggy Newton
Chairman

Barbara Smith
Co-Chairman

Harriet Stone
Co-Chairman

Section Committee

Marjorie Bucklew
Maxine Balli
Jodie Dawson
Jane McDade
Mary Reed

Sue Brigham, Commentary
Ernest Smith, Treasurer
Carley Starr, Restaurants

Photography and Digital Imaging:

Lynda Spragins

Additional Photography

Henry Bryant
Charlie Davidson
Peter Dawson

Cover

Ruth Getzen

INTRODUCTION

Wildcat Seasons is a volume of favorite recipes carefully collected from members of Wildcat Cliffs Country Club, which is located in the sparkling, cool mountain resort of Highlands, North Carolina. Since the 1870s, families have been coming to the Highlands area to escape the summer heat, bringing with them their special cuisines and imaginatively adapting those in order to savor the treasures to be gathered in the local markets, from fresh mountain trout to stone-ground grits, and from dew-laden blueberries to juicy peaches and fat yellow tomatoes.

The pristine air, lush forests, singing streams and misty waterfalls of the mountains not only instill a zest for hiking and golf but also, in turn, whet appetites and intensify the fragrances of foods. Hungry Wildcat members enjoy the superb palate of flavors presented in their club dining room as well as the profusion of culinary styles found in the many inns and restaurants in the area. Yet sometimes the most memorable dishes are the ones tasted in their private homes, perhaps on decks where hummingbirds dart near hanging flower baskets or before dry-stacked stone fireplaces with shining andirons and blazing logs.

Wildcat Seasons contains over 550 tested recipes with instructions and techniques developed over the years in the kitchens of Wildcat members, many of whom have helped put together regional cook-books in their wintertime hometowns. In addition, the Mountain Dining Section features selected recipes from several area restaurants in order to provide a complete presentation of all the marvelous foods that are part of the charm of dining in the mountains and living at Wildcat during its Seasons.

CONTRIBUTORS

We thank the Board of Directors of Wildcat Cliffs Country Club.

A special thanks and appreciation to:
Mrs. Marjorie Bucklew
Dr. and Mrs. Peter Dawson
Mrs. Helen Griffith
Mr. and Mrs. Howard Dick

Jean Aldredge
Gary Ames

Maxine Balli
Jody Bauknight
Betsey Baumrucker
Erv Baumrucker
Carol Bellows
Beth Betts
Mary Beverly
Ann Blankenship
Hilda Blitch
Mary Lee Bond
Willie Bosserman
Sue Brigham
Susie Bryan
Jean Bryant
Marjorie Bucklew
Lupe Burt

Diann Catlin
Eleanor Church
Jane Clair
Ruth Coleman
George Cooper
Petey Cooper
Gloria Creel

Cile Davidson
Fran Davis
Marti Dawes
Wilda Dick
Judy Dickinson
Anna Joyce Dietz

Anne Eason
Kate Eustis
Harriett Evans
Marilyn Evans

Ruth Farrar
Sara Flannes

Nell Gibson
Robert Goldman
Evelyn Gordon
Ada Gove
June Grant

Chuck Hammock
Jeanne Harrison
Joyce Cordell Henderson
Donna Hennessey
Marilyn Hicks
Lenny Hinds
Martha Hobbs
Leta Hodges

Rachael Jenks
Curley Johnson
June Johnson
Betty Johnston
Lou Johnston
Teri Jones

Patsy Lambert
Vivienne Lambrecht
Jeanne Lanning
Beverly Larmon
Marian Lewis
Isabel Lierman
Louisiana Entertains
Hank Lucking
Sherri Ludwig
Lorraine Lynch

Jack MaCris
Janet MaCris
Pat Mason
Marilyn McCann
Jane McDade
Ruth McDivitt
Beth McGehee
Gwen McMillan
Dottie McPherson
Marion Merritt
Martha Middleton
Shirley Miller
Alice Milton

Peggy Newton
Mary Nogueiras

Betty Paterson
Sondra Pearson
Evelyn Phillips
Terry Pullen

Judy Reed
Fern Reuter
Rose Reynolds
Sara Richards

Betty Rogers
Marguerite Rohde
Earline Roman
Tina Rood
Weezie Rosch

Wylodean Saxon
Betty Shanklin
Susan Sheehan
Veda Sherard
Barbara Smith
Dixie Smith
Ernest Smith
Fran Smith
Merv Smith
Rebecca Smith
Carley Starr

Harriet Stone
Eunice Stribling
Stanley Sullivan
Ann Swertferger

Nancy Temple
Joyce Tiller
Bonnie Tomasek
Polly Touzalin

Claire Vaughn

Bitsy Walker
Joe Walker
Martha Walker
Posey Wideman
Judy Williams

Restaurants:
Ezekiel's Barn
Lakeside Restaurant and Rosewood Market
Log Cabin Steak House
Nick's Calico Cottage
On The Verandah
Skyline Restaurant
White Goose Cafe
Chef Winslow Jones
Wolfgang's on Main
Wildcat Cliffs Country Club

ACKNOWLEDGMENTS

For the flavorful foods we enjoy, we must all thank our families and friends, as well as our favorite cooks, chefs, books and magazines, because through the years they have helped to create and enhance the recipes that we now call our own. The knowledge we have gained from them has spiced our dishes and has added zest to our cooking.

Wildcat Seasons reflects our lives here in the mountains. It contains a rich diversity of culinary tastes and styles of cooking gathered from all our geographical backgrounds and heritages. We are pleased to express grateful thanks and appreciation to the many members and friends who so generously have contributed their time, skills and efforts to make this cookbook possible. Their long, amiable hours of planning, testing, and perfecting recipes have indeed made it surpass all our expectations.

TABLE OF CONTENTS

The hummingbird symbol indicates a recipe that is quick and easy to prepare.

NOTES

Appetizers and
Beverages

APPETIZERS

BEVERAGES

BACON ALMOND SPREAD

4 strips bacon, crisply cooked and crumbled
½ cup slivered almonds
3 green onions, chopped
½ cup mayonnaise
1 cup grated sharp Cheddar cheese
¼ teaspoon salt
¼ teaspoon pepper
6 drops Tabasco

Sauté almonds and onions in bacon drippings until almonds are lightly browned and onions tender. Mix with remaining ingredients blending well; chill. Spread mixture on your favorite crackers or toast rounds and bake at 350° for 5-10 minutes until bubbly and lightly browned.

Yield: 2 cups.

Crisp stale chips or crackers in microwave on full power 45-60 seconds.

BACON SAUSAGE APPETIZER

Make ahead. Can be refrigerated for two days.

2 (8-ounce) packages breakfast sausage links
1 pound bacon
1 cup firmly packed brown sugar
¼ cup water (about)

Cut sausages and bacon slices in thirds. Wrap each piece of sausage in a piece of bacon. Secure with toothpick. Place on large baking pan and sprinkle brown sugar evenly over top. Refrigerate. When ready to bake, sprinkle a handful of water (about ¼ cup) over the sausages. Cover and bake at 350° for 45 minutes; uncover and continue baking 15 minutes. Drain well. Serve warm.

Yield: 60 pieces.

SHREDDED BARBEQUE BEEF

5 pound chuck roast
1 (3-ounce) package crab boil
½ cup butter
2-3 cloves garlic, minced
1 (14-ounce) bottle catsup
3 tablespoons liquid smoke
½ cup cider vinegar
¼ cup lemon juice
Tabasco to taste

Simmer roast and crab boil in enough water to cover the meat. Simmer until meat is very tender and separates from bone. Replenish water as necessary. Cool in liquid. Place meat on platter, remove all fat. Shred.

Sauté garlic in butter until tender; add remaining ingredients. Stir in shredded meat. Serve warm on rolls or small buns.

Yield: Serves 20-25.

BROCCOLI DIP

1 (10-ounce) box frozen chopped broccoli
1 roll Kraft Garlic Cheese
1 (10¾-ounce) can cream of mushroom soup
1 (4-ounce) can sliced mushrooms, drained
2 tablespoons butter
3 stalks celery, chopped
½ large onion, chopped
⅛ teaspoon Tabasco
⅛ teaspoon red pepper
⅛ teaspoon Worcestershire sauce

Sauté celery and onion in butter until tender; stir in drained mushrooms. Cook broccoli until almost tender; drain well. Melt cheese. Blend all ingredients together and heat through. Serve hot. Broccoli does not freeze well.

Yield: Serves 8-10.

BAKED CHEESE DIP

- **1 cup chopped pecans**
- **2 tablespoons butter**
- **1 (8-ounce) package extra sharp Cheddar cheese, grated**
- **1 (8-ounce) package sharp Cheddar cheese, grated**
- **1 (6-ounce) package mozzarella cheese, grated**
- **1 large onion, finely chopped**
- **3 cups mayonnaise**
- **8 slices bacon, crisply cooked and crumbled**
- **2 teaspoons garlic salt**
- **½ teaspoon cayenne pepper**

Place pecans in a baking pan; dot with butter and bake at 325° until toasted; set aside. In a large mixing bowl, blend cheeses with remaining ingredients; mix well. Pour into a greased 2-quart baking dish. Bake at 325° for 30 minutes. Top with pecans. Continue baking for 10 minutes. Serve warm with crackers or corn chips.

Yield: Serves 12-16.

CHICKEN CHEESE PUFFS

- **2 cups finely diced cooked chicken**
- **1 cup mayonnaise**
- **1 onion, minced**
- **¼ teaspoon dried basil**
- **¼ teaspoon dried thyme**
- **Salt and pepper**
- **¾ cup grated Cheddar or Swiss cheese**
- **½ cup Parmesan cheese**
- **Thin toast rounds or crackers**

Combine first 2 ingredients in medium bowl. Blend in onions, herbs and seasonings. Add Cheddar cheese and 2 tablespoons Parmesan cheese, blending well. Spread mixture evenly on toast rounds or crackers. Arrange on cookie sheet. Sprinkle tops with remaining Parmesan cheese. Bake at 350° 10 minutes or until lightly browned and puffy.

Yield: 2 dozen.

LAYERED CAVIAR MOLD

Portions of the gelatin mix are used in each layer (except caviar layer) so it is important to keep softened gelatin warm and liquid.

2 envelopes unflavored gelatin
½ cup cold water

Egg Layer
4 hard-boiled eggs, chopped
½ cup mayonnaise
¼ cup minced parsley
4 green onions, minced
¾ teaspoon salt
Tabasco to taste

Avocado Layer
1 medium avocado, pureed
1 medium avocado, diced
1 large shallot, minced
2 tablespoons lemon juice
2 tablespoons mayonnaise
½ teaspoon salt
Tabasco to taste

Sour Cream Layer
1 cup sour cream
¼ cup minced onion

Caviar Layer
4 ounces black or red caviar
Lemon juice

Grease a deep 9-inch springform pan with mayonnaise or spray with a no-stick cooking spray. Soften gelatin in water then microwave for 20 seconds to liquefy. Place in container over hot water; keep warm.
Egg Layer: Combine ingredients with 2 tablespoons gelatin mixture. Neatly spread into bottom of pan with spatula. Chill until set.
Avocado Layer: Combine ingredients with 2 tablespoons gelatin. Blend well and spread over egg layer. Chill until set.
Sour Cream Layer: Combine sour cream and onion with 2 tablespoons gelatin. Spread over avocado layer. Chill until set.
Caviar Layer: Strain and gently rinse caviar with cold water; drain well. Sprinkle with lemon juice. Unmold the mold carefully onto serving plate. Spread caviar on top. Serve with thinly sliced pumpernickel bread or crackers.

Yield: Serves 12-16.

BRAUNSWEIGER MOLD

- **1 pound braunsweiger**
- **1/4 cup mayonnaise**
- **2 tablespoons dill pickle juice**
- **2 tablespoons Worcestershire sauce**
- **1/4 teaspoon garlic powder**
- **1/3 cup chopped dill pickle**
- **1/4 cup chopped green onion**
- **1/2 teaspoon sugar**
- **1 (8-ounce) package cream cheese, softened and divided**

Have all ingredients at room temperature. Combine first 8 ingredients with one-third of the cream cheese, blending by hand until smooth. Do not use a blender or food processor. Chill. Line a 5-cup bowl with plastic wrap and fill with braunsweiger mixture. Refrigerate several hours. To serve, unmold onto serving plate. Remove plastic wrap and cover with topping.

Yield: Serves 12-15.

Topping

- **Remainder of cream cheese, softened**
- **2 tablespoons milk**
- **1 tablespoon mayonnaise**

Blend together and spread over mold.

Variation: Use lower fat Neufchâtel cheese in place of cream cheese.

Plan on 12 hors d'oeuvres per person.

CHICKEN CURRY BALLS

May be prepared a day in advance. Freezes well.

- **4 ounces cream cheese**
- **2 tablespoons mayonnaise**
- **2 cups chopped cooked chicken**
- **1 tablespoon curry powder**
- **1 tablespoon chopped chutney**
- **½ teaspoon salt**
- **1 cup blanched slivered almonds**
- **½ cup grated coconut**

Blend cream cheese with mayonnaise until smooth. Stir in chicken and all other ingredients except coconut. Mix well. Roll into walnut-sized balls. Roll balls in coconut. Chill.

Yield: About 3 dozen.

HERB-CHEESE BAKE

- **1 teaspoon Dijon mustard**
- **12 ounces Havarti cheese**
- **1 teaspoon dried parsley flakes**
- **½ teaspoon dried chives**
- **¼ teaspoon dried dill**
- **¼ teaspoon dried basil**
- **¼ teaspoon fennel seeds**
- **½ (17¼-ounce) package frozen puff pastry, thawed**
- **1 egg, beaten**

Spread mustard over top of cheese; sprinkle with parsley flakes and next 4 ingredients. Place cheese, mustard side down, in center of pastry. Wrap package style, trimming excess pastry. Seal seam. Place seam side down on a lightly greased baking sheet. Brush with egg. Chill 30 minutes. Bake at 375° for 20 minutes; brush with egg and bake 10 minutes or until golden brown. Serve warm with crackers, sliced apples or pears.

Yield: Serves 8-10.

JALAPEÑO CHEESE DIP

1 (8-ounce) package frozen chopped onions, thawed
2 tablespoons olive oil
2 tablespoons all-purpose flour
1 cup milk
3 (8-ounce) sticks Monterey Jack cheese, grated
1 (4-ounce) can jalapeño peppers, minced, undrained

Sauté onions in olive oil until limp. Add flour, stirring until smooth. Add milk and cook over low heat until thickened; add cheeses, stirring until blended and smooth. Stir in jalapeño peppers. Pour into a greased 2-quart baking dish. Bake at 350° for 30 minutes until lightly browned and bubbly. Serve with corn chips.

Yield: Serves 8-10.

VIDALIA ONION DIP

2 cups finely chopped Vidalia onions
2 cups grated Swiss cheese
1½ cups mayonnaise
1 teaspoon celery salt
½ teaspoon dill weed
¼ teaspoon white pepper

Combine all ingredients; place in a 2-quart shallow casserole. Bake at 350° for 30 minutes or until brown and bubbly. Serve hot with crackers or corn chips.

Yield: Serves 8-10.

Variation: Use basic recipe substituting 2 cups sharp grated Cheddar cheese for the Swiss cheese. Add 6-8 drops Tabasco.

CHEESE BACON BRUSCHETTA

- 1 baguette (French bread, unsliced)
- 2 slices bacon, cooked and crumbled
- 1 cup grated Parmesan cheese
- ½ cup mayonnaise
- ½ cup sliced green onions
- ¼ cup chopped almonds, toasted
- 2 cloves garlic, minced
- ¼ cup black olives, minced

Slice baguette into 30 (4½-inch) slices, place on foil-lined baking sheets. Bake at 400° for 5 minutes until lightly browned. Combine remaining ingredients; spread on bread slices. Bake at 400° for 5 minutes. Serve immediately.

Yield: 30 pieces.

Variation: Brush baguette slices with olive oil mixed with Italian seasonings and top with oil-packed dried tomatoes.

CURRIED CHEESE SPREAD

- 1 (8-ounce) package cream cheese, softened
- 1 (8-ounce) package Cheddar cheese, shredded
- 4 tablespoons sherry
- ½ teaspoon curry powder
- 1 (8-ounce) jar chutney, chopped
- 4 green onions, chopped, including tops

Mix first 4 ingredients together until smooth. Spread into 8-inch shallow dish. Chill until firm. To serve, spread chutney over top of cheese and cover with chopped onions. Serve with assorted crackers.

Yield: Serves 8-10.

Variation: Add ½ cup chopped nuts to cheese mixture or sprinkle over the top.

PROVENÇAL TAPENADE

Tapenade will keep up to 10 days refrigerated in a covered jar.

6 ounces goat cheese

½ baguette (French bread), sliced in ¼-½ inch pieces

Tapenade:

1 cup stuffed olives, drained

1½ cups chopped ripe olives

¼ cup chopped celery

1 clove garlic, minced

2½ teaspoons olive oil

Lightly toast baguette slices on both sides; set aside.

Prepare tapenade by placing olives, celery, garlic and olive oil in food processor using steel blade. Process ingredients gently until mixture holds together. Do not make a paste. Use more oil as necessary if mixture is too crumbly. Place in serving bowl. Chill.

Slice goat cheese to fit on baguettes. Top with a portion of tapenade and serve.

Yield: Serves 8-12.

CHEESE WAFERS

1 (8-ounce) package sharp Cheddar cheese, grated

1 cup butter, softened

2 cups all-purpose flour

½ teaspoon salt

½ teaspoon cayenne pepper

2 cups crispy rice cereal

Pecan halves (optional)

Mix cheese and butter in food processor or with electric mixer until smooth and creamy. Combine flour, salt and pepper; add to creamed mixture. Stir in crispy rice cereal until blended. Chill 2 hours. Shape dough into small balls. Place on ungreased cookie sheet; flatten with fork to ⅓ inch thickness. Top each with pecan half (optional). Bake at 350° for 10-13 minutes until brown on bottom.

Yield: 6½ dozen.

PINEAPPLE NUT CHEESE BALL

- 1 (8-ounce) package cream cheese, softened
- 2 cups chopped pecans
- 1/4 cup finely minced onion
- 1/2 medium bell pepper, minced
- 1 (8 1/4-ounce) can crushed pineapple, well drained
- 1/8 teaspoon salt

Reserve 1 cup pecans. Blend remaining ingredients together well. Form into two serving balls. Chill 1 hour until firm. Roll balls in reserved pecans and chill another hour.

Yield: Two cheese balls.

DEVILED OYSTER APPETIZER

- 1 pint small oysters
- 1 onion, minced
- 1 clove garlic, minced
- 2 tablespoons butter
- 2 egg yolks, beaten
- 3/4 cup cream
- 1 tablespoon all-purpose flour
- 1 bay leaf
- 3 stalks fresh parsley, minced
- 3 tablespoons minced chives
- 1/2 teaspoon salt
- Black pepper, Worcestershire sauce and Tabasco to taste
- 1 cup cracker crumbs
- 2 tablespoons butter

Poach oysters slightly in their own juice. Drain well; cut into small pieces. Sauté onion and garlic in 2 tablespoons butter. Mix beaten egg yolks and cream; stir in flour and add to onion mixture with bay leaf. Cook slowly for 10 minutes. Remove bay leaf and add oysters, parsley, chives and salt. Add pepper, Worcestershire and Tabasco to taste. Pour into 8-inch baking dish. Sprinkle cracker crumbs on top and dot with butter. Bake at 350° for 15-20 minutes. Serve with assorted crackers.

Yield: Serves 6-8.

SMOKED OYSTER MOUSSE

- **2 envelopes unflavored gelatin**
- **½ cup water**
- **1 (8-ounce) package cream cheese**
- **1 cup mayonnaise**
- **2 (3.6-ounce) can smoked oysters, chopped**
- **¼ teaspoon Tabasco**
- **1 tablespoon Worcestershire sauce**
- **2 tablespoons chopped parsley**
- **½ teaspoon garlic powder**

Soften gelatin in water; set aside. Combine cream cheese and mayonnaise in a saucepan. Simmer over low heat until blended and smooth. Stir in softened gelatin, oysters and all remaining ingredients. Mix well.

Spoon into well greased 3½ cup fish mold. Cover; refrigerate until set. Unmold.

Yield: Serves 12-16.

CRABMEAT APPETIZER

- **1 cup mayonnaise**
- **½ cup sour cream**
- **1 clove garlic, minced**
- **1 tablespoon dry sherry**
- **1 tablespoon minced fresh parsley**
- **1 tablespoon capers**
- **2 green onions, minced**
- **2 teaspoons lemon juice**
- **1 teaspoon chives**
- **1 teaspoon Worcestershire sauce**
- **½ teaspoon salt**
- **⅛ teaspoon cayenne pepper**
- **2 (6-ounce) cans crabmeat, rinsed, drained**
- **2 tablespoons lemon juice**

Combine all ingredients, except crabmeat and lemon juice; mix well. Toss crabmeat with lemon juice and gently stir into mixed ingredients. Cover and refrigerate 4 hours. Serve with crackers.

Yield: 3½ cups.

PESTO CHEESECAKE

- 1 tablespoon butter, softened
- ¼ cup fine dry bread crumbs
- ½ cup plus 2 tablespoons grated Parmesan cheese
- 2 (8-ounce) packages cream cheese, softened
- 1 cup ricotta cheese
- ¼ teaspoon salt
- ⅛ teaspoon cayenne pepper
- 3 large eggs
- ½ cup Pesto Sauce (see Page 283)
- ¼ cup pine nuts
- Fresh basil leaves

Rub butter on bottom and sides of 9-inch springform pan.

Mix bread crumbs with 2 tablespoons Parmesan cheese. Coat pan with bread crumb mixture.

Beat cream cheese, ricotta cheese, remaining Parmesan cheese, salt and cayenne pepper with electric mixer until smooth. Add eggs, one at a time, blending well. Transfer half of mixture to a bowl; set aside. Mix Pesto Sauce into remaining half; pour into prepared pan, smoothing top.

Carefully spoon plain mixture over pesto mixture in pan; smooth top. Sprinkle with pine nuts. Bake at 325° for 45-50 minutes until center is set. Cool. Cover tightly with plastic wrap. Refrigerate overnight.

To serve, remove from pan, garnish with basil leaves and serve with crackers.

Yield: Serves 18.

To prevent cheese from forming mold, store in a sealed container with two lumps of sugar.

CRAB BAKE

Recipe may be doubled.

- 6 ounces lump crabmeat, picked over for cartilage
- 1 cup mayonnaise
- 1 (8-ounce) package cream cheese, softened
- 3 tablespoons milk
- ½ cup minced onions
- 2 tablespoons capers
- ½ teaspoon prepared horseradish
- 4 drops Tabasco
- ½ teaspoon salt
- ½ cup grated Parmesan cheese
- ¼ cup seasoned bread crumbs

Combine mayonnaise, cream cheese and milk; mix well. Fold in crabmeat. Add remaining ingredients except Parmesan cheese and bread crumbs. Mix together and spoon lightly into a greased 4-cup baking dish. Mix Parmesan cheese and bread crumbs together; sprinkle over top of baking dish. Bake at 375° for 20 minutes until bubbly and browned. Serve with crackers.

Yield: Serves 6-8.

CRAB MELT-A-WAYS

- 6 English muffins, split
- 2 cups crabmeat, picked over for cartilage
- ½ cup butter, softened
- 1 (7-ounce) jar sharp processed cheese spread
- 2 tablespoons mayonnaise
- ½ teaspoon garlic salt
- ⅛ teaspoon salt
- Paprika

Mix butter, cheese, mayonnaise and seasonings; fold crabmeat in gently. Spread mixture generously on each muffin half. Freeze. When ready to serve, cut each muffin half into four pieces. Place on cookie sheet, sprinkle with paprika and broil for 5 minutes until bubbly.

Yield: 4 dozen.

BAKED GARLIC ROQUEFORT

- **6 whole heads garlic**
- **3 tablespoons, butter, cut into 6 slices**
- **¼ cup olive oil**
- **1 (14-ounce) can chicken broth**
- **¼ cup white wine**
- **2 teaspoons dried rosemary**
- **1 (8-ounce) package Roquefort cheese, crumbled**
- **Crusty sliced bread**

Cut ½ inch off top end of each garlic head, exposing top of garlic cloves. Remove all papery outer skin. Place garlic cut side up in glass baking dish. Top each garlic head with a pat of butter. Pour oil over all heads. Add broth and wine to dish. Sprinkle with rosemary (season with salt and pepper, optional) and bake at 375° uncovered about 1 hour 15 minutes, basting every 15 minutes with pan juices (add more broth, if necessary).

Add cheese to dish and continue baking until cheese is melted. Serve in the baking dish with garlic, cheese and juices. Dip bread in juice and spread with garlic and melted cheese.

Yield: Serves 12-15.

FROSTED HAM BALL

Wonderful way to use leftover ham. Garnish frosted ham ball with parsley, olives or nuts.

- **1 pound ground ham**
- **1 cup raisins**
- **1 onion, minced**
- **1 teaspoon curry powder**
- **¾ cup mayonnaise**
- **1 (8-ounce) package cream cheese, softened**
- **2 tablespoons milk**
- **Tabasco to taste**

Combine first 5 ingredients; mound into ball on serving plate. Blend cream cheese with milk; add Tabasco. Frost ham ball with cream cheese mixture. Chill. Serve with assorted crackers or toast rounds.

Yield: Serves 12-15.

GLAZED HAM BALLS

- 1½ pounds ground fully-cooked ham
- 1½ cups soft, torn bread crumbs
- ½ cup milk
- ¼ cup finely chopped onion
- 1 egg
- ½ cup sugar
- 2 tablespoons cornstarch
- 1 cup orange juice
- ¼ cup vinegar
- 1 cup whole cranberry sauce
- 1 cup diced fresh orange segments

Combine ham with next 4 ingredients, mixing together well. Shape into balls using 1 level tablespoon of mixture for each ball. Arrange in shallow baking dish and bake at 375° until meat is browned, turning often. Drain. Combine sugar and cornstarch in saucepan; stir in orange juice and vinegar. Cook over medium heat, stirring constantly until clear and thickened. Add cranberry sauce and orange, mixing well. Place ham balls in chafing dish and pour sauce over them; keep warm.

Yield: 3½ dozen ham balls.

Variation: Add 2-ounces cranberry liqueur to sauce just before serving.

APPETIZER MUSHROOMS

- 1 pound small mushrooms
- ½ cup butter
- 2 tablespoons black pepper
- ½ cup Worcestershire sauce

Sauté mushrooms in butter until slightly soft. Stir in black pepper and Worcestershire sauce. Simmer slowly, stirring occasionally, until liquid is absorbed. Serve warm with toothpicks.

Yield: Serves 4-6.

STUFFED MUSHROOMS

- **12 large fresh mushrooms**
- **2 tablespoons butter**
- **1 onion, finely chopped**
- **2 ounces pepperoni, diced (about ½ cup)**
- **¼ cup finely chopped bell pepper**
- **1 clove garlic, minced**
- **¼ teaspoon pepper**
- **½ cup finely crushed round buttery crackers (about 12)**
- **¼ cup grated Parmesan cheese**
- **1 tablespoon snipped fresh parsley**
- **½ teaspoon seasoned salt**
- **¼ teaspoon oregano**
- **⅓ cup chicken broth**
- **Dash of Tabasco**

Remove mushroom stems, finely chop; reserve. Melt butter in skillet; add onion, pepperoni, bell pepper, garlic and chopped mushroom stems. Sauté until vegetables are tender. Add cracker crumbs, pepper, Parmesan cheese, parsley, salt and oregano. Mix well. Stir in chicken broth and dash of Tabasco. Spoon stuffing into mushroom caps rounding tops. Place in shallow baking dish, adding about ¼ inch of water for mushrooms to sit in. Bake uncovered at 325° for 25 minutes or until thoroughly heated and browned.

Yield: 12 stuffed mushrooms.

Use a bell pepper as a cup for dips.

MUSHROOM CROUSTADES

A recipe that has been closely guarded by caterers for years. Very thin bread will be too hard to work with. Use soft white sandwich bread and shape it into buttered tins with a pestle.

- **24 thin white bread slices**
- **2 generous tablespoons butter, melted**
- **3 tablespoons minced shallots**
- **¼ cup butter**
- **½ pound fresh mushrooms, finely chopped**
- **2 tablespoons flour**
- **1 cup heavy cream**
- **1½ tablespoons minced chives**
- **1 tablespoon minced parsley**
- **½ teaspoon lemon juice**
- **½ teaspoon salt**
- **⅛ teaspoon cayenne pepper**

Cut 3-inch rounds from bread slices. Brush insides of 2 miniature muffin tins generously with butter. Gently fit bread rounds into muffin tins to form a cup. Bake 10 minutes at 400° until lightly browned; set aside. Cool.

In a heavy skillet, sauté shallots in butter for 1 minute. Stir in mushrooms; simmer until all liquid has evaporated, about 10 minutes.

Remove from heat, stir in flour. Pour cream into mushroom mixture and return to heat, stirring constantly. Bring to boil. Simmer until mixture becomes very thick.

Remove from heat; stir in remaining ingredients. Spoon into toast shells. Mix together ⅓ cup Parmesan cheese and 1 tablespoon minced parsley and sprinkle on top. Dot with butter.

Bake at 375° for 10-15 minutes until lightly browned. Serve warm.

Yield: 2 dozen.

MUSHROOM SANDWICHES

- **1 small onion, finely chopped**
- **4 tablespoons butter**
- **1 pound mushrooms, finely chopped**
- **¼ cup dry sherry**
- **½ cup cream**
- **2 tablespoons cornstarch**
- **Salt and pepper**
- **Dash of Tabasco**
- **1 loaf thin sliced white bread, crusts removed**

Sauté onion in butter until limp. Stir in mushrooms and cook until mixture is almost dry, stirring constantly. Add sherry, cream and cornstarch. Season with salt, pepper and Tabasco to taste. Cook until thickened; cool. Spread mushroom mixture between bread slices as a sandwich. Freeze sandwiches. To serve, partially thaw. Butter both sides. Cut each sandwich, making four square pieces. Put on cookie sheet and bake at 450° turning pieces over when browned. When brown on both sides, remove from oven and serve.

Yield: About 4½ dozen.

OLIVE SPREAD

- **1 (8-ounce) package cream cheese, softened**
- **2 tablespoons mayonnaise**
- **1 tablespoon milk**
- **Salt and pepper**
- **1 clove garlic, pressed**
- **2 tablespoons grated onion**
- **Dash of Beau Monde**
- **½ cup sliced ripe olives**
- **½ cup sliced toasted almonds**

Blend cream cheese, mayonnaise and milk together well. Stir in remaining ingredients; mix well. Serve with assorted crackers.

Yield: 2¼ cups.

PARMESAN STICKS

Wonderful to have on hand for those unexpected guests at cocktail time. Stores well in airtight tins or plastic bags.

- **10 slices thinly sliced bread**
- **3 tablespoons butter, melted**
- **½ cup cornflake crumbs**
- **½ cup freshly grated Parmesan cheese**
- **¼ teaspoon garlic salt**

Trim crusts from bread slices. Brush melted butter generously on both sides. Cut each slice into 4 strips. Combine crumbs, cheese and garlic salt. Roll bread sticks gently in mixture until well coated. Place on cookie sheet and bake at 325° for 10-15 minutes or until lightly browned.

Yield: 40 sticks.

SALMON PÂTÉ

Do not use a blender or food processor. The mixture should be solid enough to mold into a ball.

- **1 (14.75-ounce) can pink salmon**
- **1 (8-ounce) package cream cheese, softened**
- **¼ cup finely chopped onion**
- **1 teaspoon lemon juice**
- **2 teaspoons liquid smoke**
- **1 teaspoon prepared horseradish**
- **1 teaspoon salt**
- **1 cup chopped pecans, divided**

Drain salmon, remove skin and bones. Mix salmon with cream cheese until smooth. Add onion, lemon juice, liquid smoke, horseradish, salt and ½ cup of the pecans; mix together well. Mold into a ball; cover with remaining pecans and chill several hours. Serve with crackers.

Yield: Serves 10-15.

PÂTÉ MAISON

2 small celery stalks with leaves
4 whole peppercorns
6 cups water
1 teaspoon salt
1 pound chicken livers
1/8 teaspoon cayenne pepper
1 cup butter
1 1/2 teaspoons salt
2 teaspoons dry mustard
1/2 teaspoon nutmeg
1/4 teaspoon cloves
1/4 cup chopped onion
1 clove garlic
1/4 cup Calvados Apple Brandy or Applejack
1/2 cup currants

Add celery and peppercorns to water; add salt. Bring to a boil; reduce heat and simmer 10 minutes.

Add chicken livers; simmer gently 10 minutes. Livers should still be slightly pink inside.

Drain livers, discard celery and peppercorns. Place livers in food processor fitted with steel blade. Add remaining ingredients except currants and process until well blended and very smooth.

Stir in currants; transfer pâté to a 3-4 cup crock or terrine. Smooth top and cover. Refrigerate 4 hours. Allow pâté to stand at room temperature 30 minutes before serving.

Yield: 3 cups.

Split a flaky biscuit in half, roll out on floured surface and fill with one teaspoon of favorite filling. Fold in half and bake.

PIZZA DIP

- **1 (8-ounce) package cream cheese, softened**
- **1 (14-ounce) jar pizza sauce**
- **½ cup chopped green onions**
- **¼ cup chopped bell pepper**
- **2 cups grated mozzarella cheese**
- **½ cup chopped ripe olives**
- **1 (3-ounce) package sliced pepperoni, chopped**

Press cream cheese into bottom of a 9-inch greased pie plate; spread with pizza sauce. Layer remaining ingredients in order listed. Bake at 350° for 20 minutes. Serve with tortilla chips.

Yield: Serves 10-12.

PARTY SHREDDED PORK

- **1 (6-pound) pork roast or fresh ham**
- **⅓ cup cider vinegar**
- **¼ cup soy sauce**
- **5 cloves garlic, chopped**
- **¼ cup Worcestershire sauce**
- **1 teaspoon black pepper**
- **½ teaspoon seasoned salt**
- **¼ cup lemon juice**

Trim roast of fat and place in the middle of a large sheet of heavy duty aluminum foil. Mix remaining ingredients and pour over roast. Wrap roast tightly with foil leaving about 1-inch clearance between meat and foil. Place in deep roasting pan. Bake at 225° overnight or 8-10 hours. Meat will fall apart. Shred meat and place in chafing dish or serving platter with pan juices. Serve on small rolls or small buns with barbeque sauce if desired.

Yield: Serves 20-30.

QUESADILLAS

- **5 (10-inch) flour tortillas**
- **½ cup butter, softened**
- **1 pound grated Monterey Jack cheese**
- **8 green onions, minced**
- **½ cup minced pimientos**
- **1 (4.5-ounce) can green minced chili peppers**
- **1 tablespoon ground coriander**
- **1 teaspoon ground cumin**

Spread tortillas with butter on one side. Place on ungreased baking sheets buttered side up. Bake at 400° for 5 minutes or until barely golden. In a bowl, toss together the Monterey Jack, onions, pimientos, chili peppers, coriander and cumin. Sprinkle tortillas with cheese mixture and bake quesadillas at 400° for 5-8 minutes until cheese is bubbly. Cut into wedges.

Yield: About 40 pieces.

ROQUEFORT MOLD

- **1 envelope unflavored gelatin**
- **¼ cup water**
- **6 ounces Roquefort cheese**
- **2 (3-ounce) packages cream cheese**
- **½ cup heavy cream**
- **½ onion, grated**
- **10 black olives, minced**
- **⅛ teaspoon salt**
- **¼ teaspoon cayenne pepper**

Soften gelatin in water over low heat until dissolved. Cool. Blend cheeses together; mix well. Stir in cream, gelatin, onion, olives and seasonings. Mix together well; pour into lightly greased 3-cup mold. Chill; stirring occasionally until set.

Yield: One 3-cup mold.

SALSA DIP

Quick and easy!

- **1 (16-ounce) jar thick and chunky salsa**
- **1 cup canned black beans**
- **½ onion, minced**
- **½ cup sliced black olives**
- **½ cup whole kernel canned corn**
- **½ cup grated sharp Cheddar cheese**
- **½ cup grated Monterey Jack cheese**

Mix all ingredients together. Pour into serving bowl. Serve with tortilla chips.

Yield: 5½ cups.

SCALLOPS RUMAKI

Scallops scarce? Substitute water chestnuts.

- **Boiling water**
- **12 slices bacon**
- **24 scallops**
- **2 tablespoons soy sauce**
- **½ cup dry white wine**

Pour boiling water over bacon; let stand 5 minutes. Drain and dry. Stretch bacon as long as you can; cut each slice in half. Wrap around scallop; secure with a toothpick. Mix soy sauce and wine together. Place scallops in a shallow pan and cover with soy sauce, wine mixture. Marinate refrigerated several hours, turning occasionally. Drain and bake scallops at 350° until bacon has cooked well, about 45 minutes. Remove toothpicks and replace with fresh ones. Serve hot.

Yield: 24 pieces.

SHRIMP DIP

- ¼ cup butter
- 1 small onion, minced
- ¼ cup chopped bell pepper
- 1 cup cooked chopped shrimp
- 1 cup grated sharp Cheddar cheese
- ⅔ cup mayonnaise
- 1 teaspoon catsup
- 1 teaspoon prepared horseradish

Sauté onion and bell pepper in butter until tender. Mix with cheese in top of double boiler. Cook over boiling water until cheese melts, stirring constantly.

Stir in shrimp and remaining ingredients. Serve with corn chips or pita triangles.

Yield: 3½ cups.

SHRIMP MOLD

- 1½ tablespoons unflavored gelatin
- ¼ cup cold water
- 1 (10¾-ounce) can tomato soup, undiluted
- 1 (8-ounce) package cream cheese
- 2 cups coarsely chopped cooked shrimp
- 1 cup mayonnaise
- ¾ cup finely chopped celery
- ½ cup finely chopped onion

Soften gelatin in cold water. Heat soup in a saucepan; add gelatin and cream cheese stirring until smooth and blended. Cool. Stir in remaining ingredients. Pour into a well-greased 4-cup mold. Refrigerate overnight. Unmold; serve with assorted crackers.

Yield: One 4-cup mold.

SPINACH SQUARES

A mild, delicious appetizer that serves a crowd.

4 (10-ounce) boxes frozen chopped spinach, cooked
1 cup milk
3 eggs, beaten
1 cup all-purpose flour
1 teaspoon salt
¼ teaspoon garlic powder
½ teaspoon baking powder
2 cups shredded Monterey Jack cheese
¼ cup butter

Squeeze all water from cooked spinach.; set aside. In a large mixing bowl, combine flour, salt, garlic powder and baking powder. Stir in eggs and milk; mix well. Add spinach and cheese, blending ingredients well.

Melt butter in a 13 x 9-inch pan in a 350° oven letting butter coat the bottom of pan. Pour in spinach mixture and bake for 30 minutes. Remove from oven and let cool until baked spinach cuts easily. Cut into bite-size squares. If necessary, reheat squares and serve warm. May be frozen after baking. Reheat frozen at 350° for 15-20 minutes.

Yield: Serves 24.

Variation: For a spicier version, add 1 teaspoon nutmeg and 1½ teaspoons Tabasco.

QUICK TACO SPREAD

1 (8-ounce) package cream cheese, softened
1 (10½-ounce) can chili without beans
½ cup chopped onions
1 (8-ounce) package grated pizza cheese

Press softened cream cheese onto bottom of an 8-inch glass pie pan. Spread chili evenly over cream cheese. Add onions and top with cheese. Bake at 350° for 20-25 minutes until cheese melts and mixture is hot and bubbly. Serve with corn chips.

Yield: One 8-inch appetizer pie.

PHYLLO SPINACH SQUARES

12 sheets phyllo dough, thawed
½ cup butter, melted
2 (12-ounce) packages frozen spinach soufflé, thawed
1 (8-ounce) can water chestnuts

Arrange 6 sheets phyllo dough in the bottom of a 15 x 10-inch baking pan. Brush butter between each sheet. (Allow edges of dough to overlap sides of pan.) Spread soufflé evenly over the dough. Chop water chestnuts and sprinkle over soufflé. Top with remaining phyllo, one sheet at a time, brushing with butter between each sheet. Fold edges of phyllo toward center; brush with remaining butter. Score top layers of phyllo into 48 squares or diamonds. Bake at 400° for 30 minutes until golden brown. Cool slightly. Cut through all layers. Serve warm.

Yield: 48 appetizers.

TAMALE CHILI DIP

2 (10½-ounce) cans chili without beans
1 (13½-ounce) jar tamales
1 small onion, chopped
4 green onions, chopped
1 (8-ounce) package shredded processed cheese
½ cup chopped ripe olives
1 cup grated sharp Cheddar cheese

Pour chili in mixing bowl. Remove papers from tamales and mash into chili. Add remaining ingredients (except Cheddar cheese) and stir together. Pour into 1½-quart baking dish; top with Cheddar cheese. Bake at 350° for 25-30 minutes or until bubbly and brown. Serve with tortilla chips.

Yield: Serves 12-15.

BOILED PEANUTS (IN-SHELL)

A summer specialty when green, fresh peanuts are featured in abundance at local groceries in the mountains.

Wash peanuts thoroughly. Place peanuts in a large boiling pot; cover completely with water. Pour salt (use ¼ box salt per 5 pounds of peanuts) over top of peanuts; stir.

Bring to a boil; boil 3 hours. Test for doneness. Open peanut shell and taste test. Peanuts inside shell should be very tender. Add more water, if necessary, to cook longer. Taste test every 10 minutes until tender. Add additional salt, if needed.

FRIED DILL PICKLES

Traditionally served with fried catfish.

- **3 cups vegetable oil**
- **2 cups milk**
- **1 egg, beaten**
- **1 teaspoon Worcestershire sauce**
- **¼ cup all-purpose flour**
- **1¼ cups cornmeal**
- **1 tablespoon baking powder**
- **1 teaspoon cayenne pepper**
- **½ teaspoon salt**
- **1 quart jar dill pickles, sliced horizontally**

Heat oil in heavy frying pan. Combine milk, egg and Worcestershire sauce.

Combine flour, cornmeal, baking powder, pepper and salt.

Dip sliced pickles in milk mixture then cornmeal mixture, coating well. Repeat if necessary to coat well. Fry in hot oil until light brown.

Yield: Serves 6-8.

AGGRAVATION

"The thing that aggravates you is that you can't drink them fast enough." (A quote)

- **1½ ounces Scotch whiskey or Canadian whiskey**
- **1 ounce Kahlua coffee liqueur**
- **1 cup whole milk**
- **½ cup crushed ice**

Pour all ingredients into a blender. Blend on high speed several minutes. Serve in a silver milk punch cup (or in a paper cup).

Yield: 1 serving.

BLOODY MARY

(Tangy ice cubes)

- **4 cups Mr. & Mrs. T Rich and Spicy Bloody Mary mix**
- **6 tablespoons fresh lime juice**
- **Tabasco to taste**
- **1 cup vodka**
- **4 teaspoons Worcestershire sauce**
- **1 teaspoon garlic salt**
- **Celery salt**

Combine 1 cup of the Bloody Mary mix, 2 tablespoons lime juice and Tabasco to taste. Pour into ice cube tray; freeze overnight.

Combine vodka, Worcestershire sauce, garlic salt, remaining 3 cups Bloody Mary mix and remaining 4 tablespoons lime juice in a pitcher. Stir together. Divide the frozen ice cubes among 4 tall glasses. Pour vodka Bloody Mary ingredients into glasses. Sprinkle tops of glasses with celery salt and garnish with a celery stick, green onion or carrot stick.

Yield: 4 servings.

BRANDY MILK PUNCH

- **1½ cups milk**
- **1½ cups vanilla ice cream**
- **¾ cup brandy**
- **¼ cup sugar**
- **1½ teaspoons vanilla extract**
- **Frozen whipped topping**
- **Nutmeg**

Combine first 5 ingredients in a blender. Blend well and pour into milk punch cups and top each with dollop of frozen whipped topping. Sprinkle with nutmeg.

Yield: 2 servings.

Freeze maraschino cherries, cocktail onions, mint leaves or green olives in ice cubes for use in various beverages.

PEACH BRANDY COOLER

- **1 pint vanilla ice cream**
- **1 large peach, peeled and cubed**
- **1½ ounces peach flavored brandy**

Combine all ingredients in blender and blend until smooth.

Yield: 2½ cups.

"CREAMED" COFFEE

- 3/4 cup firmly packed brown sugar
- 2 quarts hot strong coffee
- 1/2 cup whiskey
- 1/4 cup Kahlua liqueur
- 1 pint vanilla ice cream, softened

Combine brown sugar and coffee; stir to dissolve sugar. Add whiskey. Pour into cups and top with ice cream.

Yield: 8 servings.

Hot drinks do not raise body temperature.

SUN RAY FIZZ

One of the more popular drinks at Del Monte Lodge

- 2 ounces half-and-half cream
- 2 ounces fresh orange juice
- 1 ounce Holland House Sweet-n-Sour mix
- 1½ ounces gin
- 1/2 teaspoon vanilla extract
- 1 egg white
- 2 tablespoons sugar, or less
- 3/4 cup crushed ice
- 1/4 fresh orange slice

Put all ingredients (except orange slice) in a blender and liquefy for several minutes until frothy. Pour into a cocktail glass and garnish with orange slice.

Yield: 1 serving

Del Monte Lodge
Pebble Beach, California

WARM SPICY LEMONADE

Good on a chilly night. Fat Free!

3½ cups water
½ cup fresh lemon juice
½ cup firmly packed brown sugar
10 whole cloves
8 whole allspice
2 (3-inch) cinnamon sticks

Combine all ingredients in 1½ quart glass bowl. Microwave uncovered on high 4 minutes, stirring halfway through cooking time, until hot. Let stand 15 minutes. Discard spices. Microwave uncovered on high 5 minutes or until hot.

Yield: 4 cups.

Freeze lemon peel in ice cubes for use in water glasses.

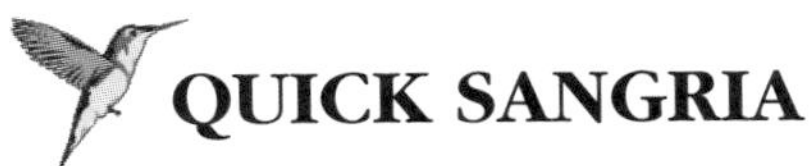

QUICK SANGRIA

2 (6-ounce) cans frozen pink lemonade, undiluted
4½ cups rosé wine, chilled
1 lime, juiced
2 cups club soda, chilled
1 lemon, thinly sliced
1 orange, thinly sliced

Combine lemonade, wine and lime juice; stir until blended. Slowly stir in soda. Pour into serving pitcher. Garnish each drink with lemon and orange slices.

Yield: 6-8 servings.

Warm citrus fruits in microwave to receive more juice.

BOURBON SLUSH

Do not dilute juice concentrates.

- **1 cup strong tea**
- **1 cup sugar**
- **1 (6-ounce) can frozen orange juice, thawed**
- **1 (3-ounce) can frozen lemonade, thawed**
- **½ cup bourbon**
- **3½ cups water**

Combine all ingredients; stir well. Pour into a plastic container and freeze for 8 hours. To serve, spoon slush into glasses.

Yield: 7 cups.

VODKA SLUSH

Do not dilute juice concentrates.

- **1 (6-ounce) can frozen orange juice concentrate, thawed**
- **1 (12-ounce) can frozen lemonade concentrate, thawed**
- **2 (6-ounce) cans frozen limeade concentrate, thawed**
- **½ cup sugar**
- **3½ cups water**
- **2 cups vodka**
- **2 (32-ounce) bottles lemon-lime drink, chilled**

Combine all ingredients, except the lemon-lime drink. Stir well; freeze 8 hours. Spoon ¾ cup slush into a glass. Add ¾ cup lemon-lime drink into glass with slush.

Yield: 16 cups.

Vodka is more flavorful if kept refrigerated.

"STYMIE"

If the addition of sweet vermouth for proper color makes the contents more than 26 ounces, have a sip!

- **1 empty (26-ounce) whiskey bottle**
- **13 ounces gin**
- **2 ounces brandy**
- **11 ounces Martini Dry Vermouth**
- **Sweet vermouth**
- **Lemon slices**

Pour gin, brandy and dry vermouth into empty whiskey bottle. Add sweet vermouth until contents are the color of whiskey. Serve with ice (on the rocks). Garnish with a slice of lemon. Normally served 2 ounces per glass. Should be prepared 48 hours before serving.

Yield: 13 (2-ounce) drinks

Royal and Ancient Golf Club of St. Andrews
Fife, Scotland

WHITE WEDDING PUNCH

- **1 (46-ounce) can pineapple juice, chilled**
- **1 cup white grape juice, chilled**
- **½ gallon vanilla ice cream**
- **3 quarts ginger ale, chilled**

Mix juices together. When ready to serve, put juices in punch bowl. Add scoops of ice cream; pour in ginger ale. Stir lightly.

Yield: 30 servings.

Use muffin tins to make extra large ice for punches.

WHISPER

A most delicious after-dinner drink!

- **1 pint (2 cups) coffee ice cream**
- **½ cup brandy**
- **½ cup white crème de cacao**
- **2 tablespoons milk**

Combine all ingredients in container of electric blender. Process until smooth. Serve immediately.

Yield: 3¼ cups.

Rinse the ice in your glass with water before pouring in carbonated beverages to stop foaming or fizzing.

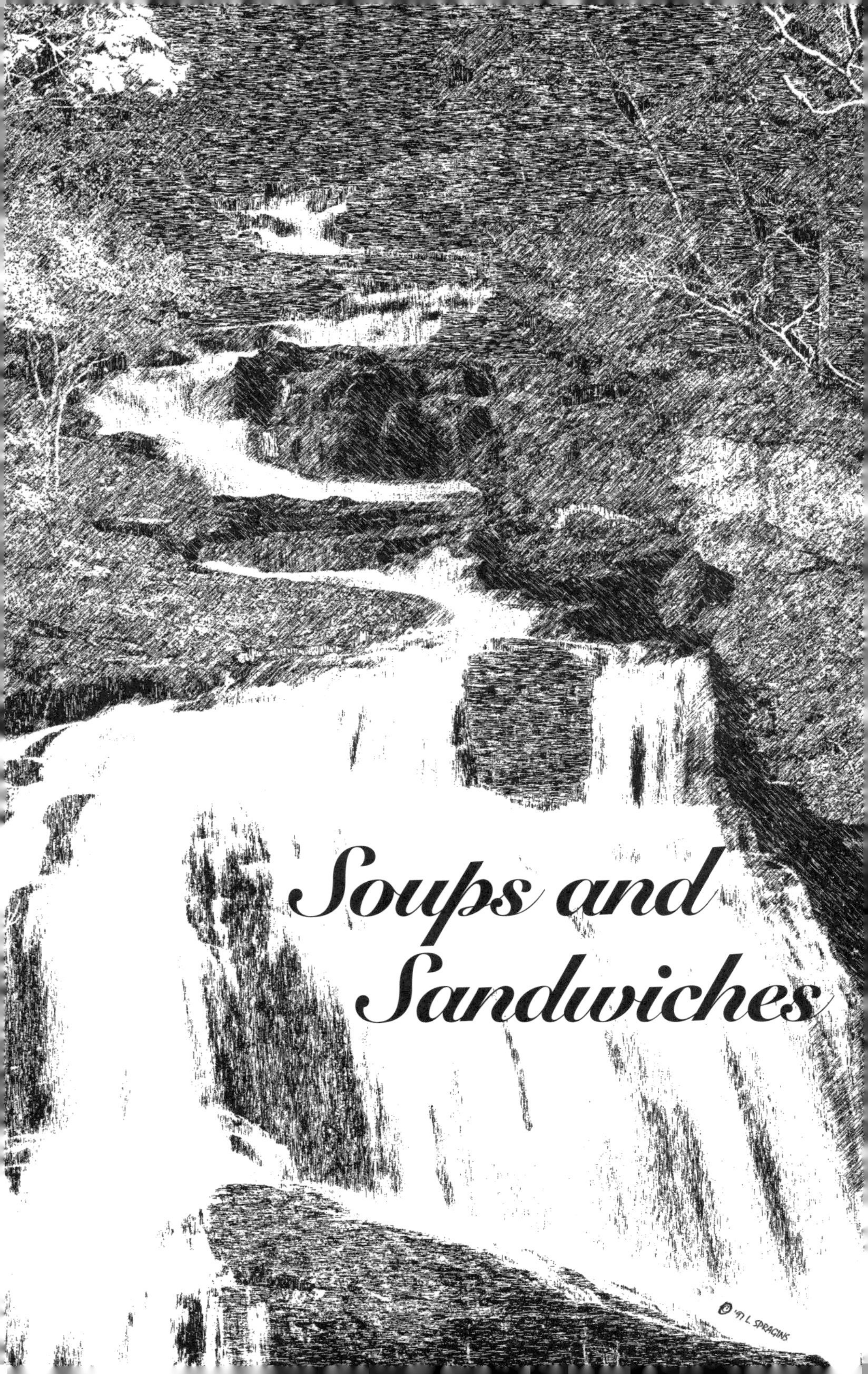

Soups and Sandwiches
© '97 L. SPRAGINS

SOUPS

SANDWICHES

CREAMY ARTICHOKE AND MUSHROOM SOUP

So good! Wonderful company soup.

- **3 tablespoons butter**
- **2 tablespoons minced onion**
- **½ cup thinly sliced fresh mushrooms (or 1 [4-ounce] can)**
- **2 tablespoons all-purpose flour**
- **1 (14½-ounce) can chicken broth**
- **2½ cups half-and-half**
- **1 (14-ounce) can artichoke hearts, drained and diced**
- **½ teaspoon salt**
- **Cayenne pepper to taste**
- **Parsley**

In heavy soup pot, melt butter; sauté onions and mushrooms for 5 minutes, stir in flour. Cook slowly for 2 minutes. Slowly add broth, then half-and-half. Heat very slowly to thicken. When thickened, add artichokes and seasonings. Garnish with parsley.

Yield: Serves 6.

EASY BROCCOLI SOUP

- **1 (10-ounce) box frozen chopped broccoli**
- **1 cup chicken broth**
- **1 onion, minced**
- **1 teaspoon nutmeg**
- **1 cup cream of onion soup**
- **1 tablespoon butter, melted**
- **1 cup sour cream**

Combine broccoli, chicken broth, minced onion and nutmeg; bring to boil over moderate heat. Simmer 5 minutes. Pour into blender, adding onion soup and butter. Blend on high speed until smooth. Add sour cream and blend a few more seconds. Serve hot or cold.

Yield: Serves 4.

BLACK BEAN SOUP

If desired, offer toppings of chopped cherry tomatoes, sour cream, jalapeño salsa along with the usual favorite topping of chopped onion.

- **1 pound dried black beans**
- **6 cups chicken broth**
- **2 cups water**
- **2 small ham hocks**
- **¼ pound salt pork**
- **1 bay leaf**
- **2 cups chopped onion**
- **½ cup chopped celery with leaves**
- **1½ cups chopped bell pepper**
- **1 large tomato, peeled and chopped**
- **1 clove garlic, minced**
- **1 (6-ounce) can tomato paste**
- **½ teaspoon pepper**
- **1 teaspoon Tabasco**
- **2 tablespoons Worcestershire sauce**
- **Rice, cooked**
- **Chopped onions**

Sort and wash beans; place in large Dutch oven or heavy soup pot. Cover with water 2 inches above beans and bring to a boil; cook 2 minutes. Remove from heat. Cover and let stand 1 hour; drain. Add chicken broth, 2 cups water, ham hocks, salt pork and bay leaf to beans; bring to boil. Cover, reduce heat and simmer 1½ hours.

Remove ham hocks and salt pork. Discard bone and fat; return ham to soup mixture. Add onion and remaining ingredients (except rice); cover and simmer 2 hours. Remove bay leaf. Partially mash beans (not all). Place ¼ cup cooked rice in each serving bowl. Spoon bean soup over rice.

Yield: 3 quarts.

MUSHROOM BARLEY SOUP

This was a favorite at Yesterday's, a Cashiers, North Carolina, restaurant in the 70's.

- **1 large onion, chopped**
- **¾ pound mushrooms, sliced**
- **½ cup butter**
- **8 cups strong chicken or beef stock**
- **½ cup medium barley**
- **2 cups milk**
- **1 cup half-and-half**
- **White pepper**
- **Salt, if needed**

In a soup kettle, cook the onions and mushrooms over moderate heat until the onion is softened. Stir in 8 cups of stock; bring to a boil. Sprinkle in barley, stirring and simmer, covered for 45 minutes. Stir in the milk and half-and-half, bring the mixture to a boil and cook at a bare simmer, covered for 30 minutes. Add white pepper sparingly, to taste. Add salt, if desired.

Yield: Serves 8.

BROCCOLI SOUP

- **2 cups water**
- **1 (16-ounce) package frozen broccoli cuts**
- **½ cup chopped onion**
- **½ cup butter, melted**
- **½ cup all-purpose flour**
- **6 cups milk**
- **4 chicken-flavored bouillon cubes**
- **1 teaspoon pepper**

Boil broccoli over medium heat; reduce heat and simmer 5 minutes; set aside (with water).

Sauté onion in butter in Dutch oven over low heat until tender. Add flour, stirring until smooth; cook 1 minute, stirring constantly. Gradually add milk and bouillon cubes; cook over medium heat, stirring constantly until thickened. Add broccoli, cooking water and pepper. Simmer 20-30 minutes, stirring occasionally.

Yield: Serves 6-8.

SPANISH BEAN SOUP

- **½ pound dried garbanzo beans (or 2 [15.5-ounce] cans)**
- **1 packet Goya Seasoning (or ham bone)**
- **2 chorizos (Spanish sausage)**
- **¼ pound smoked bacon (or salt pork)**
- **¼ pound flank steak, whole (or beef bone)**
- **1 small onion, whole**
- **1 ripe whole tomato**
- **Pinch of saffron**
- **2 medium potatoes, pared and cubed**
- **Salt to taste**

Wash dried beans, cover with cold water and soak overnight. Drain. In a soup kettle, place beans, Goya Seasoning (or ham bone), whole chorizos, bacon (or salt pork), steak (or beef bone), onion and tomato. Cover with water, bring to boil skimming off fat several times. Lower heat to medium, cover pot and simmer about 45 minutes. Add saffron, stir, cover and cook another 45 minutes until beans are tender. Remove steak (if using) and chorizos; reserve.

Remove onion, tomato, bacon (or salt pork) and bones (if using). Discard. Add potatoes and salt to pot and simmer 30-45 minutes longer. Shred reserved steak; slice chorizos and add to pot. Serve hot.

Yield: Serves 4.

Add Burgundy to minestrone or bean soups.

MODIFIED DIET SOUP

- **1 medium cabbage, cut in small chunks**
- **1 bell pepper, chopped**
- **1 onion, chopped**
- **1 (10¾-ounce) can French onion soup**
- **2 (14½-ounce) cans Italian recipe stewed tomatoes**
- **1 teaspoon garlic, chopped**
- **2 dashes Tabasco**
- **3 dashes Worcestershire sauce**
- **Salt and pepper, to taste**
- **Sprinkle of oregano**

In a Dutch oven or large soup pot, boil cabbage in just barely enough water to cover until almost tender. Add remaining ingredients. Bring to boil, lower heat and simmer 1 hour until cabbage, peppers and onions are tender. Soup gets better every day.

Yield: Serves 6-8.

CARROT SOUP

- **1 pound carrots, pared and sliced**
- **2 medium russet potatoes, pared and chopped**
- **1 medium onion, chopped**
- **3 cups chicken stock**
- **1 tablespoon curry powder**
- **2 teaspoons ground ginger**
- **1 teaspoon lemon juice**

Put all ingredients (except lemon juice) into pot and simmer 20-25 minutes or until tender; cool. Transfer all ingredients to a blender and puree. With blender on low, gradually add stock. Check seasoning. Return to pot, bring to simmer and add lemon juice. Serve hot.

Yield: Serves 4.

CHILI

Serve topped with grated cheese and chopped onion.

- 2 large onions, finely chopped
- ¼ cup shortening
- 2 pounds beef round, chopped or ground
- 1 teaspoon salt
- ½ teaspoon black pepper
- 1 teaspoon cumin
- 3 tablespoons chili powder
- 2 cloves garlic, chopped
- 1 (14-ounce) can stewed tomatoes
- 1 (8-ounce) can tomato sauce
- 1 (12-ounce) can beer
- 1 cup water
- ½ teaspoon cayenne pepper
- 3 cups canned chili beans, undrained
- 3 whole cloves
- 1 tablespoon masa harina

Sauté onions in shortening until tender; add meat and brown. Drain off fat. Add salt and seasonings; mix well. Stir in tomatoes, tomato sauce, beer, water, pepper, beans and cloves. Simmer over low heat for 1½-2 hours stirring occasionally. Stir in 1 tablespoon masa harina and serve.

Yield: Serves 6-8.

Variation: Add 1 square (1-ounce) unsweetened chocolate during last hour of cooking.

CHASEN'S CHILI

- **½ pound pinto beans**
- **5 cups canned tomatoes**
- **1 pound bell peppers, chopped**
- **1½ tablespoons vegetable oil**
- **1½ pounds onions, chopped**
- **2 cloves garlic, crushed**
- **½ cup chopped parsley**
- **1 pound ground lean pork**
- **2½ pounds coarsely ground beef**
- **2 tablespoons chili powder**
- **2 tablespoons salt**
- **1 teaspoon pepper**
- **1½ teaspoons ground cumin**

Wash pinto beans and soak overnight. Simmer in the soaking water until tender. Add tomatoes; simmer 5 minutes. Set aside.

Sauté peppers and onions in oil until tender, stirring constantly. Add garlic and parsley. Sauté pork and beef until browned (15 minutes). Add meat to onion pepper mixture. Stir in chili powder; cook 10 minutes. Add to beans; stir in spices and simmer covered 1 hour. Uncover pot and simmer another 30 minutes. Skim grease from top. Serve warm.

Yield: Serves 8.

Chasen's Restaurant
Los Angeles, California

WHITE CHILI

For a buffet, serve chili with some of the following toppings of your choice: chopped tomatoes, chopped ripe olives, guacamole, chopped green onions, crumbled tortilla chips or sour cream or offer all of them!

- **1 pound large white beans**
- **6 cups chicken broth**
- **2 cloves garlic, minced**
- **2 medium onions, chopped and divided**
- **1 tablespoon oil**
- **2 (4-ounce) cans chopped green chilies**
- **2 teaspoons ground cumin**
- **1½ teaspoons dried oregano**
- **¼ teaspoon ground cloves**
- **¼ teaspoon cayenne pepper**
- **4 cups diced cooked chicken breasts**
- **3 cups grated Monterey Jack cheese**

Combine beans, chicken broth, garlic and half of the onions in a large soup pot; bring to a boil. Reduce heat and simmer until beans are very soft, 3 hours or more. Add more chicken broth if necessary. In a skillet, sauté remaining onions in oil until tender. Add chilies and seasonings, mixing thoroughly. Add to bean mixture. Add chicken and continue to simmer 1 hour. Taste for seasonings, adding salt if necessary. Serve topped with cheese.

Yield: Serves 8-10.

CURRIED SEAFOOD CHOWDER

- **1 pound medium-size fresh shrimp, peeled**
- **3 tablespoons butter**
- **3 tablespoons all-purpose flour**
- **2 teaspoons curry powder**
- **½ teaspoon salt and pepper**
- **2 cups chicken broth**
- **1 cup clam juice**
- **3 cups half-and-half**
- **4 cups chopped potatoes (about 4 medium)**
- **1 pound grouper, cut into bite-size pieces**

Melt butter in large heavy soup pot or Dutch oven over medium heat; add flour, curry powder, salt and pepper, stirring constantly until smooth. Cook 1 minute, gradually add chicken broth, stirring until smooth. Stir in clam juice, half-and-half and potatoes; bring to boil. Reduce heat and simmer 30 minutes or until potatoes are tender. Right before serving, add fish and shrimp; cook 8-10 minutes. Stir well and serve immediately.

Yield: 3½ quarts.

NEW ENGLAND FISH CHOWDER

Traditionally, haddock or cod are used.

- **4 slices bacon (or 3 small slices salt pork), diced**
- **2 medium onions, chopped**
- **3 potatoes, pared and diced**
- **1 medium carrot, thinly sliced**
- **1 teaspoon salt**
- **½ teaspoon white pepper**
- **2 cups water**
- **1 cup clam juice**
- **1 pound fresh white fish, boned, cut in 1-inch pieces**
- **3 cups half-and-half**
- **1 tablespoon butter**

Sauté bacon until almost crisp; add onions and cook until onion is limp. Add potatoes, carrots, salt and pepper, water and clam juice. Simmer until potatoes and carrots are soft. Add fish; simmer gently until fish flakes but doesn't crumble. Add half-and-half; heat but do not boil. Add butter. Adjust seasonings.

Yield: Serves 6-8.

Add chablis to chowders.

CLAM AND CORN CHOWDER WITH DILL

- **1 medium onion, chopped**
- **½ cup chopped bell pepper**
- **2 tablespoons low-fat margarine**
- **¼ cup all-purpose flour**
- **1 teaspoon dried dill weed**
- **½ teaspoon paprika**
- **½ teaspoon Worcestershire sauce**
- **¼ teaspoon salt**
- **3½ cups vegetable juice (low sodium)**
- **1 (17-ounce) can whole kernel corn, undrained**
- **1 (6½-ounce) can minced clams, undrained**
- **1 ounce shredded Cheddar cheese (low fat or fat-free)**
- **Oyster crackers (optional)**

In large heavy saucepan, cook onion and bell pepper in hot margarine until tender but not brown, stirring often. Stir in flour, dill weed, paprika, Worcestershire sauce and salt. Add vegetable juice all at once. Cook and stir over medium heat until thickened. Stir in corn and clams. Heat through. Ladle chowder into soup bowls. Sprinkle with cheese. Top with a few oyster crackers.

Yield: Serves 4.

CRAB BISQUE

- ½ cup butter
- 1 cup finely chopped onions
- 1 cup finely chopped celery
- 2 cloves garlic, minced
- 1 tablespoon thyme
- 1 tablespoon rosemary
- 2 bay leaves
- ½ cup (or more) all-purpose flour
- 1 quart chicken broth
- ¼ cup tomato paste
- ½ cup white wine
- Salt to taste
- Dash of Tabasco
- 1 tablespoon lemon juice
- 1 tablespoon sugar
- ½ cup sherry
- 1½ cups milk
- 2 cups half-and-half
- 1 pound crabmeat
- Dash of brandy

Sauté first 6 ingredients in butter in a Dutch oven or heavy soup pot over medium heat, stirring often until onions, celery and garlic are tender. Whisk in flour until blended; gradually add chicken broth and next 6 ingredients. Bring to a boil; reduce heat and simmer on low for 1 hour, stirring frequently. Remove from heat; strain. Return to pan and blend in sherry, milk and half-and-half. Stir in crabmeat and brandy. Serve hot.

Yield: Serves 8-10 (as a first course).

EGGPLANT SOUP

Freezes well.

- 2 tablespoons butter
- 2 tablespoons oil
- 1 cup chopped onion
- ¾ cup chopped celery
- 2 pounds eggplant, peeled and diced
- 2 cups peeled, thinly sliced potatoes
- 1¼ teaspoons curry powder
- ⅛ teaspoon thyme
- ⅛ teaspoon basil
- 1 teaspoon salt
- Freshly ground black pepper
- 6-7 cups chicken stock
- Pinch of cayenne pepper
- 2 cups heavy cream

Steam onion and celery in oil and butter in tightly covered pot for 10 minutes over low heat. Add eggplant and potatoes; steam 15 minutes more until vegetables soften. Stir in next 6 ingredients. Bring to a boil; lower heat and simmer 30 minutes. Cool for 10 minutes. Puree in blender. Add cayenne and cream. Serve hot or cold.

Yield: 1½-2 quarts.

QUICK CRAB BISQUE

- 1 (10¾-ounce) can cream of mushroom soup
- 1 (10¾-ounce) can cream of celery soup
- 6-8 ounces frozen crabmeat, thawed
- 1½ soup cans of milk
- 1 cup cream
- ¼ cup sherry
- Butter to taste

Heat all ingredients (except sherry and butter); remove from heat. Add sherry and pats of butter; stir until blended.

Yield: Serves 4.

GAZPACHO

Delicious for lunch on a hot day. Gets raves!

- 1 (10¾-ounce) can tomato soup
- 1 can water
- 1 cup peeled and chopped cucumber
- ½ cup finely chopped bell pepper
- ¼ cup minced onion
- 1 tablespoon olive oil
- 2 tablespoons wine vinegar
- 1 clove garlic, minced (or ¼ teaspoon garlic powder)
- Salt and pepper to taste
- 1 tablespoon Worcestershire sauce
- 2 drops Tabasco
- Croutons
- Chopped tomatoes

Blend all ingredients (except croutons and chopped tomatoes) in blender. Serve ice cold topped with croutons and chopped tomatoes in pretty bouillon cups.

Yield: Serves 4.

LENTIL SOUP

- 1 cup dried lentils
- 1 carrot, chopped
- 1 onion, grated
- 1 (14½-ounce) can stewed tomatoes
- 1 teaspoon sugar
- 1 (24-ounce) can tomato juice
- 2 tablespoons olive oil

Wash lentils. Put in pot with ½ to 1 cup water. Bring to boil. Add carrot, onion, stewed tomatoes and sugar. Add tomato juice. Simmer 1-1½ hours. Add olive oil and cook 15 minutes more. Makes a very thick soup. To thin, add more tomato juice.

Yield: Serves 4-6.

JELLIED CONSOMMÉ MADRILÈNE

Light, cool and nice.

- 2 envelopes (1 tablespoon each) unflavored gelatin
- 2 cups tomato (or vegetable) juice, divided
- 2½ cups water
- 4 beef bouillon cubes
- ¼ cup dry sherry
- ⅛ teaspoon white pepper
- 1 cup sour cream
- 3 dashes of Tabasco
- Chives, chopped
- Cucumber or radish slices (one or two per serving)

Soften gelatin in one cup tomato (or vegetable) juice for 5 minutes. In saucepan, heat water and bouillon cubes to boiling. Add gelatin mixture, stir until beef cubes and gelatin are dissolved. Remove from heat, add remaining 1 cup juice, sherry and pepper. Chill until partially set, stirring several times. When almost firm, spoon into serving dishes. Blend sour cream and Tabasco; add a dollop to consommé and garnish with chives and a cucumber or radish slice.

Yield: Serves 8.

MAMA MIA'S ITALIAN SOUP

A crusty loaf of bread, some fruit for dessert...and mangia bene!

- **½ cup diced onion**
- **½ cup diced celery**
- **½ cup diced carrots**
- **1 tablespoon olive oil**
- **1 clove garlic, minced**
- **5 cups defatted chicken broth**
- **1 (14-ounce) can tomatoes, chopped, undrained**
- **1 (16-ounce) can kidney beans, rinsed and drained**
- **1 packed cup escarole**
- **1 cup sliced green beans**
- **½ cup diced zucchini**

In a 3-quart pot over medium heat, sauté onion, celery and carrots in olive oil 5 minutes or until lightly browned and tender. Add garlic and sauté until tender. Add broth, tomatoes with juice, kidney beans, escarole. Bring to boil over high heat; reduce heat and simmer 10 minutes.

Stir in green beans and zucchini. Cover pot and simmer 10-20 minutes or until beans are tender. Serve in soup bowls steaming hot over rice.

Yield: Serves 4-6.

Add potato slices if soup is too salty, cook a few minutes and discard potatoes.

MULLIGATAWNY SOUP

- 1/4 cup butter
- 1 medium onion, sliced
- 1 medium carrot, diced
- 1 bell pepper, diced
- 1 celery stalk, diced
- 1 medium tart apple, peeled, cored, sliced
- 1 cup chopped cooked chicken
- 1/4 cup all-purpose flour
- 2 whole cloves
- 1 teaspoon curry powder
- 1 tablespoon parsley flakes
- 1/8 teaspoon nutmeg
- 2 (10½-ounce) cans chicken broth
- 1 (16-ounce) can tomatoes
- Salt and pepper

Melt butter in a 3-quart soup or saucepan over medium heat. Add onion and sauté until softened. Blend in carrot, bell pepper, celery, apple and chicken and sauté until vegetables are tender. Stir in flour. Add cloves, curry powder, parsley and nutmeg. Blend in broth with tomatoes, breaking up tomatoes into pieces. Season with salt and pepper. Reduce heat, cover and simmer 1 hour. Discard cloves. Ladle into bowls.

Yield: Serves 6.

QUICK MUSHROOM SOUP

- 4 tablespoons butter
- 1 small onion, chopped
- 1 (4-ounce) can mushroom pieces and stems, drained
- 2 (10¾-ounce) cans cream of mushroom soup
- 2 soup cans milk
- Salt, pepper, garlic salt
- 1/4 cup sherry

Sauté onion and mushroom in butter until onion is soft. Stir in remaining ingredients, seasoning to taste. Simmer until hot (do not boil).

Yield: Serves 4.

ONION SOUP

- **½ cup butter**
- **8 large onions, thinly sliced, cut in half**
- **1 cup red wine**
- **¼ teaspoon pepper**
- **4 (10½-ounce) cans beef bouillon**
- **1½ bouillon cans water**
- **4 slices toasted French bread**
- **8 slices Provolone cheese**
- **Paprika**
- **Parsley**

Sauté onion slices in butter cooking until very tender, almost mushy (at least 30 minutes). Add wine, pepper, bouillon and water. Simmer over low heat 1 hour. Pour into oven-proof serving bowls. Top with bread (cut to fit if necessary); cover with cheese slices. Sprinkle with paprika.

Place bowls on a baking sheet or jelly-roll pan and place in oven. Broil until cheese melts and begins to turn brown. Serve immediately garnished with parsley.

Yield: Serves 8.

BAKED POTATO SOUP

- **½ cup butter**
- **½ cup all-purpose flour**
- **2 cups chicken broth**
- **2 cups milk**
- **½ teaspoon salt**
- **Dash of white pepper**
- **2 large baked potatoes, peeled and diced**
- **1 cup grated cheese**
- **¼ cup bacon, crisply cooked and crumbled**
- **2 tablespoons chopped chives (or green onions)**

Melt butter, add flour and stir until smooth. Gradually add broth and milk. Cook, stirring until thickened. Add salt and pepper and potatoes. Heat through and serve sprinkled with cheese, bacon and chives (or green onions).

Yield: 1 quart.

LOUISIANA SEAFOOD GUMBO

- **3 tablespoons vegetable oil**
- **3 tablespoons all-purpose flour**
- **1 slice bacon, diced**
- **1 medium onion, chopped**
- **1 clove garlic, minced**
- **½ cup chopped bell pepper**
- **1 cup chopped celery**
- **1 (16-ounce) can tomatoes**
- **2 cups chicken broth**
- **2 cups water**
- **5 drops Tabasco**
- **3 bay leaves**
- **1½ teaspoons salt**
- **½ teaspoon pepper**
- **1 (10-ounce) package frozen cut okra**
- **1 (6-ounce) package frozen crabmeat**
- **1 pound shrimp, cooked**
- **2 cups fresh oysters, drained**
- **1½ teaspoons gumbo filé**
- **Cooked rice**

Heat oil in a 3-quart Dutch oven or heavy pot; add flour, stirring constantly. Cook over medium heat, stirring constantly, 10-15 minutes or until roux is light brown. Stir in bacon; cook 1 minute. Add onion, garlic, bell pepper and celery; sauté until tender.

Gradually add tomatoes, broth, water, Tabasco, bay leaves, salt and pepper; simmer 1½ hours.

Add okra; cook 15 minutes, stirring occasionally. Stir in seafood; cook over medium heat 5 minutes or until oysters curl at edges. Stir in filé; serve over rice.

Yield: 4-6 servings.

BUTTERNUT SQUASH AND APPLE SOUP

- 1 small butternut squash, about 1 pound
- 3 tart green apples
- 1 medium onion, chopped
- 1/4 teaspoon rosemary
- 1/4 teaspoon marjoram
- 3 (10 1/2-ounce) cans chicken broth
- 2 soup cans water
- 2 slices white bread
- Salt and pepper
- 1/4 cup heavy cream
- 2 tablespoons chopped parsley

Cut butternut squash in half, peel and seed. Peel, core and coarsely chop apples. Pour chicken broth in heavy saucepan; add all ingredients except heavy cream and parsley. Bring to boil; lower heat and simmer uncovered 45 minutes. Let cool slightly.

Puree soup in food processor in several batches, not filling processor bowl more than a quarter full each time. Return soup to saucepan; bring to boil; reduce heat. Just before serving, add the heavy cream blending well. Serve hot with sprinkle of parsley on top.

Yield: 9 cups.

Always simmer soups; never boil them. Simmer is to cook gently at a temperature below boiling point.

SQUASH AND SHRIMP BISQUE

- **3 cups chicken stock, divided**
- **¼ teaspoon thyme**
- **¼ teaspoon basil**
- **Dash of cayenne pepper**
- **1 pound yellow squash, sliced**
- **½ cup chopped onion**
- **⅓ cup chopped bell pepper**
- **⅓ cup chopped celery**
- **2 cloves garlic, minced**
- **1 tablespoon cornstarch**
- **¼ cup cold water**
- **½ pound raw shrimp, peeled, deveined and chopped**
- **1 (14-ounce) can light evaporated milk**
- **Salt to taste**

Season 2 cups stock with thyme, basil and cayenne. Add squash, onion, bell pepper, celery and garlic. Bring to simmer and cook, covered, until squash is very tender. Put in blender and puree mixture. Return to pan. Dissolve cornstarch in water. Add this and remaining 1 cup stock to the puree; cook over low heat, stirring until smooth. Add shrimp and milk. Simmer 10-15 minutes. Correct seasoning, adding salt to taste.

Yield: Serves 6.

Add sherry to crab, lobster, shrimp or chicken bisques.

ASPARAGUS GRILL

Serve as a luncheon entrée with a fruit salad.

- **8 slices sandwich bread**
- **Butter**
- **16 slices bacon, crisply cooked (or 8 ham slices)**
- **4 slices Vidalia onion**
- **4 slices tomato**
- **16 cooked fresh asparagus spears**
- **4 slices processed American cheese**
- **Cheese Sauce**

Spread one side of each slice bread with butter. Place 4 slices bread, buttered side down, on hot griddle or large skillet. On each slice, place 4 slices bacon (or 2 slices ham), 1 slice onion, 1 slice tomato, 4 asparagus spears and 1 slice cheese. Place remaining 4 slices bread, buttered side up, on top of cheese. Cook until sandwiches are brown; turn over and brown other side. Pour cheese sauce over sandwiches and serve.

Yield: 4 sandwiches.

Cheese Sauce

- **2 tablespoons butter**
- **2 tablespoons all-purpose flour**
- **1 cup milk**
- **1 cup shredded sharp Cheddar cheese**

Melt butter in heavy saucepan over low heat. Add flour and cook 1 minute, stirring constantly. Gradually add milk; cook over medium heat until thickened and bubbly. Add cheese and stir until melted.

Yield: About 1 cup.

CHICKEN SANDWICHES

1 (10¾-ounce) can cream of chicken soup, undiluted
1½ cups diced cooked chicken
1 (4-ounce) jar chopped pimiento
¾ cup milk
3 tablespoons all-purpose flour
3 tablespoons minced onion
18 slices sandwich bread
Butter, softened
3 eggs, beaten
3 cups finely crushed potato chips

Combine soup, chicken, pimiento, milk, flour and onion in medium saucepan. Cook over low heat until thickened and bubbly. Cool thoroughly.

Trim crust from bread. Spread butter on both sides of bread. Spread ¼ cup chicken mixture on 9 slices of bread; top with remaining 9 slices. Wrap each sandwich with foil; freeze.

Remove sandwiches from freezer; slice diagonally. Dip each in beaten egg; dredge in potato chips. Arrange on baking sheet and bake at 325° for 30 minutes.

Yield: Serves 9.

CURRIED EGG SALAD

8 water chestnuts, chopped
6 hard-boiled eggs, chopped
¼-½ cup mayonnaise
1 green onion, chopped
1 teaspoon curry powder
½ teaspoon Worcestershire sauce
Salt and freshly ground pepper to taste

Combine all ingredients, blending well. Cover and refrigerate.

Yield: About 2 cups.

CHEESY EGG SANDWICHES

- **6 hard-cooked eggs**
- **2 cups shredded Cheddar cheese**
- **¼ cup chopped green onions**
- **⅔ cup mayonnaise**
- **2 tablespoons sweet pickle relish**
- **1 teaspoon prepared mustard**
- **¼ teaspoon salt**
- **¼ teaspoon black pepper**
- **¼ teaspoon garlic powder**
- **⅓ cup butter**
- **6 English muffins, split**

Peel and chop eggs; combine with all other ingredients except butter and muffins. Spread butter on each muffin half; toast. Spread egg salad mixture equally on muffin halves and broil 3 minutes or until cheese melts.

Yield: 12 open-faced sandwiches.

PIMIENTO CHEESE

- **1 (8-ounce) package sharp Cheddar cheese**
- **1 (8-ounce) package medium Cheddar cheese**
- **1 (8-ounce) processed cheese loaf**
- **1½ tablespoons sugar**
- **¼ teaspoon salt**
- **6 drops Tabasco**
- **1 (4-ounce) jar diced pimientos**
- **1 cup mayonnaise or salad dressing**

Shred both Cheddar cheeses in food processor using shredding disc. Cut cheese loaf into cubes. Remove cheese from processor. Put steel knife mixing blade in processor bowl. Add Cheddar cheeses and cubed cheese, sugar, salt and Tabasco to processor bowl and process until well mixed. Remove to mixing bowl; stir in pimiento and mayonnaise. Blend together well.

Yield: 1 quart.

PAN-FRIED GROUPER SANDWICH

- 1 (¾-pound) grouper fillet
- 1 cup buttermilk
- 1 cup all-purpose flour
- ½ teaspoon paprika
- Salt and pepper
- 2 tablespoons butter
- 2 tablespoons corn oil
- 4 soft buns, halved
- ½ cup tartar sauce
- Lettuce, tomato slices

Have butcher cut grouper fillet into 4 small fillets, removing any little bones.

Place buttermilk in shallow dish. Combine flour, paprika, salt and pepper in another bowl. Dip grouper into buttermilk then dredge in the seasoned flour; shake off excess.

Heat butter and oil in skillet over medium heat; cook fillets one or two at a time until golden brown on both sides (3 minutes a side).

Spread both sides of each bun with 1 tablespoon tartar sauce. Place cooked grouper on bottom half of each bun top with lettuce and tomato, cover with top of bun. Serve immediately.

Yield: Serves 4.

MUFFULETTA

- **3 tablespoons prepared mustard**
- **1 (8-inch) round loaf Italian bread, cut in half horizontally**
- **½ cup shredded Cheddar cheese**
- **½ cup shredded mozzarella cheese**
- **½ cup shredded provolone cheese**
- **3 ounces sliced ham**
- **3 ounces sliced salami**
- **3 ounces sliced bologna**
- **3 ounces sliced turkey**
- **1½ cups Olive Salad Mix, chilled**

Spread mustard on bread. Combine cheeses; place on bottom half of bread. Arrange meat on both halves; place on baking sheet.

Bake at 350° for 15 minutes or until thoroughly heated. Spread chilled Olive Salad Mix on bottom half; cover with top half. Cut into quarters.

Yield: Serves 2-4.

Olive Salad Mix

- **1½ cups pimiento-stuffed olives, drained**
- **1 cup ripe olives, drained**
- **1 cup chopped celery**
- **2 cloves garlic, minced**
- **1 cup mixed vegetables, drained**
- **¼ cup capers, drained**
- **⅓ cup olive oil**
- **⅓ cup white wine vinegar**

Combine all ingredients; cover and chill. Store up to 1 week.

SOUFFLÉ SANDWICHES

Serve hot with asparagus or mushroom sauce.

- **12 slices bread, crusts removed, buttered on one side**
- **6 slices ham and/or 6 slices cheese**
- **4 eggs, lightly beaten**
- **2 cups milk**
- **1 teaspoon salt**
- **1 teaspoon paprika**

Place 6 bread slices, buttered side down, in greased pan. Place slice of ham and/or cheese on each and cover with another bread slice, buttered side up. Combine eggs, milk, salt and paprika. Pour over sandwiches and refrigerate several hours or overnight. Bake at 350° for 45 minutes.

Yield: Serves 6.

Sauce

- **2 tablespoons butter**
- **2 tablespoons flour**
- **1½ cups milk**
- **1 teaspoon salt**
- **¼ teaspoon pepper**
- **½ pound mushrooms, sliced and sautéed in 3 tablespoons butter, or 1 (9-ounce) package frozen asparagus, cooked and drained**

Melt butter in saucepan and blend in flour. Gradually stir in milk. Cook, stirring constantly until smooth and thickened. Add seasonings and mushrooms or asparagus.

Yield: 2 cups.

MINI PIZZAS

These pizzas are thick with toppings. The best!

2 packages (6-inch) Boboli prebaked cheese crusts
24 slices pepperoni
4 plum tomatoes, thinly sliced
4 fresh white mushrooms, sliced
½ medium Vidalia onion, chopped
1 (8-ounce) package pizza cheese
2 tablespoons chopped fresh basil or 1 tablespoon dried
1 tablespoon olive oil
1 teaspoon red pepper flakes

Preheat oven to 500°. Arrange the 4 crusts on cookie sheet lined with aluminum foil. Brush each with olive oil and sprinkle with red pepper flakes. Cover tops with some cheese, 6 slices pepperoni, 4-5 slices of tomato, sprinkles of basil, then mushroom, onions and again with cheese. Bake at 500° for 12-15 minutes until cheese melts and pizzas are golden brown. Slice each into 4-6 wedges.

Yield: Serves 4.

Salads

SALADS

SALAD DRESSINGS

CREAMY APRICOT SALAD

- 1 (15¼-ounce) can crushed pineapple, undrained
- 1 (6-ounce) package apricot flavored gelatin
- 2 cups boiling water
- 1½ cups miniature marshmallows
- 2 (7¾-ounce) jars apricot baby food
- 1 (3-ounce) package cream cheese, softened
- 4 ounces frozen whipped topping, thawed
- 2 cups sliced bananas
- ½ cup chopped pecans or walnuts

Drain pineapple, reserving ½ cup juice; set aside. Dissolve gelatin in boiling water. Add marshmallows, stirring until slightly melted. Stir in pineapple and apricot baby food. Chill until thickened.

Combine cream cheese and reserved pineapple juice, blending until smooth. Stir in whipped topping. Fold into gelatin mixture.

Arrange banana slices in bottom of lightly oiled 12 x 8-inch glass dish. Spoon gelatin mixture over bananas. Top with pecans. Chill until firm.

Yield: Serves 12.

Grease molds with vegetable spray to ease unmolding.

ARTICHOKE AND RICE SALAD

Excellent recipe for a buffet.

- **2 (4.4-ounce) packages chicken flavored rice mix**
- **8 green onions, thinly sliced**
- **1 bell pepper, chopped**
- **3 (6-ounce) jars marinated artichoke hearts**
- **24 pimiento-stuffed olives, sliced**
- **1 teaspoon curry powder**
- **⅔ cup mayonnaise**

Prepare rice according to directions on packages, omitting the butter. Cool in a large bowl. Add onions, bell pepper and olives.

Drain artichoke hearts, reserving the marinade of one jar plus the spices in the bottom of another jar. Discard remaining marinade. Combine the marinade and reserved spices with the curry powder and mayonnaise.

Cut the artichokes in half; add to rice mixture. Toss with marinade mayonnaise dressing. Chill.

Yield: Serves 16.

Variation: Add 12 fresh mushrooms, sliced.

ASPIC STUFFED TOMATOES

- **8 large tomatoes**
- **1 (3-ounce) package raspberry gelatin**
- **2 tablespoons catsup**
- **1 tablespoon lemon juice**
- **2 teaspoons prepared horseradish**
- **1½ teaspoons Worcestershire sauce**
- **½ teaspoon salt**
- **Tabasco to taste**
- **¾ cup finely chopped celery**
- **¼ cup finely chopped onion**
- **¼ cup finely chopped bell pepper**

Cut stem ends of tomatoes off. Scoop out and reserve pulp. Drain tomato shells; set aside.

Place pulp in a blender; blend until pureed. Measure out 2 cups juicy pulp and combine with gelatin in a saucepan; bring to boil stirring to dissolve gelatin. Stir in catsup, lemon juice, horseradish, Worcestershire and salt. Chill until partially set.

Fold in vegetables.

Sprinkle insides of tomatoes with more salt. Fill with gelatin mixture. Chill until firm. Serve topped with mayonnaise on spinach leaves.

Yield: Serves 8.

EASY ASPIC

- **2 (3-ounce) boxes raspberry gelatin**
- **1¾ cups boiling water**
- **2 (8-ounce) cans tomato sauce**
- **2 tablespoons vinegar**
- **½ teaspoon salt**
- **½ teaspoon seasoned salt**
- **½ cup minced celery**
- **½ cup minced onion**
- **1 (14.5-ounce) can whole tomatoes, drained, mashed**

Dissolve gelatin in boiling water. Stir in tomato sauce, vinegar and seasonings. Chill until thickened.

When gelatin has thickened, fold in celery and onion. Mix together until well blended.

Cover inside of 5-cup mold with cooking spray or oil. Place drained and mashed stewed tomatoes evenly in mold and cover with thickened gelatin mixture. Chill until set. Unmold on lettuce-lined serving plate.

Yield: Serves 8-10.

AVOCADO CUCUMBER SALAD

- **1 (3-ounce) box lemon gelatin**
- **⅔ cup boiling water**
- **1 cup sour cream**
- **¾ teaspoon salt**
- **2 tablespoons lemon juice**
- **1 cup grated cucumber, drained**
- **1 cup diced avocados**
- **3 tablespoons minced green onions**

Dissolve gelatin in boiling water. Cool slightly. Stir in sour cream, salt and lemon juice. Chill until partially set. Fold in cucumber, avocados and green onion. Pour into 1½-quart flat dish. Chill until firm.

Yield: Serves 4-6.

COLD LIMA BEAN SALAD

- 3 (10-ounce) packages frozen Fordhook lima beans
- 1 teaspoon sugar
- ½ teaspoon salt
- ½ teaspoon prepared mustard
- ½ teaspoon paprika
- ¼ teaspoon Tabasco
- 2 tablespoons fresh lemon juice
- 2 tablespoons vinegar
- ⅓ cup olive oil
- 1 tablespoon parsley flakes
- ½ cup thin (diagonally) cut celery
- ½ cup chopped bell pepper
- ½ cup chopped green onions

Cook beans according to directions until done but firm; drain.

Mix next 9 ingredients together, blending well. Pour over hot beans and toss. Refrigerate.

To serve, mix beans with the celery, bell pepper and onions and spoon onto lettuce leaves.

Yield: Serves 8.

BROCCOLI SALAD

- 1 large bunch broccoli, cut into florets
- 5 slices bacon, crisply cooked and crumbled
- ⅓ cup raisins
- ¼ cup chopped onions
- 2 hard-boiled eggs, chopped
- ¼ teaspoon garlic powder
- ¼ teaspoon black pepper
- 1 tablespoon lemon juice
- ½ cup mayonnaise
- ¼ cup sugar
- 1 tablespoon vinegar
- 1 small head red lettuce
- 2 tablespoons chopped pimientos

Blanch broccoli in boiling water for 1½-2 minutes. Drain. Refresh in cold water; pat dry.

Combine all ingredients in mixing bowl (except lettuce and pimientos). Stir until all ingredients are blended. Chill.

Line 6 serving plates with lettuce. Place broccoli mixture on lettuce and garnish with pimientos.

Yield: Serves 6.

BLUE CHEESE PEAR SALAD

- 2 large heads Boston or Bibb lettuce
- 4 firm pears, cored and chopped
- ¾ cup crumbled blue cheese
- ¾ cup chopped walnuts
- Vinaigrette Dressing (see Page 109)

Tear lettuce into bite-size pieces; mix with other ingredients. Toss with vinaigrette dressing and serve immediately.

Yield: Serves 10-12.

CAESAR SALAD

Garlic croutons:

- **6 slices bread**
- **½ cup butter**
- **2 cloves garlic**

Dressing:

- **1 (8-ounce) bottle Caesar salad dressing**
- **1 cup sour cream**
- **¼ cup dry mustard**
- **1½ tablespoons Worcestershire sauce**
- **1 cup grated Parmesan cheese**
- **1 clove garlic, minced**
- **1 teaspoon pepper**
- **½ teaspoon anchovy paste**

- **4 heads Romaine lettuce, torn in bite-size pieces**

For croutons: Cut bread into ½-inch squares. Sauté garlic in butter for 2 minutes over medium heat. Add bread and stir until crisp and golden. Drain on paper towels.

Dressing: Combine all ingredients (except Parmesan cheese) in blender and blend well. Stir in Parmesan cheese. Let stand at room temperature. Refrigerate if not using immediately.

To serve: Place Romaine lettuce into large salad bowl. Cover with dressing and toss. Top with croutons.

Yield: Serves 8-10.

CHICKEN SALAD

- 4 cups chopped, cooked chicken or turkey
- 1 (8-ounce) can water chestnuts, drained and chopped
- 1 pound seedless grapes, halved
- 1 cup chopped celery
- 1 cup slivered almonds, toasted
- 1½ cups mayonnaise
- ½ teaspoon curry powder
- 1 tablespoon soy sauce
- 1 tablespoon lemon juice
- 1 (20-ounce) can pineapple chunks, drained
- Boston or Bibb lettuce

Combine chicken, water chestnuts, grapes, celery and ¾ cup almonds in mixing bowl; set aside.

Mix mayonnaise, curry powder, soy sauce and lemon juice together until smooth. Fold into chicken mixture and toss together well. Chill several hours. Spoon onto lettuce leaves; sprinkle with remaining almonds. Garnish with pineapple chunks.

Yield: Serves 8.

Variation: Substitute chopped cooked shrimp for chicken.

HOT CHICKEN SALAD

- 3/4 cup mayonnaise
- 2 tablespoons lemon juice
- 1/4 teaspoon Tabasco
- 1 teaspoon Worcestershire sauce
- 1 (10 3/4-ounce) can cream of chicken soup, undiluted
- 1 cup (4-ounce package) shredded Cheddar cheese
- 3 cups diced cooked chicken
- 2 hard-boiled eggs, chopped
- 1/2 cup finely chopped onion
- 1 cup chopped celery
- 1 cup chopped almonds or walnuts, toasted
- 1 cup crushed cracker crumbs
- 2 tablespoons butter, melted

Mix first 6 ingredients together. Stir in all remaining ingredients except cracker crumbs and butter. Pour into a 2-quart casserole.

Toss cracker crumbs with melted butter; set aside. Place casserole in a 350° oven and bake for 35 minutes. Sprinkle buttered cracker crumbs on top and bake 15 minutes longer.

Yield: Serves 6.

CHRISTMAS WREATH FROZEN SALAD

- **2 (3-ounce) packages cream cheese, softened**
- **1 cup mayonnaise**
- **1 cup maraschino cherries, drained, halved**
- **1 cup green maraschino cherries, drained, halved**
- **1 (20-ounce) can crushed pineapple, drained**
- **½ cup chopped pecans**
- **2½ cups miniature marshmallows**
- **1 cup whipping cream, whipped**

Combine cream cheese and mayonnaise; mix well. Stir in cherries, pineapple, pecans and marshmallows; fold in whipped cream. Pour into an 8-cup ring mold; freeze. To serve, unmold onto a lettuce-lined serving platter.

Yield: Serves 12.

FROZEN CRAB SALAD

- **1 (8-ounce) package cream cheese, softened**
- **1 cup mayonnaise**
- **1 teaspoon Tabasco**
- **⅛ teaspoon salt**
- **1 cup heavy cream, whipped**
- **2 cups crabmeat**
- **1 cup chopped celery**
- **1 cup chopped bell pepper**
- **½ cup grated carrot**
- **1 tablespoon chopped onion**

Mix softened cream cheese, mayonnaise, Tabasco and salt together; beat until smooth. Fold in whipped cream, then crabmeat, celery, bell pepper, carrot and onion.

Pour mixture into a 9 x 5-inch loaf pan. Freeze until solid, at least 6 hours. To serve, remove from freezer and allow to stand at room temperature for 15 minutes. Slice and serve on lettuce leaves.

Yield: Serves 8.

CONGEALED CRANBERRY SALAD

- 3 cups fresh cranberries
- 2 cups water
- 2½ cups sugar
- 1 (6-ounce) box lemon gelatin
- 1 cup red seedless grapes, halved
- 1 (15¼-ounce) can crushed pineapple with juice
- 1 cup chopped walnuts

In a saucepan over medium heat, cook cranberries, water and sugar together until cranberries pop open. Add lemon gelatin and stir until gelatin is dissolved. Mix in grapes, crushed pineapple with juice and walnuts. Lightly oil a 13 x 9-inch glass dish with cooking spray and pour in cranberry mixture. Chill overnight or until set. To serve, cut into squares and serve on lettuce leaves.

Yield: Serves 12-15.

CORNBREAD SALAD

- 1 (8½-ounce) package cornbread mix
- 4 medium tomatoes, peeled and chopped
- 1 bell pepper, chopped
- 1 medium onion, chopped
- ½ cup chopped sweet pickles
- 9 slices bacon, crisply cooked and crumbled
- 1 cup mayonnaise
- ¼ cup sweet pickle juice

Prepare cornbread mix according to package directions. Bake, cool and crumble; set aside.

Combine tomatoes, bell pepper, onions, pickles and bacon; mix gently; set aside.

Combine mayonnaise and pickle juice; set aside.

In a large clear serving bowl, layer half of cornbread, half of tomato mixture then half of mayonnaise. Repeat layers. Cover and chill for 2 hours.

Yield: Serves 8.

MEXICAN CORNBREAD SALAD

- 1 (6-ounce) package Mexican cornbread mix
- 1 (4.5-ounce) can chopped green chilies, undrained
- 1 (1-ounce) package ranch-style salad dressing mix
- 1 (8-ounce) carton sour cream
- 1 cup mayonnaise
- 2 (16-ounce) cans pinto beans, drained
- 1 cup chopped bell pepper
- 2 (15¼-ounce) cans whole kernel corn, drained
- 3 large tomatoes, chopped
- 10 slices bacon, crisply cooked and crumbled
- 1 (8-ounce) package shredded Cheddar cheese
- 1 cup sliced green onions

Prepare cornbread according to package directions, adding green chilies. Cool and crumble; set aside.

Combine ranch-style salad dressing mix, sour cream and mayonnaise; mix well; set aside.

Combine beans, bell pepper, corn, tomatoes, bacon, cheese and onions.

In a clear serving bowl, layer half of cornbread. Top with half of bean mixture, then half of ranch dressing mixture. Repeat layers. Cover and refrigerate 2 hours.

Yield: Serves 8.

EASY CRANBERRY SALAD

- 2 (16-ounce) cans whole cranberry sauce
- 2 cups boiling water
- 1 (15¼-ounce) can crushed pineapple, drained well
- 1 (6-ounce) box cherry or raspberry gelatin
- ½ cup chopped nuts

Dissolve gelatin in boiling water. Add cranberry sauce, pineapple and nuts. Pour into a 2-quart dish or mold. Refrigerate until set.

Yield: Serves 12.

WALDORF CRANBERRY SALAD

- 2 cups fresh cranberries
- 2 cups miniature marshmallows
- ¾ cup sugar
- 2 cups unpeeled cubed green apple
- 1 cup seedless grapes
- ½ cup coarsely chopped walnuts
- 1 cup whipping cream, whipped

Process cranberries in food processor using steel blade until coarsely ground. Combine cranberries, marshmallows and sugar in a large bowl; stir gently. Cover and chill overnight.

Stir in apple, grapes, walnuts; mix gently. Fold in whipped cream; cover and chill 1 hour or more. Serve on lettuce leaves.

Yield: Serves 6-8.

CRÈME DE MENTHE SALAD

- **2 (3-ounce) packages lime gelatin**
- **1⅓ cups boiling water**
- **2 (8¼-ounce) cans crushed pineapple, reserve juice**
- **2 cups diced canned pears**
- **6 tablespoons crème de menthe**
- **1 cup sour cream**

Dissolve gelatin in boiling water.

Drain pineapple, reserving juice; set aside. Combine pineapple juice with crème de menthe; add enough water to equal 1⅓ cups liquid. Add to gelatin. Chill until mixture starts to thicken well.

Add sour cream to gelatin and beat mixture with electric mixer until light and fluffy. Fold in drained pineapple and pears.

Pour into oiled 13 x 9-inch flat glass dish. Chill until set. Cut into squares and serve with topping.

Yield: Serves 12-15.

Topping:

- **1 (16-ounce) carton sour cream or vanilla yogurt**
- **4 tablespoons lime juice**

Blend together and drizzle over top of gelatin.

BLUE CHEESE POTATO SALAD

- **2 pounds small red potatoes, cut into 1-inch pieces**
- **½ cup crumbled blue cheese**
- **⅓ cup mayonnaise**
- **1½ tablespoons lemon juice**
- **6 slices bacon, crisply cooked and crumbled**
- **1 cup finely chopped celery**
- **1 cup walnuts, coarsely chopped and toasted**
- **½ cup chopped dill pickle**
- **¼ cup chopped bell pepper**
- **Salt and pepper**

Boil potatoes until tender; drain and cool.

In a blender, puree blue cheese, mayonnaise and lemon juice.

Mix potatoes with bacon, celery, walnuts, pickle, bell pepper and blue cheese dressing mixture. Toss until well combined. Salt and pepper to taste.

Yield: Serves 4-6.

CHEESY FRUIT SALAD

- **3 apples, unpared and chopped**
- **2 cups minced celery**
- **1 (20-ounce) can pineapple tidbits, drained**
- **8 ounces sharp Cheddar cheese, diced**
- **¾ cup slivered almonds, toasted**
- **½ cup sour cream**
- **½ cup mayonnaise**

Combine apples, celery, pineapple, cheese and almonds in a large bowl; toss gently. Combine sour cream and mayonnaise; add to apple mixture, tossing gently to coat. Serve on lettuce leaves.

Yield: Serves 6.

EGG SALAD MOLD

Best made a day ahead.

2 packages unflavored gelatin
¾ cup boiling water
3 tablespoons vinegar
1 teaspoon Worcestershire sauce
1 teaspoon salt
¼ teaspoon dry mustard
1½ cups mayonnaise
¾ cup chopped celery
⅓ cup chopped bell pepper
⅓ cup chopped pimiento
2 tablespoons chopped onion
8 hard-boiled eggs, chopped
Pepper

Dissolve gelatin in water; add vinegar, Worcestershire sauce, salt and mustard. Cool 10 minutes. Stir in mayonnaise. Add celery, bell pepper, pimiento, onion and eggs. Blend together carefully. Adjust seasonings.

Pour into a well oiled 6-cup mold or ring mold. Chill until set. Unmold and serve with Chili Mayonnaise. If using a ring mold, place Chili Mayonnaise in center.

Yield: Serves 8-10.

Chili Mayonnaise:

1 cup mayonnaise
1 tablespoon chili powder
2 teaspoons finely minced green onion tops and bell pepper

Mix ingredients well.

FRUIT AND CABBAGE SALAD

- **2 oranges, pared and sectioned**
- **2 cups chopped apple**
- **2 cups shredded cabbage**
- **1 cup seedless grapes**
- **½ cup heavy cream, whipped**
- **1 tablespoon sugar**
- **1 tablespoon lemon juice**
- **¼ teaspoon salt**
- **½ cup mayonnaise**

Place fruit and cabbage into mixing bowl. Fold sugar, lemon juice and salt into whipped cream; stir in mayonnaise. Mix gently with fruit mixture and spoon onto lettuce-lined serving bowls.

Yield: Serves 4-6.

Save pickle juice and use in potato salad and cole slaw.

5 FRUIT SALAD

- **1 cup Mandarin oranges**
- **1 cup pineapple chunks**
- **1 cup coconut**
- **1 cup small marshmallows**
- **1 cup sour cream**
- **2 bananas, sliced**

Mix oranges, pineapple, coconut, marshmallows and sour cream and refrigerate a few hours. Before serving, add bananas.

Yield: Serves 4.

GORGONZOLA WALNUT SALAD

- **4 ounces Gorgonzola cheese, crumbled**
- **¼ cup olive oil**
- **1 tablespoon vinegar**
- **½ teaspoon salt**
- **¼ teaspoon freshly ground pepper**
- **1 medium head Romaine lettuce, torn into bite-size pieces**
- **1 cup chopped walnuts, toasted**

In a food processor or blender, process first 5 ingredients slightly leaving some cheese in pieces. Combine lettuce with walnuts in salad bowl; toss with Gorgonzola cheese mixture.

Yield: Serves 8.

Lettuce should always be torn, never cut, to prevent bruising.

GRAPEFRUIT SALAD

- **1 cup boiling water**
- **1 cup sugar**
- **3 packages unflavored gelatin**
- **⅔ cup cold water**
- **1 cup grapefruit juice**
- **3 cups grapefruit sections**
- **1 teaspoon lemon juice**

Mix boiling water with sugar in saucepan over low heat. Stir until sugar is dissolved. Mix gelatin and cold water together; add to hot sugar water and stir until gelatin is dissolved. Stir in grapefruit juice. Pour into bowl and refrigerate until thickened. Fold in grapefruit sections and lemon juice; spoon into a lightly oiled 1½-quart oblong glass dish or 8 oiled individual molds and chill until set. Serve topped with Celery Seed Dressing (see Page 106).

Yield: Serves 8.

GREEK SALAD

- 1 large head iceberg lettuce
- 3 cups potato salad
- 12 sprigs watercress
- 2 tomatoes cut into 6 wedges, each
- 1 cucumber peeled, cut lengthwise into 8 fingers
- 1 avocado, cut into wedges
- 4 slices feta cheese, cubed
- 1 bell pepper, cut into rings
- 4 slices canned beets
- 4 cooked shrimp, peeled
- 4 anchovy fillets (optional)
- 12 black Greek olives
- 8 Salonika peppers or pepperoncini
- 4 radishes, sliced
- 4 whole green onions
- Oregano
- Oil and vinegar dressing

Line serving bowl with lettuce leaves, place potato salad in a mound in the center. Shred lettuce and cover potato salad. Sprinkle watercress over lettuce. Place tomato wedges around outer edge of salad, a few on top. Put cucumber between tomatoes and avocados all around circle. Place feta cheese over top of salad, bell pepper rings over all. On very top, place beets with a shrimp on each beet slice. Arrange olives, peppers, radishes and onions as desired. Cover salad with favorite oil and vinegar dressing. Sprinkle well with oregano.

Yield: Serves 4 as a main dish.

Louis Pappas' Restaurant
Tarpon Springs, Florida

Variation: Make salad easier to prepare: Place potato salad in a large serving bowl, top with shredded lettuce mixed with all other salad ingredients cut up the way you prefer. Cover with oil and vinegar dressing and serve.

HACIENDA SALAD

- 1 medium head iceberg lettuce, torn into bite-size pieces
- 1 bunch green onions, sliced
- 2 medium tomatoes, cut into wedges
- 1 avocado, chopped
- 1 (15-ounce) can ranch-style beans, drained
- 1 cup shredded Cheddar cheese
- 1 (10½-ounce) package corn chips
- 3 sprigs cilantro, chopped
- ¼ teaspoon garlic powder
- Salt and pepper
- Salsa

Combine all ingredients except salsa in a large salad bowl; toss gently. Serve with salsa or other choice of salad dressing.

Yield: Serves 8-10.

HEAVENLY SALAD

- 1 (3-ounce) package raspberry or strawberry gelatin
- 2 apples, peeled and diced
- 1 cup finely chopped celery
- 1½ cups chopped pecans
- 1 cup pineapple chunks
- 1 cup whipping cream
- 3 tablespoons sugar
- 1 teaspoon vanilla extract

Prepare gelatin according to package directions; refrigerate until firm. Whip cream; add sugar and vanilla. Place firm gelatin in mixing bowl and using beaters, whip gelatin until light and frothy. Fold whipped cream into gelatin. Fold in apples, celery, nuts and pineapple. Refrigerate until serving time.

Yield: Serves 4-6.

HORSERADISH SALAD

- 1 (3-ounce) package lemon gelatin
- 1 (3-ounce) package lime gelatin
- 2 cups boiling water
- 1 cup mayonnaise
- 3 tablespoons prepared horseradish
- 1 (15½-ounce) can crushed pineapple, undrained
- 1 (2-ounce) jar diced pimientos
- ½ cup chopped pecans

Dissolve gelatin packages in boiling water. Combine gelatin mixture, mayonnaise and horseradish blending together until smooth. Stir in pineapple with juice, pimiento and nuts. Pour into an oiled 6-cup mold and chill until firm and set.

Yield: 6 servings.

HURRICANE SALAD

This salad got its name when Hurricane Camille hit the Gulf coast. The boats from the Broadwater Hotel Marina in Biloxi, Mississippi, went to Back Bay and everyone shared what they had on board. It's good!

- 1 (15-ounce) can green peas, drained
- 1 (15-ounce) can cut string beans, drained
- 3 stems celery, chopped
- 3 shallots, chopped
- ½ bell pepper, chopped
- 1 (4-ounce) jar pimientos, drained
- ⅓ cup sugar
- ⅓ cup white vinegar
- ⅓ cup oil
- ½ teaspoon paprika
- ¼ teaspoon pepper
- ¼-½ teaspoon salt

Blend the sugar, vinegar, oil, paprika, pepper and salt. Pour over vegetables and toss. Marinate overnight.

Yield: Serves 4.

MANDARIN SALAD

- ½ head lettuce, torn into bite-size pieces
- 1 cup thinly sliced celery
- 1 (10-ounce) can Mandarin oranges, drained
- 6 green onions, chopped
- ½ cup almonds, toasted
- 2 tablespoons tarragon vinegar
- 2 tablespoons sugar
- ½ teaspoon Tabasco
- 1 teaspoon salt
- ¼ cup salad oil

Combine lettuce, celery and Mandarin oranges in large bowl.

Mix the vinegar, sugar, Tabasco, salt and salad oil together. Pour over lettuce in bowl and toss.

Serve salad on individual plates topped with green onions and almonds.

Yield: Serves 6.

MINCEMEAT SALAD

Wonderful Holiday salad.

- 1 envelope unflavored gelatin
- ¼ cup cold water
- 1 (6-ounce) package cherry gelatin
- 3½ cups boiling water
- 1 (20½-ounce) jar brandy-flavored mincemeat
- 1 (8-ounce) can crushed pineapple, drained
- 1 apple, peeled and minced
- 1 cup chopped pecans or walnuts

Soften gelatin in cold water; set aside.

Dissolve cherry gelatin in boiling water; add unflavored gelatin, stirring until gelatin dissolves. Chill until thickened. Stir in remaining ingredients; pour into lightly oiled 8-cup mold. Chill until firm.

Yield: Serves 12-14.

LUNCHEON TUNA

- 1 (3-ounce) package lemon gelatin
- 1¼ cups boiling water
- 2 teaspoons vinegar
- ½ teaspoon salt
- 1 cup mayonnaise
- 1 (9¼-ounce) can tuna, drained
- 1 hard-boiled egg, chopped
- 2 tablespoons sliced pimiento-stuffed olives
- 1 tablespoon chopped bell pepper
- ¼ cup chopped onion

Dissolve gelatin in boiling water. Add vinegar and salt; mix well. Chill until thickened. Add remaining ingredients, stirring well. Spoon mixture into an oiled 9-inch square pan. Chill until firm. Cut into squares. Top with additional mayonnaise, if desired. Serve on lettuce leaf.

Yield: Serves 9.

GREEN PEA SALAD

- 4 (10-ounce) packages frozen green peas
- 1½ pounds bacon, crisply cooked and crumbled
- 2 cups sour cream
- 2 bunches green onions, finely chopped
- Salt and pepper
- 2 bunches watercress, finely chopped

Thaw peas, do not cook; blot with paper towel. Mix bacon with sour cream, onions, salt and pepper; toss with peas. Chill. To serve, add watercress and lightly toss with peas.

Yield: Serves 8-10.

GREEN PEA TUNA SALAD

1 (10-ounce) box frozen green peas
1 cup mayonnaise
1 tablespoon lemon juice
1 teaspoon soy sauce
⅛ teaspoon curry powder
2 (6½-ounce) cans white tuna, drained, flaked
1 (3-ounce) jar cocktail onions, drained and halved
1 cup chopped celery
1 (3-ounce) can chow mein noodles

Thaw peas, do not cook; set aside. Combine mayonnaise, lemon juice, soy sauce and curry powder. Mix tuna, onions and celery with mayonnaise mixture; toss with thawed peas. Chill several hours or overnight. Top with noodles before serving.

Yield: Serves 4-6.

GERMAN POTATO SALAD

6 medium red potatoes, boiled and diced
6 hard-boiled eggs, chopped
2 stalks celery, chopped
1 small onion, chopped
½ pound bacon
½ cup sugar
2 tablespoons all-purpose flour
1 egg
½ cup cider vinegar
½ cup water
Salt and pepper

In a mixing bowl, combine potatoes, eggs, celery and onion. Add salt and pepper to taste; toss together; set aside.

Cook bacon until crisp; drain on paper towels,. Reserve drippings in skillet.

In a small bowl, mix sugar and flour together; beat in egg, vinegar and water. Pour into bacon drippings in skillet and over low heat, stir until thickened. Pour directly over potato mixture; toss gently. Spoon potato salad onto serving plate, crumble bacon and sprinkle on top. Serve at room temperature.

Yield: Serves 6.

RAMEN NOODLE SALAD

- **2 packages Ramen noodles (discard flavor packets)**
- **¾ cup butter**
- **½ cup shelled sunflower seeds**
- **¾ cup slivered almonds**
- **1 bunch broccoli spears, chopped**
- **1 small head Romaine lettuce, cut into bite-size pieces**
- **⅓ cup chopped green onions**

Break up Ramen noodles; sauté in butter with sunflower seeds and almonds until golden brown. Cool.

Mix broccoli, lettuce and onions together. Toss with noodle mixture. Chill. To serve, place broccoli lettuce mixture in salad bowl and toss with dressing.

Yield: Serves 6-8.

Dressing:

- **1 cup salad oil**
- **½ cup sugar**
- **½ cup vinegar**
- **3 tablespoons soy sauce**
- **½ teaspoon salt**

Dressing: Blend all ingredients together thoroughly; chill.

PEANUT SLAW

- **3 cups shredded cabbage**
- **1 large carrot, grated**
- **1 Granny Smith apple, grated**
- **¼ cup mayonnaise**
- **3 tablespoons cider vinegar**
- **1 teaspoon sugar**
- **Salt and pepper**
- **½ cup salted peanuts, chopped**

Toss cabbage, carrot and apple. Whisk mayonnaise, vinegar and sugar together; add salt and pepper to taste. Pour over cabbage mixture; add peanuts. Toss until combined well. Chill for 2 hours.

Yield: Serves 4-6.

SUPER SLAW

- **1 medium head cabbage**
- **2 cups seedless grapes**
- **1 cup cashews, chopped**
- **1 cup mayonnaise**
- **1 tablespoon onion juice**
- **1 teaspoon garlic powder**
- **1 teaspoon salt**
- **1 teaspoon dry mustard**
- **2 tablespoons vinegar**

Shred cabbage; add grapes and nuts. Combine mayonnaise with remaining ingredients. Stir into shredded cabbage and toss. Chill.

Yield: Serves 8.

SHRIMP SALAD WITH WHITE REMOULADE SAUCE

- **4 hard-boiled eggs**
- **1 cup mayonnaise**
- **1 tablespoon anchovy paste**
- **2 tablespoons chopped parsley**
- **2 tablespoons chopped bell pepper**
- **2 tablespoons chopped onions**
- **2 tablespoons chopped celery**
- **¼ teaspoon mashed garlic**
- **1 teaspoon Worcestershire sauce**
- **2 tablespoons Creole mustard**
- **Salt and pepper to taste**
- **2 pounds shrimp, boiled, peeled and deveined**

Place eggs and all remaining ingredients (except shrimp) into a food processor or blender and blend until smooth. Pour over shrimp; chill. Serve on lettuce in salad bowls.

Yield: Serves 8.

Variation: Shrimp may be served as an appetizer.

SPINACH RASPBERRY SALAD

- **1 (10-ounce) package frozen raspberries in syrup, thawed**
- **¼ cup sugar**
- **2 teaspoons cornstarch**
- **½ cup cranberry-raspberry juice cocktail**
- **¼ cup red wine vinegar**
- **¼ teaspoon celery salt**
- **¼ teaspoon cinnamon**
- **¼ teaspoon ground cloves**
- **1 (10-ounce) package fresh spinach, rinsed and torn**
- **½ cup chopped walnuts**
- **½ cup raisins**
- **1 cup Mandarin oranges, drained**
- **4 green onions, chopped**

Place raspberries in blender. Blend until smooth. Mash through sieve to remove seeds. Set aside.

Mix sugar and cornstarch in saucepan; stir in cranberry-raspberry cocktail, vinegar, celery salt, cinnamon, cloves and raspberries. Simmer over medium heat until thickened. Pour into glass bowl; chill.

When ready to serve, place spinach, walnuts, raisins, Mandarin oranges and green onions in a salad bowl. Drizzle with half of chilled dressing. Toss salad to coat. Pass remaining dressing.

Yield: Serves 6-8.

Crisp up cut greens by placing in freezer in metal bowl for 5-10 minutes.

CHASEN'S ORIGINAL SPINACH SALAD

- 1 pound fresh spinach, torn into bite-size pieces
- ¾ pound bacon, crisply cooked and crumbled
- 2 tablespoons bacon drippings
- ¼ cup red wine vinegar
- 3 tablespoons tarragon vinegar
- 2 cloves garlic, crushed
- ⅔ cup olive oil or salad oil
- 1 teaspoon Worcestershire sauce
- 1 teaspoon salt
- 1 teaspoon pepper

Place spinach into a bowl, chill. Combine the 2 tablespoons bacon drippings with remaining ingredients; mix well. Salt and pepper chilled spinach to taste; add crumbled bacon. Pour just enough bacon dripping vinegar dressing over spinach to coat each leaf; toss and serve. Refrigerate any remaining dressing.

Yield: Serves 6-8.

SPINACH SALAD DRESSING

- ½ cup catsup
- 2 teaspoons salt
- 1 cup oil
- 1 clove garlic, minced
- ½ cup sugar
- ½ cup cider vinegar

Mix all ingredients well and refrigerate.

Yield: 2½ cups.

LAYERED STRAWBERRY SALAD

- **¾ cup butter, melted**
- **3 tablespoons brown sugar**
- **2½ cups crushed pretzels**
- **1 cup sugar**
- **1 (8-ounce) package cream cheese, softened**
- **1 (8-ounce) carton frozen whipped topping**
- **1 (6-ounce) package strawberry gelatin**
- **1½ cups boiling water**
- **1 cup cold water**
- **1 (16-ounce) package frozen strawberries, chopped**

Combine melted butter, brown sugar and pretzels; mix together well. Spread evenly into a 13 x 9-inch glass baking dish. Bake at 350° for 10 minutes; let cool thoroughly.

Cream sugar and cream cheese until light and fluffy; fold in frozen whipped topping. Spread over cooled crust.

Pour boiling water over gelatin; stir to dissolve. Add 1 cup cold water. Chill until thickened; stir in chopped frozen strawberries. Spread over cream cheese layer. Chill until congealed or overnight. To serve, cut into squares and place on lettuce lined salad plates.

Yield: Serves 12-15.

BLUE CHEESE DRESSING

- **1 (3-ounce) package cream cheese, softened**
- **1½ ounces crumbled blue cheese**
- **1 (8-ounce) carton sour cream**
- **1 teaspoon lemon juice**
- **½ teaspoon onion salt**
- **2 tablespoons milk**

Combine cream cheese and blue cheese; stir in sour cream and remaining ingredients. Cover and chill several hours.

Yield: 1½ cups.

CELERY SEED DRESSING

Use on any fruit salad.

½ cup sugar
1½ teaspoons salt
1½ teaspoons dry mustard
½ teaspoon celery seeds
¼ cup vinegar
1 cup salad oil
1½ teaspoons grated onion

In mixing bowl, blend first 5 ingredients together with electric beaters. With beaters running, add salad oil slowly until mixture is thick. Add onion.

Yield: 1¾ cups.

CREAMY FRENCH DRESSING

⅔ cup catsup
½ cup white vinegar
¼ cup sugar
2½ teaspoons dry mustard
1 teaspoon salt
¾ teaspoon pepper
1 teaspoon Worcestershire sauce
1 cup vegetable oil

Combine all ingredients except oil and beat until smooth. Add oil ¼ cup at a time, beating after each addition. Cover and chill several hours.

Yield: 2 cups.

HONEY-MUSTARD DRESSING

- **3/4 cup plain yogurt**
- **1/4 cup mayonnaise**
- **1/4 cup honey**
- **2 tablespoons Dijon mustard**
- **2 tablespoons coarse-grained mustard**
- **1 tablespoon vinegar**

Combine all ingredients in a small bowl; cover and chill several hours.

Yield: 1½ cups.

GREEK SALAD DRESSING

- **1½ cups olive oil**
- **1/4 cup white vinegar**
- **1/4 cup lemon juice**
- **1/4 teaspoon salt**
- **1/2 teaspoon pepper**
- **1 tablespoon oregano**
- **2 cloves garlic, minced**

Combine all ingredients in a jar; cover tightly and shake vigorously. Chill several hours. Shake again before serving.

Yield: 2 cups.

GREEN GODDESS DRESSING

A cool green, this mayonnaise variation is a refreshing dressing for fresh greens or seafood salads.

- **1 clove garlic, crushed**
- **2 anchovy fillets, finely chopped**
- **3 tablespoons green onions, finely chopped**
- **⅓ cup parsley, finely chopped**
- **½ cup sour cream**
- **1 tablespoon lime or lemon juice**
- **1 tablespoon tarragon vinegar**
- **Dash of salt and pepper**
- **1 cup mayonnaise**

Blend well. Chill.

Yield: 2 cups

PENNSYLVANIA DUTCH SALAD DRESSING

Wonderful on leaf lettuce, lettuce wedges or mixed greens.

- **2 hard-boiled eggs, finely chopped**
- **1 tablespoon finely chopped parsley**
- **2 tablespoons finely chopped celery**
- **1 tablespoon grated onion**
- **3 tablespoons salad oil**
- **1½ tablespoons vinegar**
- **½ teaspoon salt**
- **⅛ teaspoon pepper**

Blend eggs, onion and oil until well mixed. Add remaining ingredients; stir well. Store in covered container in refrigerator.

Yield: 1 cup.

SALAD DRESSING

- **2 cloves garlic, crushed**
- **1 teaspoon salt**
- **1 teaspoon fresh black pepper**
- **4 tablespoons salad oil**
- **5 tablespoons olive oil**
- **3 tablespoons lemon juice**
- **2 tablespoons cider vinegar**
- **1½ heaping tablespoons grated Parmesan cheese**
- **1½ heaping tablespoons grated Romano cheese**
- **1½ heaping tablespoons crumbled blue cheese**

Combine all ingredients, mixing well. Pour into a jar or plastic container. Shake well and serve over various green salads. Keep at room temperature. Do not refrigerate.

Yield: About 1½ cups.

VINAIGRETTE DRESSING

- **3 tablespoons balsamic vinegar**
- **1 tablespoon Dijon-style mustard**
- **1 cup extra-virgin olive oil**
- **Salt and pepper**

Whisk vinegar and mustard together in a bowl; season with salt and pepper. Dribble olive oil into the bowl in a slow steady stream, whisking constantly until dressing is creamy and thickened and the oil has been incorporated. Taste to correct seasoning.

Yield: 1¼ cups.

YESTERDAY'S SALAD DRESSING

For those of you who were around here in the 70's, you probably remember this salad dressing from Yesterday's Restaurant in Cashiers, North Carolina.

1 cup mayonnaise
1 cup olive oil
1 tablespoon tarragon vinegar
1 clove garlic, crushed

Blend together and toss on your favorite green salad.

Yield: 2 cups.

Add a dash of dry mustard to oil and vinegar dressing to slow separation.

Entrées

MEAT SEASONING BLEND

- 3 tablespoons dried whole thyme
- 2 tablespoons onion powder
- 1½ tablespoons ground cumin
- 1 tablespoon pepper
- 1 teaspoon ground cloves
- 1 teaspoon garlic powder
- ½ teaspoon ground bay leaves

Combine all ingredients. Store in airtight container in a cool, dry place. Use for all types of beef, pork, veal and lamb as well as meaty soups and stews.

MARINADE À LA LENNY

Good for all cuts of meat, especially London broil.

- ⅓ cup bourbon
- 3 tablespoons soy sauce
- 3 tablespoons Worcestershire sauce
- 2 tablespoons garlic vinegar
- 2 tablespoons vegetable oil
- ½ tablespoon pickling spice
- ½ tablespoon seasoned salt flavor enhancer
- ½ tablespoon ground pepper

Mix all ingredients together; refrigerate.

Yield: 1 cup.

ENCHILADAS

- 2 pounds ground beef
- 1 large onion, chopped
- 2 teaspoons salt
- 1 tablespoon chili powder
- ½ cup Enchilada Sauce

Enchilada Sauce

- 4 tablespoons flour
- 4 tablespoons vegetable oil
- 3 cups water
- 1 (6-ounce) can tomato paste
- 4 tablespoons chili powder
- 1 tablespoon cumin
- 1½ teaspoons salt
- 2 dozen corn tortillas
- Vegetable oil
- 1 large onion, chopped
- 1 pound sharp Cheddar cheese, shredded

Brown meat and onion; add salt, chili powder and ½ cup Enchilada Sauce; set aside.

To make Enchilada Sauce, heat oil in heavy pot; add flour stirring to blend. Stir in tomato paste; add water gradually. Add chili powder, cumin and salt, cooking until thickened and smooth; keep warm.

Separate tortillas. Using tongs, dip each tortilla in hot vegetable oil until limp then into Enchilada Sauce. Place 2 tablespoons meat mixture down center and roll. Place seam side down in a 13 x 9-inch baking dish.

Pour remaining Enchilada Sauce over enchiladas; sprinkle with chopped onion and top with cheese. Bake at 375° until bubbly and cheese browns, about 25-30 minutes.

Yield: Serves 10-12.

GRILLED HAMBURGERS SUPREME

- 1/4 cup plus 2 tablespoons catsup
- 2 tablespoons molasses
- 1 1/2 tablespoons Worcestershire sauce
- 1 small onion, cut in fourths
- 1 clove garlic
- 1 teaspoon parsley flakes
- 1 teaspoon salt
- 1/2 teaspoon pepper
- 1/4 teaspoon ground nutmeg
- 1/4 teaspoon ground cinnamon
- 3 pounds ground round steak

Combine first 10 ingredients in food processor or blender and process until smooth (do not overprocess). Add to ground round, mixing well. Shape into 6 patties about 3/4-inch thick.

Grill patties 3-5 inches from slow coals for 5-7 minutes on each side or until desired degree of doneness.

Yield: Serves 6.

SWEET AND SOUR MEAT LOAF

- 1 (15-ounce) can tomato sauce
- 1/2 cup firmly packed brown sugar
- 1/4 cup cider vinegar
- 1 teaspoon prepared mustard
- 1 teaspoon salt
- 1/4 teaspoon pepper
- 2 pounds ground beef
- 1/2 pound ground pork
- 2 eggs, slightly beaten
- 1/4 cup chopped onion
- 1 cup soft breadcrumbs

Combine tomato sauce, brown sugar, vinegar and mustard; set aside. Combine the meats; add salt, pepper, eggs, onion and breadcrumbs. Stir in 1 cup of tomato sauce mixture into meat, mixing well. Place meat into a 2-quart shallow greased baking dish; form into a loaf. Pour 1/4 cup of sauce on top of loaf. Bake at 350° for 1 1/2 hours. Heat remaining sauce and serve with the meat loaf.

Yield: Serves 6-8.

ITALIAN MEAT ROLL

- 2 eggs, beaten
- 1 cup cracker crumbs
- ½ cup tomato juice
- 2 tablespoons minced parsley
- ½ teaspoon oregano
- 1 clove garlic, minced
- ½ teaspoon salt
- ½ teaspoon pepper
- 2 pounds lean ground beef
- 4 tablespoons raisins
- ½ cup minced onion
- 2 tablespoons pine nuts
- ¼ cup grated Romano cheese
- ¼ pound prosciutto, thinly sliced

Combine eggs, cracker crumbs and tomato juice; mix well. Blend with next 6 ingredients, mixing meat and ingredients well. Arrange the meat mixture on foil or wax paper into a 12 x 10-inch rectangle.

Combine raisins, onion, pine nuts, cheese and prosciutto. Spread on meat rectangle evenly. Starting from short end, carefully roll meat, using wax paper as an aid. Seal edges and ends, place roll seam side down on greased baking pan. Pour topping over meat roll. Bake at 350° for 1 hour 20 minutes. Let stand 5 minutes. Slice and serve.

Yield: Serves 6-8

Topping

- 2 cups red wine
- ½ teaspoons garlic salt
- 6 drops Tabasco
- 1 (6-ounce) can tomato paste
- ½ teaspoon dried Italian seasoning

Combine; mix well.

LASAGNA

The best lasagna recipe ever! If prepared a day ahead, it's not necessary to cook the lasagna noodles.

- **2 pounds lean ground round**
- **1 clove garlic, minced**
- **1 tablespoon minced fresh parsley**
- **1 tablespoon basil**
- **1 large onion, chopped**
- **1½ teaspoons salt**
- **1 (16-ounce) can tomatoes**
- **2 (6-ounce) cans tomato paste**
- **1 (10-ounce) package lasagna noodles**
- **2 (12-ounce) cartons cream-style cottage cheese**
- **2 eggs, beaten**
- **2 teaspoons salt**
- **½ teaspoon cayenne pepper**
- **2 tablespoons minced fresh parsley**
- **½ cup grated Parmesan cheese**
- **2½ pounds mozzarella cheese (grated or sliced)**

Brown meat; add garlic, parsley, basil, onion and salt. Cook 10 minutes; add tomatoes and tomato paste and simmer uncovered 1 hour. Cook noodles in salted water al dente.

Combine cottage cheese, eggs, salt, pepper, parsley and Parmesan cheese; mix thoroughly. Place half of the noodles in a greased 13 x 9-inch baking dish; spread with half of the cottage cheese mixture, add mozzarella cheese to cover; add half of the meat mixture. Repeat layers ending with meat. Cover top with mozzarella cheese. Bake at 375° for 40 minutes. Remove from oven and let stand at least 10 minutes before cutting into squares.

Yield: Serves 8-10.

TAMALE CASSEROLE

- **½ pound bulk pork sausage**
- **1 cup minced onion**
- **¾ cup minced bell pepper**
- **½ pound ground beef**
- **1 cup whole kernel corn**
- **1 cup ripe olives, sliced**
- **2 tablespoons water from olives**
- **1½ teaspoons salt**
- **1 teaspoon chili powder**
- **½ teaspoon garlic salt**
- **1½ cups tomato sauce**
- **2 (13½-ounce) jars beef tamales**
- **1 cup shredded sharp Cheddar cheese**

Brown sausage; remove to drain on paper towels. In 3 tablespoons sausage drippings, sauté onion and bell pepper until tender. Stir in ground beef; brown. Add sausage, corn, olives, olive liquid and seasonings; stir in tomato sauce. Simmer sauce 15 minutes. Pour into a 13 x 9-inch baking dish. Remove paper covers from tamales and arrange over top of sauce. Bake uncovered at 350° for 15 minutes. Sprinkle with cheese and bake 20 minutes until bubbly.

Yield: Serves 6-8.

PICADILLO

Cuban hash.

Olive oil
1 onion, finely chopped
1 clove garlic, crushed
1 medium bell pepper, chopped
1 pound lean ground beef
1 tablespoon capers with juice
1 (2-ounce) jar chopped pimientos, drained
2 jalapeño peppers, finely chopped
⅓ cup raisins
Salt and pepper
Pinch of allspice
12 large pimiento-stuffed olives, sliced
1½ cups crushed fresh tomatoes, or canned

Sauté onions, garlic and bell pepper in small amount of olive oil until tender; add ground beef and brown. Add all remaining ingredients; mix well. Simmer over medium-low heat 25-30 minutes. Serve over hot rice.

Yield: Serves 4-6.

SPAGHETTI SAUCE

- 4 slices bacon
- 2 pounds ground beef
- 1 large onion, chopped
- 1 large bell pepper, chopped
- 1 (12-ounce) can beer
- 1 (15-ounce) can tomato sauce
- 1½ cups water
- 1 (6-ounce) can tomato paste
- 1 bay leaf
- 1 teaspoon garlic powder
- 1 tablespoon parsley flakes
- 1 teaspoon dried basil
- 1 teaspoon dried oregano
- 1 (6-ounce) can sliced mushrooms, drained
- ½ teaspoon salt
- ½ teaspoon pepper

Cook bacon until crisp; reserve drippings. Crumble bacon; set aside.

Add ground beef, onion and bell pepper. Cook until beef is browned, stirring to crumble meat. Drain off fat; stir in beer and simmer 10 minutes. Add remaining ingredients; simmer uncovered 30-40 minutes. Remove bay leaf; stir in bacon. Spoon sauce over spaghetti.

Yield: 8 cups.

BEEF ROAST

4½ pound beef roast, cut of your choice
2 tablespoons vegetable oil
1 large onion, sliced
1 tablespoon dry mustard
1½ tablespoons light brown sugar
2 teaspoons salt
½ teaspoon pepper
¼ cup vinegar, cider or tarragon
¼ cup water

Brown meat in oil on all sides; place in roasting pan. Cover top of roast with sliced onions. Combine mustard, brown sugar, salt, pepper, vinegar and water together, mixing well; pour over roast. Cover and bake at 350° for 2½ hours until very tender. Drain off excess fat. Use pan juices for gravy (optional). Remove roast to platter. Let stand 10 minutes before slicing.

Yield: Serves 6-8.

BONELESS RIB ROAST

4-5 pound boneless rib eye roast
Worcestershire sauce
Coarse black pepper
Kosher salt

Bring roast to room temperature (important). Preheat oven to 500°. Rub roast all over with Worcestershire sauce, coarse black pepper and coarse salt.

Put roast in a foil-lined roasting pan place in a 500° oven. Bake 5 minutes to the pound (5-pound roast = 25 minutes). Turn oven off. Leave roast in oven for 2 hours counting from the time you first put it in the oven. Do Not Open Oven Door.

Meat will be evenly pink inside and you will have drippings for au jus or gravy.

Yield: Serves 8-10.

WHISKEY PLUS BEEF STEW

- 2½ pounds chuck roast, cut into cubes
- 3 tablespoons butter
- 2 tablespoons brandy
- 3 tablespoons all-purpose flour
- 2 beef bouillon cubes
- 2 tablespoons tomato paste
- 1½ cups Burgundy wine
- ¾ cup dry sherry
- ¾ cup port
- 1 (10-ounce) can beef bouillon
- ⅛ teaspoon salt
- 4 peppercorns
- 3 bay leaves
- Pinch of thyme
- 1 clove garlic, minced
- 1 (16-ounce) can white onions, drained
- 1 (16-ounce) can button mushrooms, drained

In a Dutch oven or large soup pot, brown beef cubes in butter; remove meat. Add brandy to pot and heat until vapor rises; ignite brandy and return meat to pot. Remove meat again. Over low heat, add next 3 ingredients; stir to blend. Add next 4 ingredients; mix all together well. Add beef to pot with beef bouillon, salt, peppercorns, bay leaves, thyme and garlic. Remove from heat; add onions and mushrooms. Let cool slightly and refrigerate overnight.

Pour stew into a 2-quart casserole and bake at 325° for 1 hour. Serve over rice or mashed potatoes.

Yield: Serves 6-8.

BEEF TENDERLOIN

- **1 cup port wine**
- **1 cup soy sauce**
- **½ cup olive oil**
- **½ teaspoon onion powder**
- **½ teaspoon pepper**
- **½ teaspoon garlic powder**
- **¼ teaspoon ground cloves**
- **½ teaspoon dried ground thyme**
- **5-6 pound beef tenderloin, trimmed**

Combine wine, soy sauce, oil and seasonings; mix well. Place tenderloin in a large shallow dish; pour wine mixture over top and cover tightly. Refrigerate 8 hours, turning occasionally.

Remove tenderloin; reserve marinade. Place meat on rack in roasting pan; insert meat thermometer making sure it does not touch fat. Bake at 425° for 45-60 minutes until thermometer registers 140° (rare), basting with marinade occasionally. Bake until thermometer registers 150° (medium rare) or 160° (medium). Transfer to serving platter. Let sit 15 minutes before slicing.

Yield: Serves 10-12.

Bring roasts and steaks to room temperature before cooking.

GRILLED TERIYAKI FLANK STEAK

- **¼ cup soy sauce**
- **¼ cup vinegar**
- **¼ cup honey**
- **1½ teaspoons garlic powder**
- **1½ teaspoons ground ginger**
- **¾ cup salad oil**
- **1 onion, finely chopped**
- **1½ pound flank steak**

Place steak in a shallow baking dish. Combine remaining ingredients; mixing well. Pour over steak; cover and marinate in refrigerator 4 hours, turning steak occasionally.

Remove steak from marinade, reserving marinade for basting. Grill 5 inches from hot coals about 4 minutes on each side (for rare) turning frequently and basting with marinade.

To serve, slice across grain into thin slices.

Yield: Serves 4-6.

Sprinkle meat with paprika before frying and it will turn a golden brown.

GRILLADES

Traditionally served with grits.

- **4½ pound round steak**
- **½ cup bacon drippings, divided**
- **½ cup all-purpose flour**
- **1 cup chopped onion**
- **2 cups chopped green onions**
- **¾ cup chopped celery**
- **1½ cups chopped bell pepper**
- **2 cloves garlic, minced**
- **2 cups peeled and chopped tomatoes**
- **½ teaspoon tarragon leaves**
- **1 teaspoon thyme**
- **1 cup water**
- **1 cup Burgundy wine**
- **1 teaspoon salt**
- **½ teaspoon pepper**
- **2 bay leaves**
- **½ teaspoon Tabasco**
- **2 tablespoons Worcestershire sauce**
- **3 tablespoons chopped parsley**

Cut meat into ½-inch pieces. Sauté 2-3 minutes until browned in ¼ cup bacon drippings in heavy Dutch oven; remove and set aside.

Add remaining ¼ cup bacon drippings to Dutch oven. Add flour, cook over medium heat stirring until flour is caramel colored. Add onion, green onions, celery, bell pepper and garlic; cook until tender. Add tomatoes, tarragon and thyme. Cook, stirring constantly, 3 minutes. Add water and next 6 ingredients, stirring until blended. Return meat and bring mixture to boil; cover and reduce heat. Simmer 1 hour, stirring occasionally. Uncover and simmer 30 minutes. Remove bay leaves and stir in parsley.

Yield: Serves 12.

SAUERBRATEN WITH POTATO PANCAKES

- **1 cup red wine vinegar**
- **1 cup red wine**
- **1 cup water**
- **2 medium onions, sliced, divided**
- **2 tablespoons sugar**
- **2 bay leaves**
- **2 tablespoons allspice**
- **2 teaspoons whole cloves**
- **½ teaspoon peppercorns**
- **4 pound chuck, rump or round roast**
- **1 teaspoon salt and pepper**
- **3 tablespoons all-purpose flour**
- **2 tablespoons vegetable oil**
- **½ cup finely crushed gingersnaps**
- **½ cup sour cream**

Combine first 9 ingredients (only one onion) in a large bowl; add roast, turning to coat. Add more water, if needed, to cover meat. Cover, refrigerate 3-4 days turning with wooden spoons twice daily. Do not pierce meat.

Remove meat; reserve marinade. Salt and pepper meat; coat with flour and brown in oil on all sides; set aside. Sauté remaining onion until tender; add 2½ cups marinade to the roast. Cover and simmer on low heat 4 hours until fork tender, adding more marinade if necessary, turning occasionally. Remove roast; keep warm. Whisk flour into pan drippings and any remaining marinade until smooth and thickened. Stir in gingersnaps and sour cream. Taste for seasonings; adjust. Spoon some gravy over roast; pass remainder when serving. Serve with potato pancakes.

Yield: Serves 10-12.

Potato Pancakes

- **4 medium potatoes, peeled and grated**
- **1 cup cooked, mashed potatoes**
- **¼ cup grated onion**
- **½ teaspoon caraway seeds**
- **1 teaspoon salt**
- **½ teaspoon pepper**
- **3 tablespoons butter or vegetable oil**

Combine both of the potatoes, onion, caraway seeds, salt and pepper; mix well. Heat 2 tablespoons butter in a large heavy skillet. For each pancake, spoon ¼ cup batter into skillet. Cook until brown and crisp on one side; turn over and cook until crisp. Repeat using all potato mixture, using more butter if needed.

Yield: About 12 pancakes.

BONED LEG OF LAMB IN MUSTARD CRUST

Add a few juniper berries where lamb is tied together!

- **½ cup Dijon mustard**
- **2 tablespoons soy sauce**
- **2 cloves garlic, pressed**
- **½ teaspoon ground thyme**
- **½ teaspoon rosemary**
- **¼ teaspoon ginger**
- **2 tablespoons olive oil**
- **¼ cup all-purpose flour**
- **6 pound leg of lamb, boned, rolled and tied**
- **1 cup water**

Combine mustard, soy sauce, garlic, thyme, rosemary, ginger, olive oil; whisk in flour. Place lamb on rack in shallow roasting pan. Spread mustard-flour mixture over meat evenly; set aside. Refrigerate several hours.

Pour water into roasting pan and bake at 325° about 2 hours until meat thermometer registers 145° for medium. (Maintain water level in pan during cooking.)

Let baked lamb rest 15 minutes before serving.

Yield: Serves 8.

LAMB SHANKS À LA SOUTH

- **4 medium lamb shanks**
- **1 envelope onion soup mix**
- **1 cup regular strong coffee**
- **1 cup bourbon**

Place lamb shanks in a crockpot, top with onion soup mix. Mix coffee and bourbon together and pour over soup mix. Cover crockpot and cook on low temperature 8-10 hours or cover crockpot and cook on high temperature for 5-6 hours.

Yield: Serves 4.

MARINATED LAMB CHOPS

- **6 lamb chops, 1-inch thick**
- **1 teaspoon dry mustard**
- **½ teaspoon salt**
- **¼ teaspoon paprika**
- **2 cloves garlic, pressed**
- **3 tablespoons vinegar**
- **5 tablespoons extra virgin olive oil**

Place lamb chops in baking pan. Combine remaining ingredients and pour over chops; marinate for 3-4 hours refrigerated.

Grill chops over a hot fire, basting occasionally with marinade. Cook 5 minutes on each side for medium rare.

Yield: Serves 3-6.

MARTI'S LOW COUNTRY BARBEQUE

May be served as a meat main dish or for sandwiches.

- **8 pounds boneless pork loin roast**
- **2 cups vinegar**
- **2 tablespoons crushed red pepper**

Place roast in a casserole or roasting pan. Cover tightly with foil. Bake at 250° for 7-8 hours. Remove from pan. Trim roast removing unwanted fat and shred meat (it will shred easily). Toss with pan drippings, vinegar and pepper.

Yield: Serves 24-30.

Variation: Discard pan drippings after baking and serve shredded meat with your favorite barbeque sauce.

GERMAN LOIN OF PORK

- **5 pound loin of pork roast**
- **2 quarts water**
- **2 bay leaves**
- **8 whole allspice**
- **6 whole black peppercorns**
- **6 slices bacon, cut in ½-inch pieces**
- **1½ cups chopped onion**
- **1½ cups cubed apple**
- **¼ cup firmly packed brown sugar**
- **1 bay leaf, crushed**
- **2 (16-ounce) cans sauerkraut, drained**
- **1 cup white wine**

In large pot or Dutch oven, place pork, water, bay leaves, allspice and peppercorns. Bring to boil; lower heat and simmer 1 hour. Remove pork; reserve 1 cup liquid.

Cook bacon, onion and apple until bacon is crisp and onion is tender. Stir in brown sugar, crushed bay leaf, sauerkraut and wine; add 1 cup liquid from pork. Pour into roasting pan. Place pork in center of pan on top of sauerkraut. Bake uncovered at 350° for 30 minutes. Cover and bake until pork is fork tender. Serve sliced with the sauerkraut.

Yield: Serves 8.

BEER RIBS

- **⅓ cup dark beer**
- **⅓ cup soy sauce**
- **⅓ cup Dijon mustard**
- **½ cup firmly packed brown sugar**
- **1 onion, minced**
- **1 teaspoon Worcestershire sauce**
- **4 pounds lean spareribs, halved crosswise by butcher**

Combine beer with next 5 ingredients; set aside.

In a heavy pot, cover spareribs with water, bring to a boil, adding salt to taste. Simmer ribs, skimming froth, for 20 minutes; drain. Rinse under cold water. Cut ribs into 1-rib sections and cover with beer mixture. Let marinate covered at room temperature for 2 hours (or chilled overnight). Arrange ribs in baking pan, brush with marinade and bake at 350° for 1 hour until tender and glazed.

Yield: Serves 8.

OVEN RIBS

- 6 pounds spareribs or back ribs
- ¼ cup paprika
- 2 teaspoons garlic powder
- 1 teaspoon pepper
- 1 teaspoon white pepper
- Soy sauce
- Barbeque Sauce

Place ribs in a 15 x 10-inch shallow baking pan. Combine paprika with garlic powder and peppers. Rub paprika mixture over entire surface of ribs. Cover and refrigerate several hours.

Remove pan from refrigerator and sprinkle soy sauce over ribs until ribs are covered. Baste ribs with Barbeque Sauce; cover and bake at 325° for 2 hours. Spoon barbeque sauce over ribs twice during baking. Uncover ribs; bake an additional 20-30 minutes until ribs are browned and fork tender.

Yield: Serves 4.

Barbeque Sauce

- 2 cups catsup
- 1 cup chopped onion
- ¼ cup red wine
- ¼ cup dark corn syrup
- 1 tablespoon Worcestershire sauce
- ¼ cup canola oil
- 1 teaspoon salt
- 1 tablespoon chili powder
- 2 teaspoons pepper
- ¼ cup lemon juice
- 6 drops Tabasco

Combine all ingredients in saucepan; simmer over low heat 20 minutes.

Yield: 3½ cups.

PORK TENDERLOIN

- ½ cup soy sauce
- ¼ cup bourbon
- 2 tablespoons brown sugar
- 3 pound pork tenderloin
- ⅓ cup sour cream
- ⅓ cup mayonnaise
- 1 tablespoon dry mustard
- 3 green onions, chopped

Combine soy sauce, bourbon and brown sugar; mix well. Place tenderloin in shallow pan and cover with sauce. Marinate in refrigerator several hours or overnight, turning occasionally. Reserve marinade.

Place tenderloin in baking pan and bake at 325° for 1 hour basting occasionally with marinade.

Combine sour cream, mayonnaise, mustard and onions. Refrigerate several hours for flavors to blend. Serve with sliced cooked tenderloin.

Yield: Serves 6-8.

BABY BOOMER PORK CHOPS

- 6 loin pork chops
- 2 tablespoons butter
- 1 (4-ounce) jar peach puree baby food
- Salt and pepper

Brown pork chops in butter. Place in flat 2-quart casserole baking dish. Season chops and top each with 1½ tablespoons peach puree.

Bake at 350° for 1 hour.

Yield: Serves 3-6.

LEMON PORK CHOPS

- 4 loin pork chops
- ½ teaspoon paprika
- ½ teaspoon salt
- ¼ teaspoon pepper
- ½ cup uncooked rice
- 1 medium onion
- 4 lemon slices
- 1 large bell pepper
- ¼ cup tomato juice
- 2 teaspoons sugar
- ½ teaspoon chili powder
- 1 bay leaf
- 1 teaspoon salt

Sprinkle chops with paprika and ½ teaspoon salt; brown in large hot skillet. Cut two ¼-inch slices from center of onion; separate into rings and chop remaining onion. Combine chopped onion with rice. Cut pepper into 4 rings.

Arrange chops in skillet; place lemon slice and onion slice on each chop. Arrange pepper rings around chops and fill with onion rice mixture.

Combine tomato juice, sugar, chili powder, bay leaf and salt. Pour over chops and top with remaining onion rings. Simmer for 45 minutes until chops are very tender. Serve chops topped with rice-stuffed pepper rings. Spoon sauce over top.

Yield: Serves 4.

SHERRY PORK CHOPS

6 loin pork chops
Salt to taste
Seasoned pepper to taste
2 tablespoons butter
3 tablespoons onion soup mix
1 (2½-ounce) jar sliced mushrooms, drained
½ cup sherry
1 cup sour cream
¼ cup water

Sprinkle chops with salt and pepper; brown on both sides in butter. Remove chops and place in a shallow 2-quart casserole. Combine remaining ingredients; pour over chops. Cover and bake at 350° for 1 hour.

Yield: Serves 3-6.

HAM LOAF

1 pound ground cooked ham
½ teaspoon onion powder
1 pound ground fresh pork
2 eggs, slightly beaten
¼ teaspoon salt
¼ teaspoon seasoned pepper
1 cup cracker crumbs
¾ cup firmly packed brown sugar
1½ teaspoons dry mustard
¼ cup vinegar
1 (16-ounce) can whole berry cranberry sauce

Combine first 7 ingredients; mix well. Shape mixture into a 9 x 5-inch loaf; place in a 10 x 6-inch baking dish.

Combine sugar, mustard and vinegar; mix well and spoon half over ham loaf. Bake at 350° for 1 hour and 20 minutes, basting twice with remaining sugar mixture. Top with cranberry sauce and bake an additional 10 minutes.

Yield: Serves 6-8.

TANGY PORK CHOPS

- 4 (3/4-inch) pork chops
- 1/4 teaspoon salt
- 1/4 teaspoon pepper
- 4 lemon slices
- 1/4 cup firmly packed brown sugar
- 1/3 cup catsup
- 1/3 cup water

Sprinkle pork chops with salt and pepper; arrange in a 9-inch square baking pan. Place a lemon slice on center of each chop. Top each lemon slice with 1 tablespoon brown sugar.

Combine catsup and water, mixing well. Pour sauce around chops.

Bake, uncovered, at 350° for 1 hour or until very tender.

Yield: Serves 4.

VEAL DEAL

- 4-6 veal chops
- 2 tablespoons butter
- 3/4 cup beef bouillon
- 1/4 cup dry sherry
- 1/4 teaspoon thyme
- Juice and grated rind of 1 lemon
- 1/2 cup sour cream
- 6 ounces fresh or canned mushrooms (optional)

In heavy skillet, brown chops on both sides in butter (if using mushrooms, sauté until limp). Remove meat; pour off excess fat saving crispy part of drippings. Add bouillon, sherry, thyme, lemon juice, rind and sour cream. Stir over low heat until smooth. Return meat to sauce, cover and cook slowly 30 minutes or until meat is tender. If using mushrooms, add to sauce.

Yield: Serves 4.

Variation: Substitute either pork chops or chicken breasts and follow same recipe directions.

VEAL CHOPS IN SOUR CREAM

- 4 veal loin chops, 1-inch thick
- 1/4 cup all-purpose flour
- 1 teaspoon salt
- 1/8 teaspoon pepper
- 1/4 teaspoon dried marjoram
- 1/4 teaspoon basil
- 2 tablespoons butter
- 1 teaspoon snipped chives
- 1/4 cup chili sauce
- 1/2 cup water
- 1 tablespoon all-purpose flour
- 1 tablespoon water
- 1 cup sour cream

Mix flour, salt, pepper, marjoram and basil; coat chops with this mixture. Heat butter in a skillet; sauté chops until well browned. Place in 11 x 7-inch casserole. Combine chives, chili sauce and water; pour over veal chops. Bake at 325° about 45 minutes. Remove chops and keep warm. Blend 1 tablespoon flour with water. Skim off excess fat from pan drippings; stir in flour mixture and cook until smooth and thickened; stir in the sour cream. Pass the sauce separately in a gravy boat.

Yield: Serves 4.

VEAL PAPRIKA

- 6 slices bacon, diced
- 3 1/2 pounds boneless veal shoulder, cut into 1/2-inch cubes
- 2/3 cup chopped onion
- 3 (13-ounce) cans chicken broth (5 cups)
- 3 tablespoons paprika
- 1 1/2 teaspoons salt
- 3 tablespoons flour
- 1/2 cup water
- 1 cup sour cream
- 1/2 cup toasted chopped almonds

Sauté bacon with veal and onions until meat and onion are golden brown. Add chicken broth, paprika and salt. Cover and simmer slowly (about 1 1/2 hours) until meat is tender. Blend flour and water with sour cream. Stir into veal and cook until sauce thickens, stirring constantly. Taste for seasonings. Serve over noodles or rice garnished with toasted almonds.

Yield: Serves 8.

OSSO BUCO

Veal Milanese style.

- 6 pound shin bone of veal cut
- 1 cup flour
- ½ teaspoon salt
- ½ teaspoon pepper
- ¼ cup olive oil
- 4 tablespoons butter
- 2 medium onions, chopped
- 1 clove garlic
- ½ teaspoon grated lemon rind
- 3 tablespoons chopped parsley
- 12 whole baby carrots
- 1 (15-ounce) can crushed tomatoes
- ½ teaspoon dried basil and oregano
- 1 cup white wine
- 1 cup beef or chicken broth

Have butcher saw or cut shin bone into six 2½-3 inch pieces. Mix flour, salt and pepper; roll veal in flour mixture to coat. In a heavy pot, sauté in olive oil and butter until all sides are browned. Drain most of fat.

Add all remaining ingredients to pot in order given. Cover and simmer over low heat for 1½-2 hours until very tender. Serve with rice.

Yield: Serves 6.

BRUNSWICK STEW

- **1 (3-pound) broiler-fryer chicken**
- **1 tablespoon salt**
- **2 quarts water**
- **1 pound cooked ham, cut into cubes**
- **2 large onions, chopped**
- **1 bell pepper, chopped**
- **2 tablespoons chopped fresh parsley**
- **1 (16-ounce) can stewed tomatoes, undrained**
- **1 (16-ounce) can whole kernel corn, drained**
- **1 (10-ounce) package frozen baby lima beans**
- **1 (10-ounce) package frozen okra, sliced**
- **1 teaspoon salt**
- **½ teaspoon pepper**
- **½ teaspoon dried thyme**
- **1 bay leaf**
- **1¼ teaspoons Tabasco**

Combine first 3 ingredients in a large Dutch oven; bring to boil. Cover and simmer on low heat 1 hour. Remove chicken; reserve broth. Skin, bone and coarsely chop chicken. Combine reserved chicken broth, chicken meat, ham and all remaining ingredients in a large Dutch oven or soup pot. Cover and simmer 2 hours, adding water for thinner consistency if desired. Discard bay leaf.

Yield: 1 gallon.

CHICKEN FOR TWO

- **2 chicken breast halves**
- **½ (10¾-ounce) can cream of mushroom soup, undiluted**
- **3 tablespoons dry onion soup mix**

Place each chicken breast half on a square of heavy-duty aluminum foil. Combine soup and onion soup mix; spread half on each piece of chicken. Wrap foil securely leaving some space around chicken. Bake at 350° for 1 hour.

Yield: Serves 2.

CASHEW CHICKEN

- 4 cups cooked diced chicken breast
- 2 (10¾-ounce) cans cream of mushroom soup, undiluted
- ½ cup chicken broth
- 2 cups diced celery
- ½ cup chopped green onions
- 2 (8-ounce) cans water chestnuts, sliced
- 2 tablespoons soy sauce
- 2 (3-ounce) cans chow mein noodles
- 2 cups broken cashew nuts

Combine chicken, mushroom soup and chicken broth in a large mixing bowl; blend well. Stir in celery, onions, water chestnuts and soy sauce; mix together well. Add chow mein noodles, reserving ½ cup. Add cashew nuts, reserving ½ cup. Mix together and pour into a greased 13 x 9-inch baking dish. Mix reserved noodles and cashew nuts together and sprinkle on top. Bake at 350° for 35-40 minutes or until bubbly and hot.

Yield: Serves 12.

CHICKEN AND BISCUITS

- 3 cups cooked diced chicken
- 1 (10-ounce) package frozen green peas
- 1 (10¾-ounce) can cream of chicken soup, undiluted
- ½ cup sour cream
- ½ cup milk
- ½ teaspoon salt
- ¼ teaspoon pepper
- 1½ cups shredded Cheddar cheese
- 1 (10-count) roll refrigerated buttermilk biscuits

Heat chicken, peas, soup, sour cream, milk, salt and pepper in saucepan to boiling. Place hot mixture into a 2-quart oblong shallow baking dish. Sprinkle cheese evenly over top. Place biscuits on top of cheese layer evenly (cut a couple in half to fit). Bake at 400° for 15 minutes or until biscuits are browned.

Yield: Serves 4-6.

CHICKEN BREASTS IN WINE

- 6 boneless, skinless chicken breast halves
- Salt and pepper
- 1/4 cup butter
- 1 (10 3/4-ounce) can cream of chicken soup
- 3/4 cup Sauterne or other white wine
- 1 (8-ounce) can sliced water chestnuts
- 1 (3-ounce) can chopped mushrooms
- 2 tablespoons chopped bell pepper
- 1/4 teaspoon dried thyme

Lightly season chicken with salt and pepper; brown in butter in skillet. Transfer to a shallow 2-quart baking dish. Add soup to drippings in skillet and slowly add wine, stirring until smooth. Heat to boiling and pour over chicken. Sprinkle water chestnuts, mushrooms, bell pepper and thyme over chicken. Cover with foil. Bake at 350° for 25 minutes. Remove foil and bake 20-30 minutes longer. Serve with rice.

Yield: 4-6 servings.

COMPANY CASSEROLE

- 1 (7-ounce) package wild rice
- 1 (4-ounce) can sliced mushrooms, undrained
- 1 teaspoon Worcestershire sauce
- 2 (10 3/4-ounce) cans cream of mushroom soup, undiluted
- 1 pound bulk pork sausage
- 3 cups chopped cooked chicken or turkey
- 1 1/2 cups day-old bread crumbs
- 1/4 cup butter

Cook rice according to package directions. Brown sausage; drain well. In mixing bowl, mix rice and sausage together, add soup, mushrooms, Worcestershire sauce and chicken, blend well. Pour into a 2 1/2-quart greased baking dish. Blend bread crumbs with butter and sprinkle over top of casserole. Bake at 375° for 30 minutes.

Yield: Serves 8-10.

COQ AU VIN

- ½ pound bacon
- 1 (10-ounce) package frozen pearl onions, thawed
- 3 tablespoons butter
- 6 chicken breast halves
- 1 clove garlic
- 2 tablespoons flour
- 2 tablespoons brandy
- 1½ cups red wine
- 2 tablespoons fresh minced parsley
- 1 bay leaf
- ⅛ teaspoon thyme
- ⅛ teaspoon marjoram
- ½ pound fresh mushrooms

Sauté bacon until crisp; remove. Brown onions slowly, about 10-15 minutes. Remove. Add butter and brown chicken; set aside. Add garlic and cook until soft. Add flour and stir constantly until flour is light brown; stir in brandy and red wine, cooking until smooth. Add bacon, onions, other seasonings and mushrooms; remove from heat.

Place chicken in a 2-quart casserole. Pour sauce over chicken and bake covered 1 hour; remove cover and bake 10 minutes more or until chicken is tender.

Yield: Serves 6.

APRICOT GLAZED CORNISH HENS

- **3/4 cup apricot preserves**
- **2 teaspoons grated orange rind**
- **2 tablespoons orange juice**
- **4 (1 1/4-pound) Cornish hens**
- **1/4 teaspoon paprika**
- **1/2 cup cashews**
- **2 tablespoons butter**
- **1/2 cup sliced green onions**

Combine apricot preserves, orange rind and orange juice; set aside.

Remove giblets from hens; rinse with cold water and pat dry. Close cavities and secure with toothpicks; sprinkle with paprika. Place hens, breast side up, in greased roasting pan. Bake at 350° for 1 1/2 hours basting frequently with apricot mixture during last 30 minutes.

Sauté cashews in butter until golden; set aside. Sauté onions until tender; mix with cashews and remaining apricot mixture.

Serve hens garnished with apricot mixture.

Yield: Serves 4

CORNISH HENS WITH HERBS

- **6 (1¼-pound) Cornish hens**
- **⅔ cup chopped mixed herbs (parsley, chives, rosemary, thyme, tarragon)**
- **2 limes, juiced**
- **3 tablespoons olive oil**
- **1½ tablespoons dried sage**
- **Salt and pepper**

Rinse and clean Cornish hens, removing giblets and any excess fat. Carefully lift skin from breast and stuff herbs under skin placing excess herbs in cavities of hens. Squeeze lime juice over hens; sprinkle with salt and pepper. Chill several hours. Rub olive oil and sage over hens. Place in a shallow baking pan; bake at 400° for 10 minutes. Reduce heat to 350° and continue baking for 45-50 minutes or until juice runs clear when pierced with a fork, basting often.

Twist off legs; remove breast bones and ribs. Cover with foil and keep warm in baking pan until serving time.

Yield: Serves 6.

EASY CHICKEN WITH ONIONS

- **6 skinless chicken breast halves**
- **1 (8½-ounce) can small onions, drained**
- **1 (10¾-ounce) can cream of mushroom soup, undiluted**
- **¼ cup sherry**
- **Salt and pepper**
- **1½ cups grated Cheddar cheese**

Place chicken in shallow 2-quart baking dish; add onions. Mix soup, sherry, salt and pepper; pour over chicken. Sprinkle grated cheese on top. Refrigerate. When ready to bake, place covered casserole in 350° oven for 45 minutes. Uncover and continue baking 35-45 minutes or until chicken is tender.

Yield: Serves 6.

CORNISH HENS MARBELLA

- **8 (1¼-pound) Cornish hens**
- **12 large cloves garlic, finely minced**
- **4 tablespoons oregano**
- **Salt and pepper**
- **1 cup red wine vinegar**
- **½ cup olive oil**
- **1 cup pitted prunes**
- **1 cup dried apricots**
- **1 cup pitted green olives**
- **½ cup capers**
- **4 bay leaves**
- **1 cup firmly packed brown sugar**
- **1 cup dry white wine**
- **4 tablespoons chopped fresh parsley**

Rinse hens; remove giblets and place in shallow roasting pan. Combine all ingredients (except brown sugar, wine and parsley); mix well and pour over hens. Marinate overnight.

Sprinkle brown sugar evenly over hens and pour wine around them. Bake at 350° for 1 hour 15 minutes, basting frequently until golden or juice runs clear when thigh is pierced with a fork.

Transfer hens, fruit, olives and capers to serving platter; remove bay leaves. Sprinkle with parsley and pass remaining pan drippings in sauceboat.

Yield: Serve 8.

Variation: Substitute two cut-up frying chickens for Cornish hens.

COUNTRY CAPTAIN

- **1 (3½-pound) fryer or 8 skinless breast halves**
- **½ cup all-purpose flour**
- **½ teaspoon salt**
- **½ teaspoon pepper**
- **¾ cup vegetable oil**
- **1 onion, chopped**
- **1 large bell pepper, chopped**
- **1 clove garlic, minced**
- **1 teaspoon salt**
- **½ teaspoon pepper**
- **2 teaspoons curry powder**
- **2 (14.5-ounce) cans tomatoes**
- **1 teaspoon chopped parsley**
- **½ teaspoon thyme**
- **½ cup currants**
- **1 cup almonds, toasted**

Combine flour, ½ teaspoon salt and ½ teaspoon pepper in a baggie; dredge chicken pieces, coating well. Cook in vegetable oil until browned and place in a 13 x 9-inch baking pan. Sauté onion, bell pepper and garlic in remaining vegetable oil until tender. Add seasonings, tomatoes, parsley and thyme. Pour over chicken; cover and bake at 350° for 45 minutes. Add currants; bake 15 minutes more. Sprinkle with toasted almonds. Serve with rice.

Yield: Serves 8.

DEVILISH CHICKEN

- **4 boneless, skinless chicken breast halves**
- **2 tablespoons olive oil**
- **⅓ cup finely diced onion**
- **1 clove garlic, minced**
- **¾ cup white wine**
- **½ cup chicken broth**
- **½ teaspoon cornstarch**
- **1 tablespoon Dijon mustard**
- **2 tablespoons capers**
- **Salt and pepper**

Brown breasts in olive oil; set aside, Sauté onions and garlic until limp. Add chicken, wine and chicken broth and cook until chicken is tender. Dissolve cornstarch in some of broth; add to pan. Add mustard and capers, stirring until thickened. Serve sauce over chicken.

Yield: Serves 4.

DELTA CHICKEN CASSEROLE

- **4 cups chopped cooked chicken**
- **2 bunches green onions, chopped**
- **2 stalks celery, chopped**
- **3 tablespoons butter**
- **2 (10¾-ounce) cans cream of mushroom soup, undiluted**
- **½ cup mayonnaise**
- **½ cup honey-Dijon ranch dressing**
- **1 (8-ounce) can water chestnuts, drained, thinly sliced**
- **1 (14-ounce) can artichoke hearts, drained**
- **1 cup shredded Cheddar cheese**
- **2 (3-ounce) cans sliced mushrooms**
- **½ cup white wine**
- **Salt and pepper**
- **2 teaspoons garlic with Italian herbs salad mix**
- **1½ teaspoons Louisiana hot sauce**
- **2 stacks round buttery crackers, crushed**
- **¼ cup melted butter**

Sauté green onions and celery in butter until tender. In a large mixing bowl, combine onions, celery and chicken with all remaining ingredients (except round buttery crackers and ¼ cup butter). Stir and mix together well. Pour into a greased 13 x 9-inch glass baking dish. Toss crushed crackers with ¼ cup butter and sprinkle evenly over top of casserole. Bake at 350° for 40 minutes or until bubbly and heated through.

Yield: Serves 8-10.

CHICKEN DELUXE

- 8 chicken breast halves
- ½ cup raisins
- ¼ cup vodka
- ½ cup slivered almonds
- ½ cup butter
- 1 teaspoon salt
- ½ teaspoon cayenne pepper
- 1 (10¾-ounce) can cream of mushroom soup, undiluted
- 1 (10¾-ounce) can cheese soup, undiluted
- 1 large onion, sliced

Soak raisins in vodka; set aside. Sauté almonds in butter until lightly browned; remove. Place chicken in skillet, season with salt and pepper and brown. Arrange chicken in 13 x 9-inch baking dish. Combine soups and pour over chicken. Place onion slices and raisins on top. Cover and bake at 375° for 30 minutes; sprinkle with almonds and bake 20 minutes longer.

Yield: Serves 8.

CHICKEN DIABLE

- 6 boneless, skinless chicken breast halves
- 2 medium onions, sliced
- ½ cup honey
- ⅓ cup vegetable oil
- 1 teaspoon curry powder
- 3 tablespoons Dijon mustard
- 3 tablespoons orange juice
- 1 teaspoon salt
- ¼ teaspoon pepper

Place onions on bottom of shallow 2-quart baking dish. Place chicken on top of onions. Combine remaining ingredients in saucepan and heat over medium heat until well blended. Pour over chicken. Bake at 350° for 45 minutes to 1 hour until chicken is tender, basting occasionally.

Yield: Serves 6.

DOWN-HOME CHICKEN AND RICE

- **4 cups cooked chopped chicken**
- **1 cup chopped celery**
- **2 cups cooked rice**
- **1 (10¾-ounce) can cream of chicken soup**
- **¼ cup slivered almonds**
- **½ cup chopped onions**
- **¾ cup mayonnaise**
- **1 (8-ounce) can water chestnuts, sliced**
- **1 stack round buttery crackers**
- **¼ cup butter, melted**

Combine first 8 ingredients in mixing bowl; mix together well. Pour mixture into greased 2-quart casserole. Crush crackers and mix with butter; sprinkle over top of casserole. Bake at 350° for 45 minutes.

Yield: Serves 4-6.

FIESTA CHICKEN

- **1 cup Cheddar cheese cracker crumbs**
- **2 tablespoons taco seasoning**
- **8 boneless, skinless chicken breast halves**
- **4 green onions, chopped**
- **2 tablespoons butter, melted**
- **2 cups half-and-half**
- **1 cup shredded Monterey Jack cheese**
- **1 cup shredded Cheddar cheese**
- **1 (4-ounce) can chopped green chilies, drained**
- **½ cup chicken broth**

Combine cracker crumbs and taco seasoning. Dredge chicken pieces in crumbs and place in greased 13 x 9-inch baking pan. Sauté green onions in butter in skillet until tender. Stir in cream and remaining ingredients; pour over chicken. Bake, uncovered at 350° for 45 minutes.

Yield: Serves 8.

JAMAICAN JERK CHICKEN

- 6 scallions, thinly sliced
- 2 large shallots, finely minced
- 2 large cloves garlic, finely minced
- 1 tablespoon finely minced fresh ginger
- 1 teaspoon seeded, ribbed, finely minced hot fresh chile
- 1 tablespoon ground allspice
- 1 teaspoon freshly ground pepper
- ¼ teaspoon cayenne pepper
- ½ teaspoon nutmeg
- 1 teaspoon cinnamon
- 1 tablespoon fresh thyme or 1 teaspoon dried
- 1 teaspoon salt
- 1 tablespoon dark brown sugar
- ½ cup orange juice
- ½ cup rice vinegar
- ¼ cup red wine vinegar
- ¼ cup soy sauce
- ¼ cup olive oil
- 10 chicken breast halves

Combine scallions, shallots, garlic, ginger and chile. Set aside. In a large bowl, combine allspice with next 8 ingredients; mix thoroughly. Whisk in orange juice, vinegars and soy sauce. Slowly drizzle in oil, whisking constantly. Add scallion mixture and stir to combine.

Place chicken breast halves in a 13 x 9-inch casserole. Pour sauce evenly over chicken. Cover and refrigerate overnight.

Bake uncovered at 350° for 45-50 minutes turning and basting occasionally.

Yield: Serves 8-10.

BRAISED LEMON CHICKEN

- **8 chicken pieces (thighs or boneless breasts)**
- **⅓ cup all-purpose flour**
- **1½ teaspoons salt**
- **1 teaspoon pepper**
- **2 tablespoons olive oil**
- **2 tablespoons butter**
- **2 cloves garlic, minced**
- **1 medium onion, chopped**
- **2 tablespoons minced stuffed olives**
- **1 cup diced celery**
- **1 teaspoon chili powder**
- **1 teaspoon Worcestershire sauce**
- **½ teaspoon dry mustard**
- **1 tablespoon sugar**
- **Zest and juice of 1 lemon**
- **¼ cup red wine vinegar**
- **1½ cups chicken broth, unsalted**

Mix flour with ½ teaspoon salt and ½ teaspoon pepper. Dredge chicken pieces with flour mixture; shake off excess. Heat olive oil and butter in skillet; sauté chicken pieces until golden brown. Drain. Place chicken in a 12 x 8-inch baking dish. In the same skillet, simmer garlic, onion, olives and celery until tender. Stir in remaining ingredients with remaining salt and pepper; simmer 5 minutes and pour over browned chicken. Cover and bake at 350° for 40 minutes, basting frequently. Remove cover and bake 20 minutes more. Serve with Garlic Mashed Potatoes (see Page 205).

Yield: Serves 8.

CHICKEN MARENGO

- **3 tablespoons salad oil**
- **2 cloves garlic, chopped**
- **4 green onions, chopped**
- **½ pound mushrooms, sliced**
- **1 (3 or 3½-pound) broiler-fryer, cut-up**
- **Paprika**
- **1 cup dry white wine**
- **1 tablespoon brandy**
- **1 (16-ounce) can tomatoes**
- **1 teaspoon salt**
- **1 teaspoon sugar**
- **⅛ teaspoon rosemary**
- **⅛ teaspoon marjoram**
- **½ cup sliced green olives**

In a skillet, sauté garlic, onions and mushrooms in oil until tender; remove. Place chicken in skillet and sprinkle lightly with paprika; cook until brown on all sides. Put chicken in a 2-quart casserole.

Mix sautéed mixture with remaining ingredients and pour over chicken. Bake at 350° for 1 hour. Serve with rice.

Yield: Serves 6.

CHICKEN MOZZARELLA

- **6 skinless, boneless chicken breast halves**
- **2 eggs, beaten**
- **¾ cup bread crumbs**
- **½ cup vegetable oil**
- **2 cups tomato sauce**
- **⅛ teaspoon garlic powder**
- **¼ teaspoon dried basil**
- **2 tablespoons butter**
- **1 cup Parmesan cheese**
- **1 cup mozzarella cheese**

Pound chicken to ¼-inch thickness. Dip chicken in eggs then dredge in bread crumbs. Brown in oil. Place in a 2-quart shallow casserole dish. Heat tomato sauce, garlic powder, basil and butter in saucepan; simmer 10 minutes. Pour over chicken and sprinkle with Parmesan cheese. Cover and bake at 350° for 40 minutes. Uncover and top with mozzarella cheese; bake uncovered 10 minutes.

Yield: Serves 6.

MEXICAN CHICKEN CASSEROLE

3 cups chopped chicken breast
1 large onion, chopped
1 large bell pepper, chopped
1 (10¾-ounce) can cream of mushroom soup, undiluted
1 (10¾-ounce) can cream of chicken soup, undiluted
1 pound Cheddar cheese, grated
Chili powder
Garlic salt
2 (14½-ounce) cans chicken broth
1 (10-count) dairy-case package corn tortillas
1 (10-ounce) can tomatoes and chilies, undrained

Mix onion and bell pepper; set aside. Blend the soups together; set aside. Heat chicken broth and soak tortillas in warm broth until wilted.

In a 13 x 9-inch baking dish, layer half of tortillas dripping with broth, half of chicken, onion and bell pepper. Sprinkle with chili and garlic salt then half of soups and a third of the cheese. Repeat layers making sure tortillas are dripping with broth. Bake uncovered at 375° for 30 minutes. Sprinkle top with remaining cheese and bake 10 minutes longer.

Yield: Serves 8.

MOLE POBLANO

- **4 large skinless chicken breast halves**
- **¼ cup vegetable oil**
- **1½ teaspoons salt, divided**
- **1 clove garlic, minced**
- **1 onion, chopped**
- **1 bell pepper, chopped**
- **2 tomatoes, peeled and chopped**
- **1½ teaspoons chili powder**
- **¼ teaspoon cinnamon, nutmeg, cloves, cumin**
- **1 (1-ounce) square unsweetened chocolate**
- **Grated rind of 1 orange**
- **¼ cup pine nuts or almonds**
- **2 tablespoons currants**
- **1½ tablespoons cornstarch**
- **1½ cups chicken broth**

In a large skillet, brown chicken in oil; season with 1 teaspoon salt; set aside. Sauté garlic, onion and pepper in same oil. Stir in tomatoes, seasonings, remaining salt and chocolate with all other ingredients (except cornstarch and broth). Mix well. Dissolve cornstarch in a small amount of broth; blend into remaining broth and add to sauce.

Place chicken into 1½-quart shallow baking pan. Pour sauce over chicken and bake at 350° for 45 minutes covered. Remove cover and bake for 10 minutes more or until chicken is tender.

Yield: Serves 4.

CHICKEN ENCHILADAS

- **8 chicken breast halves**
- **1 large onion, chopped**
- **1 cup grated Cheddar cheese**
- **12 corn tortillas**
- **2 cups chicken broth**
- **1 cup sour cream**
- **1 (10¾-ounce) can cream of chicken soup**
- **4 ounces taco sauce**
- **1 (4-ounce) can chopped green chilies**
- **Salt and pepper**
- **1 (16-ounce) package Monterey Jack cheese, shredded**

Simmer chicken (do not boil) slowly until tender; cut into small pieces. Combine chicken, onion and cheese. Soften tortillas, one at a time, in warm chicken broth. Fill each tortilla equally with chicken mixture; roll and place seam side down in a greased 2-quart oblong baking dish. Pour leftover broth over tortillas.

Combine sour cream and remaining ingredients (except cheese); mix well and pour over tortillas. Cover top with Monterey Jack cheese and bake at 375° for 30-40 minutes until bubbly and cheese browns.

Yield: Serves 6.

One cooked chicken breast half will yield ½ cup chopped meat.

ONION CHICKEN

- **4 boneless, skinless chicken breast halves**
- **¼ teaspoon salt**
- **¼ teaspoon pepper**
- **½ cup butter**
- **1 tablespoon Worcestershire sauce**
- **1 teaspoon dry mustard**
- **1 (2.5-ounce) can fried onion rings, crushed**

Place chicken between 2 sheets of wax paper; flatten to ¼-inch thickness using a meat mallet or rolling pin. Sprinkle with salt and pepper.

Combine butter, Worcestershire sauce and mustard; stir well. Dredge chicken in butter mixture then in crushed onion rings. Arrange chicken in a 13 x 9-inch pan; top with remaining onion rings. Drizzle with remaining butter. Bake at 350° for 35 minutes.

Yield: Serves 4.

CHICKEN PAPRIKA

- **1 chicken, cut into pieces**
- **¼ cup olive oil**
- **All-purpose flour**
- **Paprika**
- **2 (10¾-ounce) cans cream of celery soup, undiluted**
- **1 (10¾-ounce) can cream of mushroom soup, undiluted**
- **1½ cups sherry**

Sprinkle chicken pieces lightly with flour and brown in olive oil over medium heat.

Mix soups and sherry and pour into a greased 13 x 9-inch baking pan. Place chicken parts over soups and heavily top with paprika. Cover with foil and bake at 350° for 1½-2 hours or until tender. Serve with rice or noodles.

Yield: Serves 4.

CHICKEN PASTA

This versatile dish can be served cold or hot.

- **¾ cup mayonnaise**
- **¾ cup buttermilk**
- **¼ cup grated Parmesan cheese**
- **2 teaspoons basil**
- **2 green onions, chopped**
- **8 ounces corkscrew pasta, half spinach, half plain**
- **1 (16-ounce) package frozen mixed vegetables, cooked**
- **3 cups chopped cooked chicken**

In a large mixing bowl, combine mayonnaise, buttermilk, Parmesan cheese, basil and green onions; set aside. Cook pasta according to package directions; drain and cool. Stir chicken, pasta and cooked vegetables into mayonnaise mixture tossing until well coated. Cover and chill 1 hour or overnight. Serve cold.

To serve hot: Mix ingredients as directed and pour into a greased 2½-quart casserole baking dish. Bake at 350° for 30 minutes or until casserole is hot and bubbly.

Yield: Serves 8-10.

CHICKEN PHYLLO

- **8 ounces phyllo dough (10-12 sheets), thawed**
- **1 cup chopped celery**
- **¾ cup chopped onion**
- **2 tablespoons butter**
- **2 cups chopped cooked chicken**
- **2 tablespoons chicken broth**
- **2 teaspoons parsley flakes**
- **½ teaspoon salt**
- **½ teaspoon ground nutmeg**
- **¼ teaspoon pepper**
- **1 egg, beaten**
- **6 tablespoons butter, melted**
- **Béchamel Sauce**

Sauté celery and onion in butter until tender. Add chicken and chicken broth. Cook over low heat until broth is absorbed. Stir in parsley, salt, nutmeg, pepper and egg. Remove from heat; set aside.

Stack half the sheets of phyllo dough, brushing with butter between each layer. Spoon 1¼ cups chicken mixture over phyllo dough to within 1 inch of edges. Turn one short side over filling, about 1 inch; fold in long sides. Roll jelly-roll style starting with folded short side. Place seam side down on a lightly greased shallow baking pan. Repeat with remaining phyllo and chicken mixture. Brush each roll with melted butter. Score each roll into 3 or 4 portions. Bake at 350° for 40 minutes or until rolls are brown and crisp. Cut rolls where scored. Spoon Béchamel Sauce over rolls.

Yield: Serves 6-8.

Béchamel Sauce

- **¼ cup butter**
- **¼ cup all-purpose flour**
- **¼ teaspoon salt**
- **2½ cups chicken broth**
- **4 egg yolks**
- **3 tablespoons lemon juice**

Melt butter in saucepan over low heat; add flour and salt, stirring until smooth. Cook 1 minute, stirring constantly. Gradually add chicken broth; cook over medium heat, stirring until thickened and bubbly. Remove from heat. Beat yolks until thick and lemon-colored. Gradually stir about a quarter of the hot mixture into yolks; add to remaining hot mixture, stirring constantly. Add lemon juice. Cook 2 minutes, stirring constantly.

Yield: 2½ cups.

PIZZA CHICKEN

Tasty dish that is low in fat.

- **4 skinless chicken breast halves**
- **1 (6-ounce) can tomato juice**
- **4 teaspoons Parmesan cheese**
- **1 tablespoon oregano**
- **Salt and pepper**

Place chicken breasts in 1½-quart baking pan. Cover chicken with tomato juice; sprinkle Parmesan cheese and oregano over top. Lightly salt and pepper. Bake at 350° for 45 minutes or until chicken is tender.

Yield: Serves 4.

CHICKEN POT PIE

- **½ cup butter, melted**
- **3 tablespoons all-purpose flour**
- **3 cups chicken broth**
- **1 cup milk**
- **3 cups diced cooked chicken**
- **½ teaspoon salt**
- **½ teaspoon pepper**
- **1 (16-ounce) can mixed vegetables, drained**
- **1 (16-ounce) can green peas**
- **Pastry for 9-inch pie**

Combine butter and flour in saucepan over low heat; gradually add chicken broth and milk, stirring constantly until thickened. Stir in chicken, salt, pepper and mixed vegetables. Mix well. Pour into a greased 13 x 9-inch baking dish. Roll pastry on lightly floured surface, cut into strips 1 inch wide and arrange in lattice design over chicken. Bake at 350° for 30 minutes or until pastry is brown.

Yield: Serves 6.

CHICKEN BREASTS PRIMAVERA

- **6 large mushrooms, sliced**
- **4 tablespoons butter, divided**
- **Salt**
- **Freshly ground pepper**
- **6 boneless, skinless chicken breast halves**
- **All-purpose flour**
- **2 teaspoons vegetable oil**
- **¾ cup chicken bouillon**
- **1 cup whipping cream**
- **½ lemon, juiced**
- **2½ tablespoons minced fresh dill**
- **½ cup cooked green peas (optional)**

Sauté mushrooms in 2 tablespoons butter until tender; season with salt and pepper to taste. Reserve. Season chicken breasts with salt and pepper, dredge each lightly with flour. Heat remaining 2 tablespoons butter and oil in skillet. Add chicken breasts and brown on both sides. Add a little bouillon, lower heat and simmer covered 6 minutes adding bouillon as necessary. Add cream and lemon juice to skillet and cook until cream is reduced by half. Stir in mushrooms and dill and cook until chicken is tender. Pour in peas and serve hot.

Yield: Serves 4-6.

YUMMY BAKED CHICKEN

- **6 boneless, skinless chicken halves**
- **½ teaspoon seasoned salt**
- **1 (10¾-ounce) can cream of chicken soup, undiluted**
- **½ cup mayonnaise**
- **½ cup grated sharp Cheddar cheese**
- **½ cup dry stuffing mix**

Place chicken breasts in a shallow 2-quart baking dish. Sprinkle with seasoned salt. Mix soup, mayonnaise and cheese together. Pour over chicken. Bake at 350° for 30 minutes uncovered. Sprinkle chicken with stuffing mix and bake uncovered 15 minutes longer. Serve with rice.

Yield: Serves 6.

SICILIAN CHICKEN

4 boneless, skinless chicken breast halves
Olive oil
2 cloves garlic, chopped
1 cup diced celery
3 tablespoons white vermouth
2 tablespoons capers
1 tablespoon tomato paste
½ cup chicken broth
¼ teaspoon thyme
½ cup sliced green olives
½ teaspoon cornstarch (optional)

Brown chicken in olive oil; remove. Sauté garlic and celery until tender, adding more olive oil if needed. Add chicken and remaining ingredients (except cornstarch). Cover and slowly simmer for 40 minutes or until chicken is tender. Thicken sauce with cornstarch if necessary.

Yield: Serves 4.

SUPER CHICKEN CASSEROLE

Doubles easily. Delicious.

2 cups chopped chicken
1 cup cooked rice
1 cup diced celery
¼ cup chopped onion
1 (8-ounce) can water chestnuts, thinly sliced
½ cup slivered almonds
1 cup sour cream
1 cup cream of chicken soup, undiluted
1 (2-ounce) jar chopped pimiento, drained
Salt and pepper to taste
1 cup coarsely ground corn flakes
½ cup melted butter, divided

Sauté celery and onion in half of the butter until tender. In a large mixing bowl, combine celery and onion with all remaining ingredients (except corn flakes and remaining butter). Pour into a greased 1½-quart casserole. Mix corn flakes with butter and sprinkle evenly on top. Bake at 350° for 40 minutes or until slightly browned and bubbly.

Yield: Serves 4.

CHICKEN SPAGHETTI

Plan on a half-cup cooked chopped chicken per breast half.

5 cups cooked chopped chicken breast
1 cup chopped celery
1 cup chopped onion
1 cup chopped bell pepper
½ cup chopped green onion
½ cup butter
1 (10¾-ounce) can cream of mushroom soup, undiluted
1 (10¾-ounce) can cream of celery soup, undiluted
1 (10¾-ounce) can cream of chicken soup, undiluted
1 cup white wine
1 pound processed cheese loaf, cubed
1 cup sliced black olives
1 (8-ounce) can water chestnuts, sliced
1 (6-ounce) can sliced mushrooms
Salt, pepper, Tabasco
¾ pound thin spaghetti
1 cup grated Parmesan cheese

Sauté celery, onion, green onion and bell pepper in butter until tender. In a large saucepan, mix soups and next 5 ingredients; stir over medium heat until well blended and cheese melts. Fold in chicken, cooked celery, onions and bell pepper; add salt, pepper and Tabasco to taste.

Cook spaghetti al dente according to package directions. Do not overcook. Combine drained spaghetti with chicken mixture, tossing together well. Divide equally between two well-greased 12 x 8-inch glass baking pans. Sprinkle tops with Parmesan cheese.

Bake at 350° for 35-40 minutes until bubbly and thoroughly heated.

Yield: Serves 16.

GLEN ACRES BRAISED DUCK

- **2 ducks, halved**
- **2 tablespoons vegetable oil**
- **2 tablespoons sherry**
- **2 tablespoons tomato paste**
- **3 tablespoons all-purpose flour**
- **½ cup bouillon**
- **½ cup dry red wine**
- **1 teaspoon salt**
- **¼ teaspoon pepper**
- **½ pound fresh mushrooms, thinly sliced**
- **1 bay leaf or 1 teaspoon marjoram**

Remove and discard wings. Brown ducks in oil in large heavy skillet until deep brown. Pour in sherry, turning ducks over a minute or two; remove ducks; set aside.

Lower heat; stir in tomato paste and flour. Gradually add bouillon and red wine, stirring constantly. Bring to boil; add remaining ingredients; mix well.

Place ducks in a shallow roasting pan and cover with tomato paste, bouillon, mushroom mixture. Bake at 325° for 2-3 hours or until ducks are tender. Remove ducks to platter; cover to keep warm. Degrease pan drippings; reheat and pass with ducks. Serve with wild rice garnished with crabapples.

Yield: Serves 4.

TURKEY BREAST

5-7 pound turkey breast
¼ cup vegetable oil
2 tablespoons salt
2 tablespoons pepper
1 cup cider vinegar
1 oven bag-turkey size

Place turkey in baking bag and follow directions for preparing bag. Mix oil, salt, pepper and vinegar and pour over turkey. Seal bag. Place in a shallow roasting pan. Bake at 300° for 3½-4 hours. Reserve and refrigerate drippings for other uses (gravies, sauces, etc.).

Yield: One turkey breast.

TENDER TURKEY

1 uncooked turkey
1 teaspoon salt
2 stalks celery, chopped
1 onion, chopped
1 apple, chopped
½ cup butter
2 cups boiling water

Spread salt inside turkey cavity. Mix celery, onion and apples and place in turkey cavity.

Preheat oven to 450°. Place turkey on rack in roasting pan; rub all over with butter. Pour boiling water all around turkey; cover tightly. Bake 2 hours for 14 pounds or less and 2½ hours for more than 14 pounds. Turn off heat. Do Not Open Oven Door. Leave turkey in closed oven 8 hours. Turkey will be tender with lots of drippings. Refrigerate and reheat before serving.

Yield: One baked turkey.

CORNBREAD SAUSAGE DRESSING

Serve with chicken or turkey dinners.

1 cup chopped pecan
7 slices bread, torn
6 cups cornbread crumbs
4 cups chicken broth
1 onion, chopped
3 stalks celery, chopped
¼ cup butter, melted
½ pound bulk pork sausage (optional)
½ teaspoon salt
½ teaspoon pepper
4 eggs, beaten

Toast chopped pecans; set aside.

Place torn bread and cornbread crumbs into a large bowl. Pour chicken broth over crumbs and bread; stir well.

Sauté onion and celery in butter until tender; add to crumb mixture.

Brown sausage in heavy skillet; drain. Stir sausage, pecans and remaining ingredients into cornbread mixture. Spoon into a lightly greased 13 x 9-inch baking dish. Bake at 350° for about 45 minutes.

Yield: Serves 8-10.

A 3-pound chicken will yield 3 cups cooked chopped chicken meat.

FRIED FARM-RAISED CATFISH

8 catfish fillets
1 teaspoon salt
Tabasco
1 teaspoon pepper
2 cups cornmeal mix
4 cups vegetable oil

Lightly salt fillets on both sides; rub fillets with Tabasco. Mix pepper and cornmeal together. Dredge fillets in cornmeal mixture; drop into oil heated at 375°, two fillets at a time. Cook until golden brown, turning once.

Yield: Serves 8.

FAVORITE AMANDINE

2 pounds catfish, grouper or other favorite fish fillets
1 teaspoon salt
½ teaspoon pepper
1 cup self-rising flour
½ cup melted butter
½ cup slivered almonds
2 tablespoons chopped fresh parsley

Sprinkle serving-size fillets with salt and pepper; dredge in flour. Sauté in melted butter. When fish is brown on one side, turn carefully; brown other side. Total cooking time is 7-10 minutes depending on thickness of fish. Remove from pan; keep warm.

Sauté almonds in pan until lightly browned; add parsley. Serve over fish.

Yield: Serves 4-6.

PECAN CRUSTED CATFISH

- **4 green onions, minced**
- **2 cloves garlic, minced**
- **4 tablespoons teriyaki sauce**
- **1 teaspoon dried basil**
- **1 tablespoon chopped fresh cilantro**
- **6 (6-ounce) catfish fillets**
- **3 cups bran flakes**
- **1½ cups pecans**
- **1 cup fresh bread crumbs**
- **1 tablespoon pepper**
- **Salt**
- **All-purpose flour**
- **3 eggs, beaten**
- **⅓ cup plus 1 tablespoon butter**
- **6 tablespoons olive oil**

Combine first 5 ingredients. Place fish in flat glass baking dish. Spoon onion-garlic mixture over both sides of fish. Cover and refrigerate 2 hours.

Finely grind bran flakes in food processor. Add pecans; process until finely ground. Transfer to large bowl. Mix in bread crumbs and pepper; season with salt. Place flour in second large bowl. Pour eggs into third large bowl. Remove fish from marinade. Coat fish with flour; shake off excess. Dip fish into eggs then coat with pecan mixture, pressing to adhere.

Melt butter with oil in heavy large skillet over medium heat. Add fish and cook until golden brown and cooked through, about 5 minutes per side.

Yield: Serves 6.

Add 1 teaspoon peanut butter to hot oil for frying fish. It eliminates the fishy smell.

CATFISH PARMESAN

- **12 small catfish fillets**
- **1 cup dry bread crumbs**
- **¾ cup Parmesan cheese**
- **¼ cup chopped parsley**
- **1 teaspoon paprika**
- **½ teaspoon oregano**
- **¼ teaspoon basil**
- **2 teaspoons salt**
- **½ teaspoon pepper**
- **½ cup melted butter**
- **Lemon wedges**

Pat fillets dry. Combine bread crumbs, Parmesan and seasonings; mix well. Dip fish in melted butter; roll in crumb mixture.

Arrange fish in well-greased 13 x 9-inch baking dish. Bake at 375° for 25 minutes or until fish flakes easily when tested with a fork. Serve with lemon wedges.

Yield: Serves 6.

CLAMS CASINO

- **1 dozen clams in shell**
- **¼ cup minced onion**
- **¼ cup minced bell pepper**
- **2 tablespoons butter**
- **¼ cup chopped pimiento**
- **3 slices bacon, cut into fourths**
- **Lemon**
- **Parsley**

Pry open shells (discard any open shells). Discard top shell. Loosen meat from bottom shell. Drain shells and meat on paper towels.

Sauté onion and bell pepper in butter until tender; stir in pimiento. Return clams to shell and arrange in shallow baking pan. Spoon 1 tablespoon onion mixture onto each clam, top with bacon. Bake at 375° for 15-20 minutes until bacon is browned. Garnish with lemon and parsley.

Yield: 6 first course servings.

Variation: Substitute oysters for clams and follow same directions.

CLAMS MORNAY

- 1 quart clams
- 3 tablespoons butter, melted
- 3 tablespoons all-purpose flour
- ¾ cup milk
- ¼ cup clam juice
- 2 egg yolks, beaten
- Salt
- Tabasco
- ¼ cup bread crumbs
- 1 tablespoon butter, melted
- ¼ cup Parmesan cheese

Simmer clams in their own liquid until edges curl. Drain; reserve ¼ cup liquid. Finely chop clams.

Combine butter and flour over low heat. Add milk and ¼ cup clam juice, stirring constantly until thickened. Add yolks gradually a little at a time. Add salt and Tabasco to taste, stir in clams.

Spoon into 4 individual scallop or clam shells. Mix bread crumbs, butter and Parmesan cheese; sprinkle over top. Broil 3-4 inches from heat until bubbly and browned.

Yield: Serves 4.

NAGS HEAD CRAB AND SHRIMP CASSEROLE

- 1 pound lump crabmeat, drained
- 1 pound medium shrimp, cooked, shelled, deveined
- ¼ cup chopped celery
- ¼ cup chopped bell pepper
- ¾ cup mayonnaise
- 1 teaspoon lemon juice
- 2 teaspoons Worcestershire sauce
- ½ teaspoon salt
- ½ cup buttered bread crumbs

Pick over crabmeat removing all bits of cartilage; set aside. Combine celery, bell pepper, mayonnaise, lemon juice, Worcestershire sauce and salt; mix well. Fold in crabmeat and shrimp.

Place mixture in a 1½-quart deep baking dish. Top with buttered crumbs. Bake at 400° for 20-30 minutes.

Yield: Serves 4-6.

BAKED CRAB

- 1 (6-ounce) can fancy white or select claw crabmeat
- 1 (3-ounce) can sliced mushrooms or ½ pound fresh
- 1 small onion, grated
- ½ bell pepper, chopped
- 2 tablespoons butter
- 2 tablespoons all-purpose flour
- 1 cup chicken broth or milk
- 2 egg yolks, beaten
- 2 tablespoons sherry
- Salt and cayenne pepper
- ¼ cup grated Cheddar cheese

Sauté mushrooms, onion and bell pepper in butter until tender; stir in flour. Add chicken broth or milk gradually, stirring constantly until thickened. Add egg yolks and sherry. Pour into 4 (4-ounce) ramekins. Sprinkle with cheese and bake at 375° until golden brown, about 15-20 minutes.

Yield: Serves 4.

CREOLE CRAB PIE

- 1 unbaked (9-inch) pie crust
- 1 cup chopped bacon
- 2 tablespoons chopped green onion
- 1 pound crabmeat, picked over for cartilage
- 3 eggs, beaten
- 2 cups milk
- ½ teaspoon salt
- Cayenne pepper to taste

Bake pie crust at 350° until very light brown; set aside.

Sauté bacon and green onion until bacon is crisp; add crabmeat, mixing gently. In a bowl, mix eggs, milk, salt and cayenne pepper.

Spread crabmeat mixture evenly in bottom of pie crust. Pour egg milk mixture over crabmeat. Bake at 350° for 25-30 minutes until pie is set and crust is brown.

Yield: Serves 8.

CRAB IMPERIAL

- 2 slices white bread, crusts removed
- 2 eggs, beaten
- 1/4 cup mayonnaise
- 1 teaspoon prepared mustard
- 1/2 teaspoon chopped parsley
- 1/2 teaspoon salt
- 1/8 teaspoon pepper
- Dash of Worcestershire sauce
- 1 pound crabmeat, picked over for cartilage, drained
- 1 tablespoon butter
- 1 tablespoon all-purpose flour
- 1/2 cup milk
- 1/4 teaspoon salt
- 1/4 teaspoon pepper
- Dash of Worcestershire sauce
- Paprika

Cut bread into small pieces. Combine next 7 ingredients; fold in bread and crabmeat. Spoon mixture into 4 (6-ounce) baking dishes; set aside.

Melt 1 tablespoon butter; add flour, stirring until smooth. Gradually add milk; cook over medium heat stirring constantly until thickened. Stir in salt, pepper and Worcestershire sauce. Spoon 2 tablespoons white sauce on top of crabmeat in baking dishes. Sprinkle with paprika and bake at 350° for 20 minutes. Garnish with parsley.

Yield: Serves 4.

MARYLAND CRAB CAKES

Use just plain white bread; it works because it virtually has no character, it disappears without a trace! Recipe doubles easily.

- **1 large egg**
- **2 tablespoons mayonnaise**
- **3 slices white bread, crusts removed, cut in ½-inch pieces**
- **Dash of Worcestershire sauce**
- **1 heaping teaspoon honey mustard**
- **1 teaspoon Old Bay seasoning**
- **1 pound fresh crabmeat, well picked over for cartilage**
- **Peanut oil**

Combine egg and mayonnaise; add bread, Worcestershire sauce, honey mustard and Old Bay seasoning. Mix with crabmeat; let stand at room temperature 1 minute.

Form into 6 cakes. In a heavy skillet, cook cakes in 1-inch deep hot oil about 3 minutes per side until browned. Drain. Serve with additional honey mustard, if desired.

Yield: Serves 4.

CRAWFISH ÉTOUFFÉE VILLE PLATTE

- **¾ cup butter**
- **2 tablespoons all-purpose flour**
- **3 medium onions, chopped**
- **1 bell pepper, chopped**
- **2 stalks celery, chopped**
- **2 cloves garlic, crushed**
- **½ cup diced canned tomatoes with chilies**
- **2 pounds peeled crawfish tails, with fat**
- **⅓ cup chopped scallions**
- **⅓ cup chopped parsley**

Melt butter in Dutch oven or heavy pot; stir in flour until light brown. Add onion, bell pepper, celery and garlic. Cover and simmer slowly 30 minutes, stirring occasionally until vegetables are tender and slightly browned. Add tomatoes and simmer 15-30 minutes.

Thirty minutes before serving, add crawfish tails (if commercially packed, make sure to get all of the fat out of bags and into the pot). Cook over medium heat 10-15 minutes. Add scallions and parsley. Serve over rice.

Yield: Serves 4-6.

CRAWFISH MONICA

- **1 pound pasta of choice**
- **½ cup butter**
- **¾ cup chopped green onions**
- **1 pound peeled crawfish tails**
- **1 tablespoon Cajun Magic Seafood Seasoning**
- **2 cups half-and-half**

Cook pasta according to package directions; drain. Melt butter in large saucepan, sauté onions. Add crawfish tails and Cajun Magic; sauté 1 minute. Add half-and-half and cook over medium heat 5-10 minutes until sauce thickens. Add pasta, toss well, heat and serve.

Yield: Serves 6.

Variation: Substitute 1½ pounds shrimp for crawfish; follow same directions.

CRAWFISH MONSEIGNEUR

A delicious dish without a lot of chopping preparation.

1½ pounds crawfish tails
½ cup butter or crawfish fat
1 (10¾-ounce) can cream of celery soup
½ teaspoon cayenne pepper
3 tablespoons butter
3 tablespoons all-purpose flour
¾ cup milk
1 (8-ounce) can sliced mushrooms
⅓ cup chopped green onion tops
1 (4-ounce) jar chopped pimientos
1 teaspoon salt
¼ teaspoon cayenne pepper
¼ teaspoon black pepper
4 dashes Tabasco
¼ cup white wine

Place crawfish, butter (or crawfish fat), soup and cayenne in a 3-quart pot. Cover and cook over medium heat for 5 minutes, stirring occasionally; set aside.

In a saucepan, melt 3 tablespoons butter; add flour, blending well. Gradually add milk and cook over moderately high heat, stirring constantly, until thickened. Reduce heat to simmer, stir in mushrooms, onion tops, pimiento, salt, cayenne and black peppers, Tabasco and wine. Stir until well blended and cook 2 minutes. Pour over crawfish mixture; mix well. Cover and simmer 5 minutes. Serve over rice.

Yield: Serves 6.

FRIED OYSTERS

½ cup finely crushed saltine cracker crumbs
⅛ teaspoon salt
¼ teaspoon pepper
12 ounces fresh oysters
Vegetable oil

Combine cracker crumbs, salt and pepper. Dredge oysters in crumbs. Place on a baking sheet and freeze until firm. Heat 1-inch oil in heavy skillet. Fry frozen oysters until golden brown. Drain on paper towels.

Yield: Serves 2.

OYSTER CASSEROLE

After pouring cream mixture over top of casserole, use a fork to poke through so that the liquid mixes in well.

3 cups saltine cracker crumbs
½ cup butter, melted
2 pints oysters
½ cup half-and-half
2 tablespoons sherry
1 teaspoon pepper
½ teaspoon salt
1 teaspoon Worcestershire sauce
1 teaspoon cayenne pepper
4 tablespoons butter

Combine cracker crumbs with butter, mixing until crumbs are well coated. Sprinkle one third of crumbs into a greased 9 x 9-inch casserole baking dish.

Drain oysters reserving ¼ cup liquid. Spoon half of oysters evenly over cracker crumbs. Repeat layers.

Combine cream, sherry, reserved oyster liquid and seasonings; pour over oysters. Sprinkle with remaining third of cracker crumbs. Dot top with butter and bake at 400° for 30 minutes.

Yield: Serves 4-6.

OYSTERS ROCKEFELLER CASSEROLE

Serve as a first course or as an appetizer.

3 green onions with tops
¼ cup chopped celery
1 teaspoon tarragon
1 teaspoon chervil
3 sprigs parsley
½ cup chopped frozen spinach, drained
2 tablespoons soft, fresh bread crumbs
Salt, pepper, Tabasco, Worcestershire sauce, garlic to taste
½ cup butter, melted
1 pint (24) oysters, drained

Place all ingredients (except butter and oysters) into a food processor or blender and process until finely ground. Mix processed ingredients with butter.

Arrange drained oysters in bottom of greased 8 x 8-inch casserole dish. Spoon ground mixture evenly over top. Bake at 450° for 15 minutes until hot and bubbly. Serve immediately.

Yield: Serves 6.

SCALLOPS

3 tablespoons butter
½ pound fresh mushrooms, sliced
½ cup chopped onion
1½ cups shredded Gruyère cheese
1 cup mayonnaise
¼ cup white wine
¼ cup chopped fresh parsley
1 pound bay scallops
½ cup buttered bread crumbs

Sauté mushrooms and onion in butter until tender. Remove from heat and stir in cheese, mayonnaise, wine, parsley and scallops.

Place in a 1½-quart baking dish. Top with buttered crumbs. Bake at 350° for 20 minutes until bubbly and hot.

Yield: Serves 4.

BOILED SHRIMP

Shrimp are not hard to cook!

- Shrimp should be firm and white when cooked properly.
- Pink is not cooked. A shrimp turns pink immediately when immersed in hot water.
- Boil shrimp in the shell to reduce shrinkage.
- If you are served a limp translucent shrimp, don't eat it!

Follow this formula for boiling shrimp:

3 cups water for:

1 pound medium-large shrimp in shell
2 tablespoons shrimp boil mix
½ lemon, sliced
½ teaspoon salt

Bring water, shrimp boil mix, lemon and salt to a rolling boil. Add shrimp. Bring to another rolling boil. Boil 4 minutes. Remove from heat. Drain. Chill. Peel and devein.

SHRIMP SAUCE

Recipe doubles well. Wonderful with "peel and eat" shrimp.

½ cup butter
¼ cup catsup
¼ cup Worcestershire sauce
1 lemon, juiced
Salt and pepper
⅛ teaspoon Tabasco

Heat all ingredients; mix well. Serve warm in small individual serving bowls for dipping.

Yield: 1 cup.

TARTAR SAUCE

- **1 cup mayonnaise**
- **1 tablespoon chopped onion**
- **¼ cup sweet pickle relish**
- **1 tablespoon lemon juice**

Combine all ingredients, mixing well.

Yield: 1¼ cups.

FRIED SHRIMP

- **2 pounds medium-large fresh shrimp, peeled**
- **4 eggs, beaten**
- **⅔ cup spicy French dressing (optional)**
- **2 tablespoons lemon juice**
- **1 teaspoon onion powder**
- **1⅓ cups saltine cracker crumbs**
- **⅓ cup white cornmeal**
- **⅔ cup corn flake crumbs**
- **Vegetable oil**

Butterfly shrimp (optional) by cutting along outside curve almost through; remove vein. Flatten shrimp. Combine eggs, French dressing, lemon juice and onion powder, pour over shrimp. Cover and refrigerate 3 hours.

Combine crackers, cornmeal and corn flake crumbs. Remove shrimp from marinade; discard marinade. Dredge shrimp in crumb mixture. Fry in deep hot oil (375°) until golden.

Yield: Serves 4-6.

BOURBON STREET SHRIMP

- **1/4 cup butter**
- **6 large mushrooms, sliced**
- **1 (10 3/4-ounce) can shrimp soup**
- **1/2 teaspoon soy sauce**
- **1/4 teaspoon pepper**
- **1/4 cup sherry or Pernod**
- **1 cup sour cream**
- **1 1/2 pounds shrimp, cooked, deveined and split lengthwise**

Sauté mushrooms in butter until tender. Stir in soup, soy sauce, pepper and sherry or Pernod. Cook, stirring until hot, bubbly and smooth. Stir in sour cream and shrimp. Heat until bubbly. Spoon over cooked rice.

Yield: Serves 6.

SHRIMP CHIPPEWA

- **1 pound medium shrimp, peeled, deveined**
- **2 tablespoons all-purpose flour**
- **1 teaspoon Creole seasoning mix**
- **4 tablespoons butter**
- **1 medium onion, chopped**
- **4 green onions, chopped**
- **1 clove garlic, minced**
- **1 cup sliced mushrooms**
- **1/3 cup white wine**
- **2/3 cup cream**
- **Salt and pepper**
- **Chopped parsley**
- **8 ounces fettuccine, cooked, drained**

Combine flour and Creole seasoning mix; dust over shrimp; set aside.

Sauté onion, green onions and garlic in butter until tender; add mushrooms. Stir in shrimp, gradually add wine and cream, stirring until smooth. Cook over medium heat 5-8 minutes; add pasta. Sprinkle parsley over each serving.

Yield: Serves 4.

SHRIMP DISH FOR A PARTY

A good buffet dish for a festive occasion.

10 pounds shrimp, cooked, peeled and deveined
¼ cup butter, melted
2 onions, chopped
1 cup chopped celery with tops
½ cup chopped fresh parsley
2 lemons, juiced
½ teaspoon nutmeg
1 cup butter, melted
1 cup all-purpose flour
3 cups half-and-half
3 cups sour cream
2 cups white wine
1 cup water
2 teaspoons Creole seasoning
4 (4-ounce) can sliced mushrooms, drained
Salt and pepper to taste

Sauté onions, celery and parsley in ¼ cup butter until onions and celery are soft; add lemon juice and nutmeg. Stir in shrimp; set aside.

In a large pot or Dutch oven, combine butter and flour; stir until blended. Over low heat, gradually add half-and-half, sour cream, white wine and water, stirring constantly until smooth and thickened. Add Creole seasoning and mushrooms; season with salt and pepper. Simmer slowly for 10 minutes; stir in shrimp mixture. Refrigerate overnight. Heat at serving time. Add more wine if too thick.

Yield: Serves 30-40.

SHRIMP MARENGO

- ½ pound bacon, diced
- 2 cloves garlic, minced
- 1 cup chopped onion
- 1 cup chopped celery
- 1 pound mushrooms, sliced
- 4½ cups Italian-style plum tomatoes
- 1 (6-ounce) can tomato paste
- 1½ teaspoons rosemary
- 1¼ teaspoons basil
- 1 bay leaf
- 1 tablespoon salt
- ¼ teaspoon freshly ground black pepper
- 1 tablespoon sugar
- 3-4 drops Tabasco
- 3½ pounds raw shrimp, shelled and deveined
- 2 bell peppers, seeded and cut into large cubes
- Chicken stock
- All-purpose flour, if needed

Sauté bacon in large skillet until crisp; remove and set aside. Add garlic and onion to bacon drippings; sauté until tender and golden. Add celery and mushrooms; cook 5 minutes. Return bacon to skillet. Add tomatoes, tomato paste and all seasonings. Bring to a boil and simmer, uncovered, for 20-30 minutes. Add shrimp and bell pepper. Simmer 10-15 minutes. If mixture is too thick, it may be thinned by adding chicken stock. If too thin, add 2 tablespoons flour mixed with ⅓ cup chicken stock. Serve with rice.

Yield: Serves 8.

SHRIMP PRIMAVERA

- **1 pound tortellini pasta with cheese stuffing**
- **1 pound linguine pasta**
- **2 tablespoons olive oil**
- **2 pounds medium shrimp, cooked, shelled, deveined**
- **2 cups cauliflower florets**
- **2 cups julienne zucchini**
- **1½ cups sliced carrots**
- **½ cup julienne red bell pepper**
- **1 medium red onion, sliced into thin rings**
- **½ cup chopped parsley**
- **¼ pound snow peas, blanched**
- **Dressing**

Cook pastas separately according to package directions, al dente. Drain. While still warm, toss together with olive oil. Add all remaining ingredients; toss well. Chill. Cover with Dressing and mix together well. Serve chilled.

Yield: Serves 12-15.

Dressing:

- **1 (1-ounce) ranch salad dressing mix**
- **¾ cup milk**
- **1 cup mayonnaise**
- **2 tablespoons chopped fresh dill**
- **2 tablespoons Dijon mustard**
- **2 tablespoons horseradish**
- **1 tablespoon lemon juice**
- **Salt and pepper**

Combine salad dressing mix and mayonnaise. Add remaining ingredients; mix well.

Yield: 2 cups.

SHRIMP RICE CASSEROLE

- 1 pound medium shrimp, cooked, peeled and deveined
- 1 (6¼-ounce) package long-grain and wild rice, cooked
- 1 (10¾-ounce) can cream of shrimp soup, undiluted
- ½ pound fresh mushrooms, sliced
- 1 tablespoon butter
- ½ cup sour cream
- ½ cup mayonnaise

Combine shrimp, rice, cream of shrimp soup and mushrooms. Grease a 2-quart baking dish with the tablespoon of butter; pour in shrimp rice mixture. Mix sour cream and mayonnaise and spread on top. Bake at 350° for 30 minutes.

Yield: Serves 4.

SHRIMP AND PASTA LARMON

- 1 (9-ounce) package angel hair pasta
- 1 cup butter
- 4 cloves garlic, minced
- Salt and pepper
- ½ cup chopped fresh parsley
- 2 pounds large shrimp, peeled and deveined
- ½ cup Romano cheese

Cook pasta according to package directions; drain and place in large mixing bowl.

Sauté garlic in butter; add seasonings, parsley and shrimp. Stir and cook over moderate heat 5-8 minutes. Toss with pasta, mixing well. Add Romano cheese and toss. Serve immediately.

Yield: Serves 6.

SHRIMP AND CRAB RICE

- **1 (6¼-ounce) package long grain and wild rice**
- **1 cup diced bell pepper**
- **1 cup diced onion**
- **1 cup sliced celery**
- **2 tablespoons butter**
- **1½ pounds shrimp, cooked, peeled, deveined**
- **1 teaspoon curry powder**
- **1 teaspoon Worcestershire sauce**
- **¾ cup mayonnaise**
- **Salt and pepper**
- **½ cup white wine**
- **1 (8-ounce) can sliced water chestnuts, drained**
- **1 pound crabmeat, picked over for cartilage**
- **1 medium pimiento, chopped**

Cook rice according to package directions; set aside. Sauté bell pepper, onion and celery in butter until tender; add to cooked rice. Combine rice mixture with all remaining ingredients. Pour into a greased 13 x 9-inch baking dish. Bake at 350° covered for 45 minutes until thoroughly heated. Sprinkle with minced parsley and serve.

Yield: Serves 8.

One pound uncooked in-shell shrimp yields about 20.

NEW ORLEANS SNAPPER

- **1 egg, beaten**
- **1 cup milk**
- **4 red snapper fillets (about 2½ pounds)**
- **2 tablespoons butter, melted**
- **Salt and pepper**
- **½ cup all-purpose flour**
- **1 cup vegetable oil**
- **1 (14-ounce) can artichoke hearts, drained and quartered**
- **4 large mushrooms, sliced**
- **¼ cup butter, melted**
- **1 teaspoon Worcestershire sauce**
- **1 teaspoon lemon juice**
- **1 teaspoon vinegar**
- **½ cup sliced almonds, toasted**

Combine egg and milk; mix well. Brush fillets with 2 tablespoons butter; sprinkle with salt and pepper. Dip fillets in egg mixture; dredge in flour.

Fry fish in hot oil until golden brown (5 minutes per side). Drain well; keep warm.

Sauté artichokes and mushrooms in butter; add Worcestershire sauce, lemon juice and vinegar and simmer 1 minute. Spoon mixture over fish. Sprinkle with almonds.

Yield: Serves 4.

SEAFOOD LASAGNA

8 lasagna noodles
1 cup chopped onion
2 tablespoons butter
1 (8-ounce) package cream cheese, softened
1½ cups cream-style cottage cheese
1 egg, beaten
2 teaspoons basil
2 (10¾-ounce) cans cream of mushroom soup
⅓ cup milk
⅓ cup dry white wine
1 pound shrimp, cooked, peeled, deveined and halved
1 (7½-ounce) can crabmeat, drained, cartilage removed
½ cup Parmesan cheese
1 cup shredded sharp processed American cheese

Cook lasagna noodles according to package directions; drain.

Sauté onion in butter until tender, stir in cream cheese, cottage cheese, egg, basil and salt and pepper. Set aside.

Combine soup, milk and wine. Stir in shrimp and crabmeat.

Place 4 noodles in bottom of greased 13 x 9-inch baking dish. Spoon half cottage cheese mixture over noodles. Top with half shrimp crabmeat mixture. Repeat layers. Sprinkle with Parmesan cheese. Bake uncovered at 350° for 45 minutes. Top with American cheese and bake 5 minutes more until cheese has melted. Let stand 15 minutes before serving.

Yield: Serves 12.

SEAFOOD CASSEROLE

Casserole may be divided and baked in two smaller dishes. Freezes well. Wonderful company dish.

- **2 (10¾-ounce) cans cream of mushroom soup, undiluted**
- **½ cup mayonnaise**
- **1 onion, chopped**
- **¾ cup whole milk**
- **3 pounds shrimp, cooked, peeled and deveined**
- **1 pound crabmeat, rinsed, drained, picked for cartilage**
- **1 (3-ounce) can water chestnuts, drained and sliced**
- **1⅓ cups long-grain rice, cooked according to package directions**
- **1½ cups diced celery**
- **3 tablespoons minced parsley**
- **Salt, pepper, nutmeg, cayenne pepper**
- **¾ cup slivered almonds**
- **Paprika**

In a large mixing bowl, combine ingredients in order given (except almonds and paprika). Fold and mix together; check seasonings. Pour into a 15 x 10-inch greased baking pan. Sprinkle top with almonds and paprika. Bake at 350° 35-40 minutes or until hot and bubbly.

Yield: Serves 10-12.

MOUNTAIN TROUT

- 4 (1-pound) mountain trout, cleaned
- 2 cups buttermilk
- 1 teaspoon Tabasco
- 2 cups all-purpose flour
- 2 teaspoons salt
- 2 cups peanut oil
- Lemon wedges

Combine buttermilk and Tabasco in a 2-quart baking dish. Place whole trout (head removed) into buttermilk and let marinate refrigerated several hours.

Mix flour and salt. Remove trout from marinade allowing some buttermilk to cling. Roll in flour until well coated. Heat oil in a heavy skillet until hot, not smoking. Cook trout 3 minutes per side, turning once, until nicely browned. Drain on paper towels.

Yield: Serves 4.

BAKED MOUNTAIN TROUT

You may use your favorite salad dressing instead of the Caesar to make this recipe a family favorite.

- 2 pounds boned trout fillets
- ½ cup Caesar salad dressing
- 1 cup crushed potato chips
- ½ cup grated sharp Cheddar cheese

Dip fillets in salad dressing. Place fillets in baking pan in single layer, skin side down.

Combine crushed chips and cheese. Sprinkle over each fillet. Bake at 400° for 12-15 minutes until trout has cooked and flakes easily.

Yield: Serves 2-4.

Variations:

- Substitute crushed cheese crackers for potato chips.
- Substitute any fish fillet of choice for trout.

Vegetables
SPRAGINS
DAVIDSON

VEGETABLES

ASPARAGUS BAKE

- **4 (15½-ounce) cans long green asparagus, drained**
- **3 (10¾-ounce) cans cream of mushroom soup, undiluted**
- **2 cups grated Cheddar cheese**
- **1 teaspoon pepper**
- **½ cup toasted almonds**
- **½ cup Italian bread crumbs**
- **2 tablespoons butter**

In a well-buttered 13 x 9-inch casserole, layer half of asparagus, half of mushroom soup, pepper and half of cheese. Repeat layering. Mix almonds with bread crumbs and sprinkle over top. Dot with butter and bake at 350° for 35-40 minutes.

Yield: Serves 8.

Open asparagus cans from bottom or you may break tips.

ASPARAGUS BUNDLES

- **2 sheets phyllo dough, cut lengthwise in half**
- **¼ cup butter, melted**
- **20 thin asparagus tips, 3 inches long**
- **4 scallions (white and green parts) trimmed to 3 inches**
- **Salt and freshly ground pepper**

Lightly brush both sides of a half sheet of phyllo with butter. Arrange 5 asparagus and 1 scallion in a bundle along one short edge of the dough; there will be a 1-inch margin on either side.

Season asparagus with salt and pepper. Fold in the edges of phyllo and roll up. Place bundle on cookie sheet; brush with butter. Repeat with remaining ingredients to make 3 more bundles.

Bake at 375° for 12-15 minutes until phyllo is golden brown. Serve hot.

Yield: Serves 4.

ASPARAGUS CASSEROLE

2 (10½-ounce) cans green asparagus tips
1 (10¾-ounce) can cream of asparagus soup, undiluted
1 (10¾-ounce) can cream of mushroom soup, undiluted
2 soup cans milk
½ pound grated sharp Cheddar cheese
1 (8-ounce) package stuffing mix (not cornbread type)
3 tablespoons butter, divided
½ teaspoon paprika
Salt and pepper

Grease 8 x 11-inch casserole; line bottom with ½ cup of stuffing mix. Place 1 can of asparagus in a line over stuffing mix. Combine soups, milk, salt and pepper to taste. Pour half of soup mixture over top of asparagus; dot with half of butter. Repeat layers. Sprinkle top with grated cheese and paprika. Bake at 350° for 45 minutes.

Yield: Serves 6-8.

BAKED BEANS

6 slices bacon
1 large onion, chopped
1 (1-pound) can baked beans
1 (1-pound) can kidney beans, drained
1 (1-pound) can lima beans, drained
½ pound sharp Cheddar cheese, shredded
½ cup firmly packed brown sugar
⅓ cup catsup
2 teaspoons Worcestershire sauce

Cook 4 slices bacon until crisp, crumble and set aside. Sauté onions in bacon drippings until tender. Combine the remaining ingredients; stir in the crumbled bacon and onion. Pour into a 3-quart casserole and top with remaining two slices bacon.

Bake at 350° for 30-40 minutes or until heated thoroughly and bubbly.

Yield: Serves 12.

BOURBON BAKED BEANS

- **1 apple, finely chopped**
- **½ cup chopped onion**
- **½ cup raisins**
- **4 slices bacon, crisply cooked and crumbled**
- **½ cup chili sauce**
- **1 cup firmly packed brown sugar**
- **½ cup bourbon whiskey**
- **2 (28-ounce) cans pork and beans**
- **2 slices bacon, uncooked**

Combine all ingredients except uncooked bacon; stir well. Spoon mixture into a greased 2-quart casserole. Arrange bacon slices on top. Bake uncovered at 350° for 1 hour.

Yield: Serves 6-8.

BAKED LIMA BEANS

To avoid soaking beans overnight, place them in large pot with 2 inches of water covering beans. Cover pot and bring to rolling boil. Turn off heat and let beans stand 1 hour. Beans will now be ready to cook.

- **1 pound dried baby lima beans**
- **2 teaspoons salt, divided**
- **½ cup butter, softened**
- **¾ cup firmly packed brown sugar**
- **1 tablespoon dry mustard**
- **1 tablespoon molasses**
- **1 cup sour cream**

Soak beans in water overnight. Drain; cover with water, add 1 teaspoon salt and cook until tender (about 1 hour). Do not overcook. Drain and rinse under hot water. Place beans back in cooking pot and mix in butter, brown sugar, mustard, molasses and remaining 1 teaspoon salt, stirring gently. Fold in sour cream and pour into a greased 2-quart casserole dish. Bake uncovered at 350° for 1 hour.

Yield: Serves 8.

DANISH LIMAS

- 2 (10-ounce) packages frozen lima beans
- ½ cup chopped celery
- ¼ cup chopped onion
- 1 cup sour cream
- ½ cup blue cheese, crumbled
- ¼ cup chopped pimiento
- 4 slices bacon, crisply cooked and crumbled

In saucepan, cook lima beans, celery and onion in water for 20 minutes until tender; drain well. Stir in sour cream and blue cheese. Cook stirring over low heat until mixture is heated through and cheese is melted. Do not boil. Stir in pimiento. Serve topped with crumbled bacon.

Yield: Serves 8.

NELL'S GREEN BEANS AND SHOEPEG CORN

- ½ cup chopped onion
- ½ cup chopped celery
- ¼ cup chopped bell pepper
- 1 (12-ounce) can shoepeg corn
- ½ cup grated sharp Cheddar cheese
- 1 (10¾-ounce) can cream of celery soup
- 1 (16-ounce) can French-cut green beans
- 1 (8-ounce) carton sour cream
- ½ cup butter
- 1 stack round buttery crackers, crushed

Combine first 8 ingredients. Pour into a well-greased 13 x 9-inch baking pan. Melt butter and mix with crushed crackers. Sprinkle buttered crackers on top of casserole. Bake at 350° for 45 minutes.

Yield: Serves 6-8.

LOUISIANA RED BEANS 'N' RICE

1 pound dried red kidney beans
1 ham bone, with meat on it
2 cups chopped onion
½ cup chopped bell pepper
1 cup chopped celery
2 cloves garlic, minced
3 tablespoons butter
1 tablespoon salt
½ teaspoon red pepper
Tabasco to taste
1 pound smoked sausage, sliced (Kielbasa)
Green onions, chopped

Wash, pick over beans. Cover with cold water and soak overnight; drain. Pour beans in Dutch oven or large soup pot; cover with 3 inches water. Sauté onion, bell pepper, celery and garlic in butter until tender. Stir onion mixture into beans. Add salt, red pepper, and Tabasco to beans; simmer for 4 hours until beans are soft. Sauté sliced sausage in skillet until brown; add to beans and cook over low heat 1 hour. Serve over cooked rice; garnish top with chopped green onions.

Yield: Serves 8-10.

Steamed Rice

4 cups water
2 teaspoons salt
2 cups long-grain rice
½ teaspoon salad oil

In a heavy saucepan, bring water and salt to a boil. Stir in rice and oil, reduce heat to low and simmer tightly covered for 20 minutes or until liquid is absorbed. Place rice in a colander over simmering water, cover with a dish towel and allow to steam until served.

Add a small amount of sugar to vegetables to bring out more flavor.

SMOTHERED GREEN BEANS

- **3 slices bacon**
- **2 tablespoons butter**
- **1 cup chopped onion**
- **1 pound fresh green beans**
- **2 cups water**
- **Salt and cayenne pepper**
- **12 small new potatoes, peeled**

In a Dutch oven or large pot, cook bacon until slightly crisp; remove and set aside. Add butter to bacon drippings and sauté onion until tender. Chop bacon and add to pot. Add beans, water and seasonings to taste. Lower heat, cover and cook for 20 minutes. Add potatoes; cover pot and cook over medium heat until potatoes are tender.

Yield: Serves 6.

BROCCOLI-CHEESE CASSEROLE

- **2 (10-ounce) packages frozen chopped broccoli**
- **1 (10¾-ounce) can cream of mushroom soup**
- **1 cup mayonnaise**
- **2 tablespoons lemon juice**
- **Grated rind of 1 lemon**
- **2 eggs, beaten**
- **½ cup butter, divided**
- **1½ cups grated sharp Cheddar cheese**
- **2 green onions, chopped**
- **1 stack round buttery crackers, crushed**

Partially cook broccoli, drain and set aside. Mix mushroom soup, mayonnaise, lemon juice, lemon rind and eggs together well; stir in ¼ cup butter, cheese and onions. Fold cooked broccoli into mushroom soup mixture and spoon all into a well greased 2-quart casserole. Mix crackers with remaining ¼ cup butter and sprinkle on top. Bake at 350° for 40-45 minutes or until hot and bubbly.

Yield: Serves 6-8.

BROCCOLI SUPREME

- **1 egg, slightly beaten**
- **1 (10-ounce) package frozen chopped broccoli, partially thawed**
- **1 (8½-ounce) can cream-style corn**
- **1 tablespoon grated onion**
- **¼ teaspoon salt**
- **Dash of pepper**
- **3 tablespoons butter**
- **1 cup herb-seasoned stuffing mix**

In mixing bowl, combine egg, broccoli, cream-style corn, onion, salt and pepper. In small saucepan, melt butter; add stuffing mix, tossing to coat. Stir ¾ cup of the stuffing mix into vegetable mixture. Turn into ungreased 1½-quart casserole. Sprinkle with remaining ¼ cup stuffing mix. Bake uncovered in 350° oven for 35-40 minutes.

Yield: Serves 4-6.

SMOTHERED CABBAGE

- **1 large or 2 small heads cabbage**
- **6 tablespoons butter**
- **2 cups chopped onion**
- **1 cup chopped bell pepper**
- **½ cup chopped celery**
- **½ cup diced ham**
- **1 tablespoon chopped garlic**
- **Salt, cayenne and black pepper, to taste**

Cut the cabbage in fourths and remove the tough white center. Parboil until slightly tender. Drain and chop the cabbage. In a saucepan, melt the butter and sauté the onions, bell pepper, celery and ham for 3-4 minutes. Add the cabbage and garlic. Season with salt, cayenne and black pepper. Cover and cook over low heat, stirring occasionally for 15-20 minutes until all is wilted or "smothered down."

Yield: Serves 6-8.

CARROT SOUFFLÉ

- **1 cup sugar**
- **3 tablespoons all-purpose flour**
- **1 teaspoon baking powder**
- **½ cup butter, melted**
- **2 cups cooked, mashed carrots (about 1½ pounds)**
- **3 large eggs**
- **1 teaspoon vanilla extract**

Combine all ingredients, except eggs and vanilla, in mixing bowl. Add eggs one at a time, beating on high speed of electric beater after each addition. Stir in vanilla and beat well.

Pour into a greased 9 x 9-inch baking pan and bake at 350° for 1 hour or until crust forms.

Yield: Serves 6-8.

CELERY CASSEROLE

- **4 cups ½-inch slices celery**
- **4 cups water**
- **½ cup (scant) sugar**
- **4 tablespoons butter**
- **1 (10¾-ounce) can cream of chicken soup, undiluted**
- **1 cup dry cornbread stuffing mix**

Combine celery, water and sugar in large saucepan; cook on medium heat 5 minutes or until celery is barely tender. Drain; cool. Grease 1½-quart shallow casserole with some of the butter. Toss celery with chicken soup and pour into casserole.

Sprinkle cornbread stuffing mix on top. Dot with remaining butter. Bake at 350° for 30 minutes until bubbly and heated through. Do not overcook.

Yield: Serves 6-8.

Variations:

- Add ½ cup shredded Cheddar cheese to soup.
- Substitute 1 cup chopped pecans for cornbread stuffing mix.

GREEN CORN TAMALE CASSEROLE

A tasty side dish with Mexican dinners.

- **2 (4-ounce) cans whole green chilies**
- **6 cups fresh corn kernels (or canned white corn kernels)**
- **⅔ cup yellow cornmeal**
- **4 tablespoons butter, melted**
- **4 teaspoons sugar**
- **2 teaspoons salt**
- **2 cups shredded Cheddar cheese**

Rinse chilies; cut into strips. Combine next 5 ingredients in food processor until corn is finely blended. Butter a 2-quart casserole. Pour half corn mixture into dish, top with chili strips and cover with the cheese. Pour remaining corn mixture over cheese, spreading evenly. Cover and bake at 350° for 1 hour. Serve with salsa.

Yield: Serves 6-8.

SCALLOPED CORN

- **1 (15¼-ounce) can whole kernel corn, drained**
- **1 (15-ounce) can cream-style corn**
- **¼ cup milk**
- **¼ cup crushed round buttery crackers**
- **¼ cup chopped onion**
- **2 eggs, beaten**
- **1 (2-ounce) jar chopped pimientos, drained**
- **½ teaspoon salt**
- **¼ teaspoon pepper**
- **4 tablespoons Parmesan cheese**
- **2 tablespoons butter**

Combine all ingredients except Parmesan cheese and butter, mixing well. Pour into a greased 1½-quart casserole. Sprinkle top with cheese; dot with butter. Bake uncovered at 350° for 40-45 minutes until center is almost set. Let stand 5 minutes before serving.

Yield: Serves 6.

SCALLOPED CORN AND TOMATOES

Serve with turkey or chicken.

- 2 (14½-ounce) cans tomatoes, drained, chopped
- 1 (15¼-ounce) can whole kernel corn, drained
- 1 (14¼-ounce) can cream-style corn
- 2 eggs, slightly beaten
- ¼ cup all-purpose flour
- 2 teaspoons sugar
- ½ teaspoon pepper
- 1 medium onion, finely chopped
- ⅓ cup butter
- ½ teaspoon garlic powder
- 4 cups soft bread crumbs
- ½ cup grated Parmesan cheese

Combine tomatoes with next 6 ingredients; blend well; set aside. Sauté onions in butter until tender and mix with garlic powder, bread crumbs and Parmesan cheese. Pour tomato corn mixture into a greased 2-quart casserole dish; top with bread crumb mixture. Bake uncovered at 350° for 1 hour or until brown and set.

Yield: Serves 12.

CORN PUDDING

- 2 (15-ounce) cans creamed corn
- ½ cup butter, melted
- ½ cup all-purpose flour
- 2 tablespoons sugar
- 6 eggs, slightly beaten
- ½ teaspoon salt
- 1 cup whole milk

Combine all ingredients, mixing well. Pour into a greased 2½-quart oblong baking dish. Bake at 350° for 1 hour, stirring twice during the first 30 minutes.

Yield: Serves 6-8.

SILVER QUEEN CORN PUDDING

- **2 cups fresh silver queen corn, cut from cob**
- **¼ cup all-purpose flour**
- **1 tablespoon sugar**
- **1 teaspoon salt**
- **2 cups half-and-half**
- **3 large eggs, beaten**
- **⅛ teaspoon ground nutmeg**
- **¼ cup butter, melted**

Place corn over a bowl and slice kernels off with a sharp knife. With a table knife, scrape cobs well to get remaining kernels and juice. Stir in flour, sugar and salt; mix well. Blend in eggs, butter and nutmeg. Gradually blend in cream. Pour into a lightly greased 1½-quart casserole. Place casserole in larger flat baking pan with water (so that corn casserole is sitting in 1 inch of water). Bake at 350° for 1 hour (or until set in the middle and a silver knife inserted comes out clean).

Yield: Serves 4-6.

BAKED HERBED EGGPLANT

- **1 (1½-pound) eggplant, unpeeled**
- **¼ cup olive oil**
- **⅛ teaspoon each: basil, thyme, oregano**
- **1 teaspoon salt**
- **½ teaspoon minced garlic**
- **Black pepper to taste**
- **2 tablespoons butter, melted**
- **1 tablespoon chopped parsley**
- **¼ cup bread crumbs or toasted wheat germ**

In a small pan, mix olive oil, basil, thyme, oregano, salt, pepper and garlic. Wipe eggplant and cut into eight round slices. Brush on both sides with oil herb mixture. Place on cookie sheet and bake for 15 minutes at 375° then turn slices over and bake 15 minutes longer. Melt butter in oil herb pan; stir in parsley and bread crumbs. Spoon over top of each eggplant slice. Broil until brown (2-3 minutes).

Yield: Serves 4.

EGGPLANT CASSEROLE À LA MORRISON'S

- **1 large eggplant**
- **Salt and pepper**
- **1 cup coarsely crushed cracker crumbs**
- **½ onion, finely chopped**
- **4 tablespoons bacon drippings**
- **2 eggs, beaten**
- **½ cup butter, melted**
- **1 cup finely crushed cracker crumbs**

Peel eggplant; cut into cubes. Boil until tender; drain well. Place eggplant in mixing bowl, add salt, pepper and coarsely chopped cracker crumbs. Sauté onion in bacon drippings until tender; add to eggplant mix. Stir beaten eggs into eggplant, beating by hand until well mixed. Pour mixture into greased 1½-quart casserole. Mix melted butter with finely crushed cracker crumbs and sprinkle over top of casserole. Bake at 375° for 30 minutes.

Yield: Serves 4.

EGGPLANT PARMESAN

- **1 large eggplant**
- **1 (28-ounce) jar chunky garden style tomato sauce**
- **1 (8-ounce) package mozzarella cheese (6 slices)**
- **Freshly grated Parmesan cheese**
- **Olive oil**

Peel eggplant and slice into ¼-inch slices. Sauté in olive oil until browned on both sides. Grease a 2-quart casserole. Prepare layers as follows: eggplant, sprinkled with Parmesan cheese, covered with tomato sauce, sprinkled with Parmesan cheese then mozzarella cheese slices. Repeat layers 3 times. Bake covered at 325° for 45-50 minutes. Remove cover last 5 minutes of baking time.

Yield: Serves 4-6.

MUSHROOM SOUFFLÉS

Quickly rinse mushrooms in a colander or wipe them clean. Never immerse mushrooms in water.

- **1 pound fresh mushrooms, chopped**
- **¼ cup chopped onion**
- **6 tablespoons butter, divided**
- **6 tablespoons all-purpose flour**
- **2 cups milk**
- **½ cup shredded Cheddar cheese**
- **¼ teaspoon salt**
- **⅛ teaspoon pepper**
- **Tabasco**
- **6 eggs, separated**
- **Shrimp and Almond Sauce**

Sauté mushrooms and onion in 3 tablespoons of the butter until tender; remove mushroom onion mixture and set aside. In the same skillet, combine remaining 3 tablespoons butter and all of flour; stirring constantly, cook 1 minute. Gradually add milk cooking over medium heat, stirring constantly, until thickened. Stir in cheese, salt, pepper and Tabasco (a few drops); cool. Combine mushroom mixture and egg yolks; stir into cheese mixture blending well. Beat egg whites until stiff peaks form; fold into mushroom mixture.

Pour into 6 lightly greased (10-ounce) custard cups. Place in large shallow pan and add water around cups so that they are sitting in 1 inch of water. Bake at 325° for 45 minutes or until knife inserted in soufflé comes out clean. Remove and invert onto plates (or serving platter). Top each soufflé with Shrimp-Almond Sauce.

Yield: 6 soufflés.

Shrimp and Almond Sauce

- **1 (10¾-ounce) can cream of shrimp soup, undiluted**
- **1 (3-ounce) package cream cheese, softened**
- **¾ cup milk**
- **1 tablespoon lemon juice**
- **1 (2-ounce) package sliced almonds, toasted**
- **¼ cup dry sherry**

Combine cream of shrimp soup, cream cheese, milk and lemon juice in small saucepan; cook over low heat until thoroughly heated. Stir in almonds and sherry.

Yield: 2 cups.

MUSHROOMS IN CREAM

Serve as a vegetable side dish with beef or chicken. Reserve stems for soup.

- **20-24 large mushrooms**
- **½ cup butter, softened**
- **2 tablespoons chopped fresh parsley**
- **1½ teaspoons chopped chives**
- **2 green onions, minced**
- **½ teaspoon salt**
- **½ teaspoon lemon juice**
- **1 cup heavy cream**

Remove stems from mushrooms; place mushrooms in a shallow 2½-3-quart baking dish. Mix butter, parsley, chives, onions, salt and lemon juice. Stuff mushroom caps. Pour cream evenly over top. Bake at 450° for 10 minutes.

Yield: Serves 8.

ONION RINGS

Very crisp, thin and delicious.

- **3 large Vidalia onions, thinly sliced**
- **1 egg, beaten (optional)**
- **3 cups milk**
- **3 cups self-rising flour**
- **Vegetable oil**

Separate onions into rings. Mix egg with milk in a large bowl. Place as many onion rings as possible into milk to soak. Place flour in another large bowl.

When ready to prepare, remove onions from milk, dredge in flour to coat, shake off excess. Cook in deep hot vegetable oil in batches until light brown. Drain on paper towels. Keep warm until all onions are cooked.

Yield: Serves 6.

SAVORY BAKED ONIONS

- **4 large Vidalia onions**
- **1½ cups chili sauce**
- **⅛ teaspoon salt**
- **½ cup brown sugar**
- **¼ cup butter or margarine**

Peel and cut onions in half crosswise. Place in single layer in 2-quart oblong casserole, cut side up. Heat chili sauce, salt, sugar and butter. Spoon over onions. Bake at 400° for 35-40 minutes until tender and glazed.

Yield: Serves 8

If you need half of an onion, use the top half. The root stays fresher longer in the refrigerator.

BAKED VIDALIA ONIONS

Delicious side dish with any meat entrée.

- **4 medium Vidalia onions**
- **¼ cup butter, melted**
- **1 (10¾-ounce) can cream of chicken and broccoli soup, undiluted**
- **½ teaspoon pepper**
- **¼ cup dry sherry**
- **1½ cups grated sharp Cheddar cheese**

Cut each onion into 6 wedges without cutting all the way through. Place in a greased 2-quart square casserole. Pour melted butter over onions. Mix soup, pepper and sherry together; spread over onions. Sprinkle cheese evenly over top. Bake covered at 375° for 1 hour 15 minutes, uncover and continue to bake another 10 minutes. Carefully remove onions from casserole, topping each serving with sauce from baking pan.

Yield: Serves 4.

BLACK-EYED PEAS

- **1 (1-pound) package dried black-eyed peas**
- **6 cups water**
- **4 slices bacon**
- **1 tablespoon salt**
- **1 tablespoon sugar**
- **1 tablespoon white vinegar**
- **½ teaspoon pepper**
- **¼ teaspoon garlic powder**
- **1 cup chopped onion**

Sort and wash peas; place in a large pot. Cover with water 2 inches above peas. Bring to a rolling boil for 2 minutes; remove from heat and let stand for 1 hour. Drain. Add 6 cups water and remaining ingredients to peas. Bring to boil; reduce heat and simmer for 1½ hours or until peas are tender.

Yield: Serves 8-10.

GARLIC POTATOES WITH MUSHROOMS

- **3 pounds medium new potatoes**
- **6 thick slices bacon, crisply cooked and crumbled**
- **2 tablespoons chopped chives**
- **½ pound mushrooms, sliced**
- **Salt and freshly ground pepper**
- **½ cup plus 1 tablespoon butter, melted**
- **2-3 cloves garlic, pressed**

Wash and slice potatoes ¼-inch thick. Layer potato slices in a shallow 3-quart glass baking dish. Sprinkle with bacon and chives. Add sliced mushrooms and season with salt and pepper. Add pressed garlic to butter and pour over potatoes and mushrooms. Cover with foil and bake at 350° for 45 minutes. Continue baking uncovered until potatoes are tender, about 10-15 minutes.

Yield: Serves 6.

MINTED PEAS

1 (10-ounce) package frozen green peas
½ teaspoon salt
¼ teaspoon pepper
1 tablespoon butter
⅓ cup mint jelly

Cook peas until crisply tender; blend in other ingredients. Simmer to heat well and blend flavors. Serve immediately.

Yield: Serves 4.

GARLIC MASHED POTATOES

2 complete heads of garlic
3 tablespoons olive oil
8 large potatoes, peeled and quartered
½ cup butter, softened
1 cup half-and-half
½ cup sour cream
2 teaspoons salt
1 teaspoon pepper
½ teaspoon dried parsley
½ teaspoon ground rosemary
½ teaspoon ground thyme

Gently peel outer skins from garlic heads. Cut one quarter off tops of each head; discard. Place garlic heads on sheet of foil; drizzle with olive oil. Wrap tightly and bake at 375° for 1 hour or until garlic has softened. Remove from oven; cool. Squeeze garlic paste from each clove into a bowl; set aside.

Boil potatoes until tender; drain. Return pan to heat shaking pan to dry potatoes; add garlic paste. Mash potatoes with butter adding half-and-half and sour cream until fluffy. Stir in seasonings. Serve immediately.

Yield: Serves 8-10.

HASH BROWN POTATO CASSEROLE

Recipe doubles easily.

- **1 pound frozen hash-brown potatoes, thawed**
- **½ cup butter, melted**
- **1 (10¾-ounce) can cream of chicken soup**
- **1 cup shredded Cheddar cheese**
- **½ cup chopped onion**
- **1 teaspoon salt**
- **1 tablespoon sugar**
- **½ teaspoon pepper**
- **1 (8-ounce) carton sour cream**
- **2 cups crushed corn flake crumbs**
- **¼ cup butter, melted**

Blend all ingredients (except corn flake crumbs and ¼ cup butter) in large mixing bowl. Pour into a greased 2½-quart casserole. Mix corn flake crumbs and butter together and sprinkle over casserole. Bake at 350° for 45-50 minutes until casserole is browned and bubbly.

Yield: Serves 6.

Variations:

- Substitute cream of potato soup for cream of chicken soup.
- Substitute ½ cup freshly grated Parmesan cheese in place of crushed corn flake crumbs and ¼ cup butter.

PARMESAN POTATO FINGERS

- **¼ cup all-purpose flour**
- **¼ cup Parmesan cheese**
- **2 tablespoons parsley flakes**
- **¾ teaspoon salt**
- **⅛ teaspoon pepper**
- **⅓ cup butter**
- **6 medium potatoes**

Combine flour, cheese, parsley, salt and pepper in a plastic bag. Cut each potato lengthwise into eighths. Drop cut potatoes, a few at a time, into plastic bag, shaking to coat. Melt butter in a 13 x 9-inch casserole dish. Place coated potatoes in single layer in butter. Bake uncovered at 375° for 1 hour. Turn potatoes once after 30 minutes.

Yield: Serves 8-10.

ITALIAN POTATO PIE

- **2 pounds potatoes, peeled and sliced**
- **½ cup butter, softened**
- **½ cup low-fat sour cream**
- **½ cup chopped chives (optional)**
- **Salt and pepper**
- **12 ounces shredded mozzarella cheese**
- **3 tomatoes, peeled and sliced**
- **1 teaspoon basil**
- **1 teaspoon oregano**
- **½ cup grated Parmesan cheese**
- **½ cup butter, melted**

Boil potatoes until tender; drain and mash. Stir in softened butter, sour cream, chives, salt and pepper. Beat together until fluffy. Spread potatoes into a buttered and lightly floured 9½-inch deep glass pie pan forming a shell. Arrange 6-ounces mozzarella cheese over potatoes; top with tomato slices. Sprinkle with basil and oregano. Top with remaining mozzarella. Cover mozzarella with Parmesan cheese and drizzle top with butter. Bake at 400° for 20-25 minutes. Cool slightly and serve.

Yield: Serves 6-8.

JUDY'S CHEESY POTATOES

- **5 large baking potatoes, unpeeled**
- **3 (8-ounce) packages shredded sharp Cheddar cheese**
- **Salt and pepper to taste**
- **3 (8-ounce) cartons sour cream**
- **2 (12-ounce) packages bacon, crisply cooked and crumbled**
- **1 (0.12-ounce) jar dried chives**

Wash potatoes; slice into ¼-inch pieces horizontally. Simmer in water to cover until tender. Drain. Arrange potato slices in a 13 x 9-inch baking dish. Top with remaining ingredients in order given. Bake at 350° for 30 minutes or until hot and heated thoroughly.

Yield: Serves 8-10.

SWEET POTATO CASSEROLE

- **2 cups mashed sweet potatoes**
- **1 teaspoon vanilla extract**
- **½ cup raisins**
- **¼ teaspoon salt**
- **1¼ cups sugar**
- **½ cup butter, melted**
- **2 tablespoons baking powder**
- **3 eggs, beaten**

Blend all ingredients together thoroughly. Pour into a 2-quart oblong baking dish. Bake at 400° for 20-25 minutes until set. Remove from oven and cover potatoes with Topping. Return to oven 10 minutes or until lightly browned.

Yield: Serves 6-8.

Topping:

- **3 tablespoons butter, softened**
- **¼ cup brown sugar**
- **1¼ cups corn flake crumbs**
- **¼ cup chopped nuts**

Variations:

- Add ⅔ cup mashed ripe bananas to sweet potatoes before baking.
- Add ¼ cup bourbon to potatoes before baking.
- Instead of Topping, cover potatoes with marshmallows.

Peel asparagus stalks with a potato peeler up to bottom of tips.

POTATO PANCAKES À LA BAUMRUCKER

- **1 medium onion**
- **6 large potatoes**
- **2 eggs**
- **1 teaspoon salt**
- **¼ teaspoon pepper**
- **1½ teaspoons caraway seeds**
- **Vegetable oil**

Coarsely grate onion and potatoes using food processor; mix together and drain well until all water is removed. Place in mixing bowl and mix eggs, salt, pepper and caraway seeds into potato onion mixture, blend well and keep drained of water.

In electric skillet set at 450° or a large skillet over medium high heat, add vegetable oil to depth of ¼ inch. When oil is ready, spoon ¼ cup batter into skillet. Pancake should be same size and thickness of regular pancake. Cook until brown on one side; turn and cook until crisp. Repeat until all mixture is used. Add more oil when needed. Drain on paper towels and keep warm until ready to serve.

Yield: Serves 6.

SPINACH CASSEROLE

- **2 (10-ounce) packages frozen chopped spinach**
- **1 (10¾-ounce) can cream of mushroom soup**
- **½ cup mayonnaise**
- **1½ cups shredded sharp Cheddar cheese**
- **2 tablespoons minced onion**
- **½ teaspoon salt**
- **¼ teaspoon pepper**
- **1 cup cracker crumbs**
- **3 tablespoons butter**

Cook spinach according to package directions; drain well to remove all water. Add next 6 ingredients; mix together well. Pour into a lightly greased 1½-quart casserole. Top with cracker crumbs; dot with butter and bake at 350° for 40 minutes.

Yield: Serves 6-8.

SPINACH BACON CASSEROLE

- **3 (10-ounce) packages frozen chopped spinach**
- **4 (10-ounce) packages frozen Welsh rarebit**
- **2 pounds bacon, crisply cooked and crumbled**
- **2 (8-ounce) cans water chestnuts, drained, sliced**
- **1 (2.8-ounce) can French fried onions, crumbled**

Partially cook spinach; drain well, pressing out all water. Combine drained spinach, bacon and water chestnuts, mixing together gently but well; set aside.

Thaw rarebit in top of double boiler or microwave. Place half of rarebit on bottom of greased 13 x 9-inch glass baking dish. Spoon spinach mixture evenly over rarebit; top with remaining rarebit. Sprinkle with crumbled fried onions. Bake at 350° for 30 minutes or more until hot and bubbly.

Yield: Serves 8-10.

BUTTERNUT SQUASH CASSEROLE

- **2 cups cooked butternut squash, drained**
- **¾ cup sugar**
- **½ cup butter**
- **1 (5-ounce) can evaporated milk**
- **1 teaspoon lemon extract**
- **2 eggs, beaten**

Beat squash until smooth. Blend in remaining ingredients; mix well. Pour into 1½-quart casserole dish. Bake at 350° for 60 minutes or until set.

Yield: Serves 4-6.

SPINACH WITH ARTICHOKES

- **1 (14-ounce) can artichokes, drained**
- **1 (8-ounce) bottle French salad dressing**
- **4 tablespoons vegetable oil**
- **4 tablespoons all-purpose flour**
- **2 cups milk**
- **1 (8-ounce) package grated sharp Cheddar cheese**
- **2 (10-ounce) packages frozen chopped spinach**
- **½ teaspoon salt**
- **½ teaspoon pepper**
- **4 drops Tabasco**
- **½ teaspoon ground nutmeg**
- **1 cup Parmesan cheese**

Drain artichokes, cut in half; marinate in French dressing overnight. Heat oil in saucepan over medium heat; add flour stirring until well blended. Gradually add milk stirring until thickened; add Cheddar cheese and blend well. Remove from heat; set aside. Cook spinach according to package directions; cool slightly and squeeze to remove all water. In mixing bowl, mix spinach and cheese sauce together. Stir in salt, pepper, Tabasco and nutmeg, blending well. Arrange artichokes on bottom of 2½-quart oblong baking dish. Pour spinach mixture over artichokes; top with Parmesan cheese. Bake at 350° for 40-45 minutes until casserole is bubbly and cheese slightly browned.

Yield: Serves 6-8.

SPAGO'S RATATOUILLE

- ½ cup extra-virgin olive oil
- 1 pound onions, cut into 1-inch cubes
- 1 pound eggplant, peeled and cut into 1-inch cubes
- 1 pound yellow pepper, cored, seeded and cut into 1-inch squares
- 1 pound plum tomatoes, trimmed, seeded and cut into 1-inch cubes
- ½ pound zucchini, peeled and cut into 1-inch cubes
- 2 cloves garlic, minced
- Leaves of 1 large sprig thyme
- 1 teaspoon salt
- ½ teaspoon white pepper
- 2 tablespoons sherry vinegar
- 4 basil leaves
- 3 scallions, white parts only, cut into thin rounds

Heat ¼ cup of the olive oil in a large skillet and sauté onion over medium high heat until translucent. Stir in remaining vegetables, garlic, thyme, salt and pepper. Lower heat and cook covered for 30 minutes, stirring occasionally. Transfer to a serving bowl and let cool to room temperature. Toss with vinegar and remaining olive oil. When ready to serve, sprinkle with scallions and basil.

Yield: Serves 8.

Celery juice is an effective stress reducer.

COMPANY SQUASH

- **8 medium-size yellow squash**
- **½ cup chopped onion**
- **1 (8-ounce) carton sour cream**
- **1 teaspoon salt**
- **½ teaspoon pepper**
- **¼ teaspoon basil**
- **1 cup soft bread crumbs**
- **½ cup grated medium Cheddar cheese**
- **⅓ cup butter, melted**
- **½ teaspoon paprika**
- **8 slices bacon, crisply cooked and crumbled**

Trim ends off squash, chop and cook with onion in boiling salted water until tender; drain and mash. Combine squash, sour cream, salt, pepper and basil; pour into a greased 2-quart casserole. Combine bread crumbs, cheese, butter and paprika; sprinkle over squash. Top with bacon. Bake at 325° for 30 minutes.

Yield: Serves 6-8.

CREOLE SUMMER SQUASH

- **½ bell pepper, chopped**
- **1 medium onion, chopped**
- **2 tablespoons vegetable oil**
- **2 fresh tomatoes, peeled and chopped**
- **5-6 medium-small yellow squash**
- **½ clove garlic, mashed**
- **Salt and pepper**
- **Parmesan cheese**

In a large skillet, sauté pepper and onion in vegetable oil until tender; add tomatoes, squash and garlic. Do Not Add Water. Simmer on low until squash is tender, stirring occasionally to prevent sticking. Salt and pepper to taste. Sprinkle each serving with Parmesan cheese.

Yield: Serves 4.

FRIED GREEN TOMATOES

- **4 large green tomatoes (about 2 pounds)**
- **¼ cup sugar**
- **½ cup plain white cornmeal**
- **¼ cup all-purpose flour**
- **1 teaspoon salt**
- **¼ teaspoon pepper**
- **3 tablespoons bacon drippings**
- **6 tablespoons vegetable oil**

Remove a thin slice from tops and bottoms of tomatoes; cut tomatoes into ¼-inch thick slices. Layer tomatoes in a small deep dish. Sprinkle each layer with sugar; let stand 1 hour. Drain, reserving liquid. Mix cornmeal, flour, salt and pepper together in shallow pan. Dredge tomatoes in the mixture. Heat bacon drippings and oil in large cast-iron skillet over medium heat. Fry tomatoes 2-3 minutes on each side until golden. Drain on paper towels. Drain off all but 1 tablespoon pan drippings; add reserved sugar liquid, heat and drizzle over tomatoes.

Yield: Serves 6.

SCALLOPED TOMATOES

- **4 cups peeled, chopped tomatoes**
- **1 cup chopped onion**
- **1 cup cheese cracker crumbs**
- **1½ teaspoons sugar**
- **½ teaspoon salt**
- **1 (8-ounce) carton sour cream**
- **1½ cups seasoned croutons**
- **1 tablespoon butter, melted**

Layer half each of tomatoes, onion, cracker crumbs, sugar and salt in a greased 1½-quart casserole. Repeat layers. Bake at 325° for 20 minutes. Spread sour cream over top; sprinkle croutons over sour cream. Drizzle melted butter over croutons. Bake 10 minutes more. Serve warm.

Yield: Serves 6.

MARILYN'S TOMATO PIE WITH WORLD'S BEST PIE CRUST

We suggest you prebake the pie crust at 375° for 10 minutes before using in this recipe.

- **3 medium tomatoes, peeled and sliced**
- **1 cup mayonnaise**
- **1 cup shredded Cheddar cheese**
- **1 tablespoon dried basil or 11 fresh basil leaves**
- **¼ cup chopped onion**
- **1 tablespoon minced bell pepper**

Arrange half of tomatoes in pie crust. Combine mayonnaise, cheese, basil, onion and bell pepper, mixing well. Spread half of mixture over tomato slices. Repeat layers. (If using fresh basil, tuck leaves among tomato slices.) Bake at 375° for 30-35 minutes until top is slightly browned.

Yield: Serves 8.

World's Best Pie Crust

- **1½ cups all-purpose flour**
- **1 teaspoon salt**
- **1½ teaspoons sugar**
- **½ cup vegetable oil**
- **2 tablespoons milk**

Combine all ingredients, mixing well. Place in a 9-inch pie pan. Use fingers to form into a pie shell. Pierce with fork.

Tomatoes keep longer stored stem down.

OVEN-ROASTED VEGETABLES WITH ROSEMARY AND GARLIC

2 cups carrots
2 cups eggplant
2 cups squash
2 cups parboiled potatoes (boil 7 minutes)
2 cups golden bell pepper
2 cups red onion
½ cup olive oil
2 tablespoons chopped garlic
2 tablespoons chopped rosemary leaves
Salt
Freshly ground pepper
Sprigs of rosemary for garnish

Cut vegetables into 1½-inch cubes, adding any other vegetables that are in season and look appealing. Toss with olive oil, chopped garlic and rosemary. Add salt and pepper to taste. Turn oven to highest setting and preheat for 15 minutes. Place vegetables one layer deep on a sheet pan and oven-roast for 20 minutes or until almost done. Finish cooking under broiler until edges are blackened and caramelized. Do not stir during cooking. Remove from pan and serve at room temperature with sprigs of rosemary for garnish.

Yield: Serves 6.

Sprinkle French fries with flour before frying.

VEGETABLE MEDLEY

- **4 small yellow squash, sliced**
- **3 small zucchini, sliced**
- **1 Vidalia onion, sliced**
- **3 stalks celery, sliced**
- **2 tomatoes, thickly sliced**
- **Salt**
- **Lemon pepper**
- **½ teaspoon sugar**
- **Olive oil**
- **Parmesan cheese**

Layer sliced vegetables with tomatoes on top in an 11 x 9-inch casserole. Sprinkle with salt, lemon pepper and sugar. Drizzle with olive oil and sprinkle with Parmesan cheese.

Cover tightly with foil. Bake at 350° for 40 minutes. Remove foil and bake 10 minutes longer.

Yield: Serves 4-6.

SONDRA'S VEGETABLE CASSEROLE

- **1 (12-ounce) can English peas**
- **1 (16-ounce) can mixed vegetables**
- **2 cups grated sharp Cheddar cheese**
- **1 cup chopped onion**
- **2 cups water chestnuts, drained and sliced**
- **1 cup mayonnaise**
- **1 cup crushed round buttery crackers**
- **½ cup butter, melted**

Drain vegetables and combine with all ingredients except round buttery crackers and butter. Pour into a greased 2-quart casserole. Cover with crackers; pour butter over crackers and bake at 350° for 30 minutes or until hot and bubbly.

Yield: Serves 4-6.

ZUCCHINI CASSEROLE

- **4 medium zucchini, unpeeled**
- **10 tablespoons biscuit baking mix**
- **2 eggs, beaten**
- **1 cup chopped canned mushrooms**
- **¾ cup butter, softened**
- **½ cup chopped onion**
- **1 clove garlic, minced**
- **1 cup grated Swiss cheese**
- **½ cup cracker crumbs**

Coarsely grate zucchini; add biscuit baking mix, eggs, mushrooms, butter, onion and garlic. Mix ingredients together well. Pour into a buttered 1½-quart casserole. Top with Swiss cheese mixed with cracker crumbs. Bake at 350° for 45 minutes.

Yield: Serves 6.

Add hot milk to potatoes when mashing; it keeps them from becoming soggy.

Eggs, Pasta, Rice

EGGS

GRITS

PASTA

RICE

BACON AND EGG CASSEROLE

- 1 cup fresh bread crumbs
- 12 hard-boiled eggs, sliced
- 1 pound bacon, crisply cooked and crumbled
- 2 tablespoons bacon drippings
- 4 cups sour cream
- 2 (4-ounce) cans mushroom stems and pieces, drained
- 2 teaspoons salt
- 4 teaspoons chopped parsley
- 4 teaspoons chopped chives
- ½ teaspoon paprika
- 1½ cups grated cheese

Sprinkle bread crumbs over bottom of greased 13 x 9-inch baking dish; top with sliced eggs. Mix remaining ingredients (except cheese) and pour over eggs. Sprinkle with cheese. Bake at 350° for 30-35 minutes until bubbly.

Yield: Serves 10-12.

EASY SPINACH PIE

- ½ cup sliced green onions
- 2 cloves garlic, minced
- 1 tablespoon butter
- 1 (10-ounce) package frozen chopped spinach, thawed, drained
- ½ cup creamed cottage cheese
- ½ cup biscuit baking mix
- ½ cup milk
- 3 eggs, beaten
- 1 teaspoon lemon juice
- ¼ teaspoon pepper
- 3 tablespoons grated Parmesan cheese
- ¼ teaspoon ground nutmeg

Sauté onions and garlic in butter until tender. Stir in well drained spinach. In greased quiche dish, layer spinach then cottage cheese. In a blender, mix biscuit baking mix, milk, eggs, lemon juice and pepper for 15-20 seconds. Pour over cottage cheese. Sprinkle top with Parmesan cheese and nutmeg. Bake at 350° for 35-40 minutes or until knife inserted in center comes out clean.

Yield: Serves 8.

BREAKFAST CASSEROLE

An old reliable recipe that is great for company and a wonderful dish to have on hand. It will keep 2 days refrigerated before baking.

- **1 pound bulk sausage, browned, drained and crumbled**
- **10 slices white bread, crusts removed**
- **4 tablespoons butter, softened**
- **1 onion, minced**
- **2 cups grated Cheddar cheese**
- **6 eggs**
- **2½ cups whole milk**
- **1 teaspoon salt**
- **⅛ teaspoon paprika**
- **1 teaspoon dry mustard**
- **1 teaspoon Worcestershire sauce**

Butter bread on both sides. Place 5 slices bread in a 13 x 9-inch casserole, spread half the sausage, onions and cheese over bread. Place other 5 slices bread on top followed by rest of sausage, onions and cheese. Lightly beat eggs and milk together; add remaining ingredients and blend. Pour over layers in casserole. Cover and refrigerate overnight. Bake at 350° for 1 hour.

Yield: Serves 8-10.

Variation: Substitute 3 cups chopped cooked ham for sausage.

1 pound hard cheese yields 4-5 cups grated.

CHILE RELLEÑOS

- **2 (4-ounce) cans whole green chilies**
- **1 (8-ounce) package Monterey Jack cheese, cut into strips**
- **5 eggs**
- **⅔ cup milk**
- **6 tablespoons all-purpose flour**
- **¾ teaspoon baking powder**
- **1 cup shredded Cheddar cheese**
- **¼ cup sliced black olives**

Rinse chilies, pat dry with paper towel. Slit down one side and remove seeds. Cut Monterey Jack cheese into strips just a bit shorter than chilies. Place a cheese strip into each pepper, folding over to enclose cheese. Place chilies side by side in a well greased 2-quart oblong baking dish.

Beat eggs until foamy; beat in milk, flour and baking powder until smooth. Pour over chilies covering all surfaces. Sprinkle with Cheddar cheese. Bake at 350° for 40 minutes or until set in the middle. Remove from oven; let stand 10 minutes. Garnish with sliced olives. Serve with salsa.

Yield: Serves 8.

Stale eggs float in water; fresh eggs sink.

DEVILED EGG BAKE

Do not overheat or reheat; egg whites will be rubbery.

12 large hard-boiled eggs
4 teaspoons prepared mustard
6 tablespoons sour cream
½ teaspoon salt
½ teaspoon pepper
4 tablespoons butter
1 cup chopped bell pepper
⅔ cup chopped onion
½ cup chopped pimiento
1½ cups sour cream
2 (10¾-ounce) cans cream of mushroom soup
1½ cups shredded sharp Cheddar cheese

Halve eggs lengthwise; remove yolks. Blend yolks, mustard, sour cream, salt and pepper. Fill whites; set aside. In a large skillet, melt butter, sauté bell pepper and onions until tender. Stir in pimiento, sour cream and soup. Remove from heat; mix well. Pour half of mixture into a 13 x 9-inch baking dish. Arrange eggs stuffed side up in single layers lengthwise. Spoon remaining sauce over eggs. (Sauce will thin out when heated.) Sprinkle cheese on top. Bake at 350° for 20 minutes or until heated and bubbly.

Yield: Serves 12.

Cottage cheese stays fresh longer when stored upside down.

EGGS HUSSARDE

- 4 slices Canadian bacon
- 1¾ cups Marchands de vin Sauce
- 4 eggs, poached
- ¾ cup Hollandaise Sauce (see Page 226)
- 2 English muffins, split and buttered
- Paprika

Sauté Canadian bacon in butter until lightly browned. Toast muffins. For each serving, place a slice of bacon on muffin half; cover with Marchands de vin Sauce. Place a poached egg on each muffin half and cover with Hollandaise Sauce. Sprinkle each with paprika.

Yield: Serves 4.

Marchands de vin Sauce

- ¾ cup butter
- ⅓ cup finely chopped mushrooms
- ½ cup minced cooked ham
- ⅓ cup finely chopped shallots
- ½ cup finely chopped onions
- 2 tablespoons minced garlic
- 2 tablespoons all-purpose flour
- ½ teaspoon salt
- ¼ teaspoon pepper
- 3 drops Tabasco
- ¾ cup beef bouillon
- ½ cup red wine

In a large skillet, melt butter and sauté mushrooms, ham, shallots, onions and garlic until tender. Add flour, salt, pepper and Tabasco; blend well. Stir in bouillon and wine. Simmer over low heat 35 minutes.

Yield: 2 cups.

Variation: Substitute Cheese Sauce (see Page 282) for the Hollandaise Sauce.

Egg whites should be at room temperature before beating.

EGGS SARDOU

A Louisiana favorite and a good brunch dish. Recipe can be doubled.

- **1½ tablespoons butter**
- **1 (10-ounce) package frozen chopped spinach**
- **1 tablespoon flour**
- **¼ cup cream**
- **½ teaspoon salt**
- **¼ teaspoon pepper, sugar and ground nutmeg**
- **4 artichoke bottoms**
- **4 eggs, poached**

Cook spinach according to package directions; drain well. Melt butter in skillet; add spinach and stir 3 minutes. Sprinkle flour over spinach stirring constantly; add cream. Cook over low heat 5 minutes. Add seasonings. Place artichoke bottoms in hot water bath; let sit to keep warm.

To serve, place spinach on each serving plate. Top with two artichoke bottoms; top each with a poached egg and cover with Hollandaise Sauce.

Yield: Serves 2.

Hollandaise Sauce

- **½ cup butter**
- **3 egg yolks**
- **2 tablespoons lemon juice**
- **¼ teaspoon salt**
- **⅛ teaspoon white pepper**
- **½ teaspoon prepared mustard**

Heat butter until it bubbles; set aside. Place remaining ingredients in blender (or food processor) and mix on low for 5 seconds. Slowly add hot butter in a steady stream, blending until mixture thickens.

Yield: ¾ cup.

OVERNIGHT SCRAMBLED EGGS

- **1 cup cubed ham or Canadian bacon, chopped**
- **¼ cup chopped green onions**
- **3 tablespoons butter, melted**
- **12 large eggs, beaten**
- **1 (4-ounce) can sliced mushrooms, drained**
- **Cheese Sauce**
- **¼ cup melted butter**
- **2¼ cups soft bread crumbs**
- **⅛ teaspoon paprika**

In a large skillet, sauté ham and green onions in butter until onions are tender. Add eggs and cook over medium high heat, stirring to form large, soft curds. When eggs are set, stir in mushrooms and Cheese Sauce. Spoon into a greased 13 x 9-inch baking dish. Mix melted butter and crumbs; spread over egg mixture and sprinkle with paprika. Cover and chill overnight.

Remove from refrigerator; let stand at room temperature 30 minutes. Bake uncovered at 350° for 30 minutes or until well heated.

Yield: Serves 12.

Cheese Sauce:

- **2 tablespoons butter**
- **2½ tablespoons flour**
- **2 cups milk**
- **½ teaspoon salt**
- **⅛ teaspoon pepper**
- **1 cup shredded processed cheese loaf**

Melt butter in heavy saucepan over low heat; blend in flour, cook 1 minute. Gradually add milk; cook over medium heat, stirring until thickened. Add salt, pepper and cheese. Stir until cheese melts.

Yield: 2½ cups.

Add 1 teaspoon cold water to egg whites before beating to increase volume.

POTATO CRUST QUICHE

Crust:

- **3 medium potatoes, peeled and grated**
- **1 egg, beaten**
- **2 tablespoons all-purpose flour**
- **½ cup chopped onion**
- **¼ teaspoon salt**
- **¼ teaspoon pepper**

Filling:

- **4 eggs**
- **1 cup chopped onion**
- **1 cup chopped broccoli**
- **1 cup chopped ham or turkey**
- **3 tablespoons all-purpose flour**
- **⅛ teaspoon ground nutmeg**
- **¼ teaspoon salt**
- **1 cup grated Cheddar cheese**

Mix potatoes, egg, flour, onion, salt and pepper together. Press evenly into a well greased quiche pan. Bake crust at 400° for 25 minutes.

For filling, mix first 7 ingredients together. Pour into potato crust and top with cheese. Bake at 375° for 40 minutes or until set.

Yield: Serves 6-8.

CREAMY GRITS

- **2 cups water**
- **2 tablespoons butter**
- **½ cup uncooked grits**
- **1 cup half-and-half, divided**
- **1 teaspoon salt**

Bring water and butter to boil; stir in grits. At medium heat, return to boil. Reduce heat; cook 10-15 minutes, stirring occasionally until thickened. Stir in ½ cup cream and salt. Simmer 10 minutes, stirring occasionally. Add remaining cream and simmer 10 minutes, stirring occasionally. Serve immediately.

Yield: Serves 2.

CHEESE GRITS

- **1 cup uncooked grits**
- **½ cup butter**
- **1½ tablespoons Worcestershire sauce**
- **2 cups grated Cheddar cheese**
- **3 eggs, separated**
- **⅔ cup whole milk**
- **1 clove garlic, minced**
- **Tabasco**

Cook grits according to package directions. While hot, add butter, Worcestershire sauce and cheese. Stir until blended. Add egg yolks, mixing well. Blend in milk, garlic and Tabasco. Beat egg whites until stiff peaks form. Fold egg whites gently into grits mixture. Pour into greased 2½-quart casserole dish. Bake at 350° for 35-40 minutes or until set.

Yield: Serves 6.

FIESTA GRITS SOUFFLÉ

- **1 cup uncooked grits**
- **4 cups boiling water**
- **1 teaspoon salt**
- **2 cups shredded sharp Cheddar cheese**
- **½ cup chopped onion**
- **1 clove garlic, minced**
- **2 tablespoons melted butter**
- **⅓ cup finely chopped jalapeño peppers**
- **4 eggs, separated**

Stir grits into boiling water; add salt. Cook 10-20 minutes until grits have thickened. Remove from heat; add cheese, stirring until melted. Set aside.

Sauté onion and garlic in butter until tender; add to grits. Stir in peppers. Beat egg yolks slightly and add to grits, mixing well.

Beat egg whites until stiff; fold into grits. Spoon mixture into a greased 2-quart casserole. Bake at 350° for 45-50 minutes.

Yield: Serves 6-8.

GRUYÈRE CHEESE GRITS

- **4 cups milk**
- **½ cup butter, divided**
- **1½ cups shredded Gruyère cheese**
- **1 teaspoon salt**
- **1 cup uncooked regular grits**
- **⅛ teaspoon pepper**
- **⅓ cup grated Parmesan cheese**

Place milk in a large heavy saucepan; bring to a boil. Add ¼ cup butter and Gruyère cheese; stir until cheese melts. Slowly add grits; boil until thickened, stirring constantly. Stir in salt and pepper. Over low heat, beat mixture with electric beaters on low speed 5 minutes. Remove from heat; pour mixture into lightly greased 8-inch square pan. Melt remaining butter; add Parmesan cheese, mixing well. Spread over top of grits mixture. Bake at 400° for 30 minutes.

Yield: Serves 8.

To help prevent cheese from forming mold, store in a sealed container (refrigerated) with two lumps of sugar.

SAUSAGE GRITS

- **1 pound bulk pork sausage**
- **1 medium onion, chopped**
- **3 cups hot cooked grits**
- **2½ cups grated Cheddar cheese**
- **3 tablespoons butter**
- **3 eggs, beaten**
- **1½ cups milk**
- **Parsley for garnish**

Brown sausage and onion; drain well. Spoon sausage and onion into a greased 2-quart baking dish. Combine the hot grits, cheese and butter, stirring until cheese and butter melt. Combine eggs and milk; stir into grits. Pour over sausage. Bake at 350° for 1 hour. Garnish casserole with parsley.

Yield: Serves 4-6.

CANNELLONI ITALIANO

Bellissimo!

12 cannelloni shells
3 cups tomato sauce
1 teaspoon Italian seasoning
½ teaspoon salt
2 tablespoons grated Parmesan cheese
¼ cup diced onion
1 teaspoon minced garlic
2 tablespoons olive oil
1 (10-ounce) package frozen chopped spinach, thawed and drained well
1 pound ground beef
½ teaspoon salt
5 tablespoons Parmesan cheese
2 tablespoons whipping cream
2 eggs, slightly beaten
½ teaspoon oregano
6 tablespoons butter
6 tablespoons all-purpose flour
1 cup milk
1 cup whipping cream
½ teaspoon salt
½ teaspoon pepper
2 tablespoons butter

Cook cannelloni shells according to package directions. Drain; set aside.

Combine tomato sauce, Italian seasoning, salt, 2 tablespoons Parmesan cheese; cook over low heat, stirring constantly, until heated. Spread 1 cup tomato mixture in greased 13 x 9-inch baking dish; set remaining sauce aside.

Sauté onion and garlic in olive oil until tender. Add drained spinach and cook, stirring for 10 minutes; set aside.

Brown ground beef; discard pan drippings. Stir in spinach mixture, salt, 5 tablespoons Parmesan cheese, 2 tablespoons whipping cream, eggs and oregano; mix well. Stuff cannelloni shells with meat, spinach mixture and place on tomato sauce in baking dish.

Melt 6 tablespoons butter in heavy saucepan over low heat; add flour, stirring until smooth. Gradually add milk and whipping cream; cook over low heat stirring constantly until thickened. Stir in salt and pepper. Pour over cannelloni. Spoon remaining tomato sauce over cream sauce. Dot with 2 tablespoons butter. Bake uncovered at 375° for 20-30 minutes until hot and bubbly.

Yield: Serves 6.

SPINACH-STUFFED SHELLS

- 24 jumbo macaroni shells
- 1 (32-ounce) jar spaghetti sauce with mushrooms
- 1½ pounds lean ground beef
- 1 (10-ounce) package frozen spinach, thawed, drained
- 2 cups ricotta cheese
- 2 cups shredded mozzarella cheese
- 1 small onion, diced
- ½ cup grated Parmesan cheese
- 2 tablespoons chopped parsley
- 1 teaspoon oregano
- Tabasco
- ⅛ teaspoon nutmeg
- ¼ cup Parmesan cheese

Cook macaroni shells according to package directions; drain and set aside.

Brown meat; add to spaghetti sauce. Spoon 1 cup spaghetti meat sauce into a greased 13 x 9-inch baking dish; set remaining sauce aside.

Combine next 9 ingredients; mix well. Stuff each shell with 1½ tablespoons spinach mixture; arrange in baking dish. Spoon remaining spaghetti sauce over shells. Sprinkle with ¼ cup Parmesan cheese. Cover and bake at 350° for 30-40 minutes.

Yield: Serves 6-8.

Briefly rinse cooked pasta in hot water to reduce stickiness.

PASTA CRAB DELIGHT

- 2¼ cups uncooked seashell macaroni
- 1 (8-ounce) package cream cheese
- 1 (8-ounce) carton sour cream
- 1 cup cottage cheese
- ½ cup chopped green onions
- ½ cup chopped fresh parsley
- 2 (6-ounce) cans crabmeat, drained, picked
- 2 medium tomatoes, peeled and sliced
- 1½ cups shredded Monterey Jack cheese

Cook macaroni according to package directions; drain.

Combine cream cheese, sour cream, cottage cheese, green onions and parsley; mix well.

Layer half each of macaroni, cheese mixture and crabmeat in a greased 2-quart oblong baking dish. Repeat; top with tomato slices. Bake at 350° for 25 minutes; sprinkle with cheese and bake another 5 minutes.

Yield: Serves 6.

GORGONZOLA PASTA WITH SALMON

- 1½ cups heavy cream
- ½ pound Gorgonzola cheese, cubed
- 1 (16-ounce) package angel hair pasta
- ½ pound smoked salmon, sliced
- ¼ cup capers, drained
- 2 tablespoons chopped parsley

Heat cream and cheese very slowly until cheese melts. Cook pasta according to package directions, al dente; drain. Mix pasta with cream mixture; top with salmon, capers and parsley.

Yield: Serves 4-6.

FETTUCCINE PRIMAVERA

- 1 cup broccoli florets
- 1 cup sliced zucchini
- ½ cup diced bell pepper
- ½ cup chopped onion
- ½ teaspoon dried basil
- ¾ cup butter
- 2 fresh tomatoes, peeled and cut into small wedges
- ½ cup sliced mushrooms
- 1 teaspoon salt
- 1 (12-ounce) package fettuccine noodles
- Parmesan cheese

Sauté broccoli, zucchini, bell pepper, onion and basil in butter over medium heat until vegetables are tender. Stir in tomatoes, mushrooms and salt; simmer 5-10 minutes. Keep warm.

Cook fettuccine according to package directions; drain. Toss with vegetables. Serve with Parmesan cheese.

Yield: Serves 5.

FETTUCCINI WITH ALMONDS

- ¾ pound fettuccine or pasta of choice
- 5 tablespoons olive oil, divided
- 4 cloves garlic, minced
- 3 tablespoons fresh bread crumbs
- ½ cup chopped almonds
- 3 tomatoes, peeled and sliced into ¼-inch strips
- ½ cup chopped fresh basil
- 1 teaspoon salt
- ½ teaspoon pepper

Cook fettuccine in salted water, al dente. Drain.

Heat 3 tablespoons olive oil in skillet; over medium heat, sauté garlic 1 minute. Add bread crumbs and almonds; cook until golden (about 3 minutes).

Stir in remaining olive oil, tomatoes, basil, salt and pepper. Cook 1 minute. Stir in pasta and toss with sauce until heated through.

Yield: Serves 4.

MACARONI AND CHEESE

A real comfort food.

- **1 (8-ounce) package elbow macaroni (or seashell)**
- **½ cup chopped onion**
- **¼ cup chopped bell pepper**
- **¼ cup chopped pimiento**
- **1 tablespoon butter**
- **1 pound medium sharp Cheddar cheese, grated**
- **1 (10¾-ounce) can cream of mushroom soup, undiluted**
- **1 cup mayonnaise**
- **1 (2½-ounce) jar sliced mushrooms, drained**
- **1 sleeve round buttery crackers, crushed**
- **3 tablespoons butter**

Cook macaroni according to package directions; drain. Sauté onion and bell pepper in butter until tender; stir in pimiento and cook 1 minute.

Combine macaroni, onion mixture and all remaining ingredients (except crackers and butter); toss well. Spoon into lightly greased 2-quart baking dish. Mix crackers with butter and sprinkle over top. Bake at 350° for 30-40 minutes until bubbly and golden.

Yield: Serves 6-8.

Variation: Add 1 tablespoon blue cheese with the Cheddar.

One cup uncooked pasta yields 2 cups cooked.

NOODLE PUDDING

Delicious side dish with chicken or seafood.

- ½ pound cooked broad egg noodles
- ⅓ cup sugar
- 3 eggs
- 1 cup milk
- 2 teaspoons vanilla extract
- ½ cup butter, melted
- ½ teaspoon salt
- 1 cup sour cream
- 1 cup cottage cheese
- 4 tablespoons white raisins
- 6 ounces dried apricots
- 8¾ ounces crushed pineapple, drained
- 8¾ ounces sliced peaches, drained
- 1 cup cornflake crumbs
- ½ cup sugar
- 1 teaspoon cinnamon
- 3 tablespoons butter

Place apricots in hot water to plump; set aside. Beat eggs and sugar together; add milk, vanilla, butter, salt, sour cream and cottage cheese. Mix well. Fold in noodles, raisins, plumped apricots, pineapple and peaches. Pour into a greased 13 x 9-inch baking dish.

Stir cornflake crumbs, sugar and cinnamon together and sprinkle over top of casserole; dot with butter, cover and bake at 350° for 30 minutes. Uncover casserole and bake another 30 minutes.

Yield: Serves 8.

BLT PASTA

- **¾ pound fusilli or pasta of choice**
- **½ pound bacon**
- **24 cherry tomatoes, halved**
- **1 teaspoon salt**
- **1 teaspoon pepper**
- **2 bunches arugula, stems removed, leaves cut into strips**
- **3 tablespoons butter, melted**
- **2 tablespoons olive oil**
- **3 green onions, chopped with tops**
- **Parmesan cheese**

Cook pasta in salted water until just done. Drain, reserving ½ cup pasta water; set aside.

Cook bacon in large skillet until crisp, drain on paper towel. Pour off all but 1 tablespoon bacon drippings. Add tomatoes, pasta water, salt and pepper; sauté 1 minute. Add arugula and stir until just wilted, about 1 minute.

Over medium heat, combine bacon and pasta with tomato mixture. Add butter and olive oil and toss until heated through. Sprinkle with chopped onions. Serve with Parmesan cheese.

Yield: Serves 4.

ROTINI ROMANO

- **1 bell pepper, cut into strips**
- **1 large onion, chopped**
- **2 cups sliced fresh mushrooms**
- **1 (3-ounce) package pepperoni, sliced**
- **½ cup white wine**
- **2 tablespoons olive oil**
- **2 teaspoons Italian seasoning**
- **1 (12-ounce) package rotini pasta**
- **1½ cups shredded mozzarella cheese**
- **1 (32-ounce) jar spaghetti sauce**
- **¼ cup grated Romano cheese**

Combine bell pepper, onion, mushrooms and pepperoni in a large bowl. Add wine, olive oil and Italian seasoning, toss gently. Marinate at room temperature for 1 hour.

Cook rotini according to package directions; drain. Add to marinated vegetables; stir in mozzarella cheese, tossing gently.

Spoon into greased 13 x 9-inch baking dish. Pour spaghetti sauce over pasta completely covering pasta. Cover and bake at 350° for 25 minutes. Sprinkle with Romano cheese; bake another 5 minutes.

Yield: Serves 6.

Al dente—very slightly undercooked.

PASTA WITH SAUSAGE SAUCE

Try different types of pastas with this sauce. Fusilli is a favorite.

- **1 pound bulk pork sausage**
- **1 clove garlic, minced**
- **1 (6-ounce) can tomato paste**
- **1½ cups water**
- **1 (27-ounce) can spaghetti sauce**
- **½ teaspoon salt and pepper**
- **1 tablespoon basil**
- **1 tablespoon oregano**
- **1¼ pounds pasta of choice**

Sauté sausage and garlic until sausage is browned. Add all remaining ingredients. Simmer over low heat for 2 hours, add additional water if necessary.

Cook pasta according to package directions; drain. Toss with sausage sauce.

Yield: Serves 8.

VERMICELLI AND MUSHROOMS

- **¾ cup chopped onion**
- **1 clove garlic, minced**
- **½ cup butter, melted, divided**
- **1 pound fresh mushrooms, sliced**
- **1 (10-ounce) package frozen peas, thawed**
- **1½ tablespoons lemon juice**
- **1 teaspoon salt**
- **¼ teaspoon pepper**
- **¼ teaspoon oregano**
- **1 (12-ounce) package vermicelli**
- **Grated Parmesan cheese**

Sauté onion and garlic in ¼ cup butter 3 minutes. Add mushrooms, cook 5 minutes, stirring often. Stir in peas, lemon juice, salt, pepper, oregano; cook over low heat 5 minutes.

Cook vermicelli according to package directions; drain. Toss with remaining ¼ cup butter. Spoon mushroom mixture over vermicelli. Serve with Parmesan cheese.

Yield: Serves 4.

RIGATONI WITH VODKA SAUCE

Great served alone or as a side dish.

- **2 tablespoons butter**
- **1 onion, chopped**
- **2 cloves garlic, minced**
- **1 (16-ounce) can plum tomatoes, chopped, with juice**
- **3 ounces prosciutto ham, chopped**
- **½ cup vodka**
- **¾ cup heavy cream**
- **1 cup Parmesan cheese, divided**
- **8 ounces rigatoni pasta**
- **Salt, pepper and Tabasco to taste**

Sauté onion and garlic in butter until tender. Add chopped tomatoes, juice and prosciutto; simmer 10 minutes. Add vodka and simmer 5 minutes. Stir in cream and ½ cup Parmesan cheese; simmer 4 minutes.

Cook pasta according to package directions, al dente; drain and add to sauce, tossing to coat well. Season to taste. Serve sprinkled with remaining Parmesan cheese.

Yield: Serves 4.

ITALIAN SPAGHETTI SAUCE

- **1 large onion, chopped**
- **4 cloves garlic, minced**
- **¼ cup olive oil**
- **1 pound lean ground beef**
- **1 (28-ounce) can tomatoes**
- **1 (15-ounce) can tomato puree**
- **½ teaspoon salt**
- **½ teaspoon pepper**
- **1 teaspoon oregano**
- **3 tablespoons minced fresh basil**
- **1 teaspoon sugar**
- **1 teaspoon Italian seasoning**
- **1 cup red wine**

Sauté onion and garlic in olive oil until tender; add ground beef and cook until browned. Add next 8 ingredients; cover and simmer 1 hour, stirring occasionally. Add wine and stir to blend.

Serve over pasta sprinkled with Parmesan cheese.

Yield: Serves 4-6.

CHRISTMAS EVE SPAGHETTI

Served in Italy on Christmas Eve, ingredients have religious connotation for the Italians: nuts for life, raisins for the sweetness of the Christ child, anchovies (little fish) for Christianity.

- **3 tablespoons olive oil**
- **1 clove garlic, minced**
- **1 (2-ounce) flat can anchovy fillets**
- **1½ tablespoons pine nuts (pignoli)**
- **1 tablespoon seedless raisins**
- **1 (2-ounce) bottle capers, drained**
- **1 (6-ounce) jar pitted green olives, drained and quartered**
- **1 (9-ounce) can pitted ripe olives, drained and quartered**
- **1 (7-ounce) can tomato paste with basil**
- **¼ cup chopped fresh parsley**
- **¼ teaspoon dried oregano**
- **½ teaspoon dried basil**
- **2 (16-ounce) cans Italian plum tomatoes**
- **1¾ cups water**
- **Salt and pepper to taste**
- **1¼ pounds spaghetti pasta**

Sauté garlic in olive oil. Remove from heat. Add canned anchovies, oil and all, pine nuts, raisins, well-drained capers, olives, tomato paste, parsley and spices. Simmer over low heat stirring constantly for 5 minutes. Put plum tomatoes into blender and liquefy. Add to mixture with water and salt and pepper to taste.

Cover and simmer 1 hour. Cook spaghetti pasta according to package directions, al dente. Drain. Toss with sauce.

Yield: Serves 4-6.

CHEESE RICE SOUFFLÉ

- 2 tablespoons butter
- 2 tablespoons all-purpose flour
- 1 cup milk
- ¼ teaspoon salt
- 1 cup shredded Cheddar cheese
- 3 eggs, separated
- 1 cup cooked rice
- ¼ teaspoon cream of tartar

Melt butter in heavy saucepan over low heat; add flour and cook 1 minute, stirring constantly. Gradually add milk; cook over medium heat, stirring constantly until thickened. Add salt and cheese, stir until cheese melts. Remove from heat; cool slightly.

Beat egg yolks slightly; stir into cheese sauce along with rice.

Combine egg whites and cream of tartar, beating until stiff but not dry; fold into rice mixture. Pour into a lightly greased 1½-quart casserole or soufflé dish. Bake at 325° for 40 minutes or until soufflé is golden brown.

Yield: Serves 4-6.

OLÉ RICE

- 1 large onion, chopped
- 1 medium bell pepper, chopped
- 2 tablespoons butter
- 2 teaspoons chili powder
- 1 (10¾-ounce) can tomato soup
- 1 (1-pound) can tomatoes
- 1 teaspoon salt
- ½ teaspoon pepper
- 4 cups cooked rice
- ¾ cup grated Cheddar cheese

Sauté onion and pepper in butter until tender. Blend in all remaining ingredients (except cheese). Pour into greased 2-quart casserole. Top with cheese and bake at 375° for 30 minutes or until cheese has lightly browned and casserole is thoroughly heated.

Yield: Serves 6.

GARDEN RICE

Very colorful dish, delicately seasoned.

- 1 bunch green onions, chopped
- 1 small bell pepper, chopped
- 1½ pounds sliced zucchini or yellow squash
- ¾ cup butter, melted, divided
- 1 (12-ounce) can Mexicorn, drained
- 1 teaspoon lemon pepper
- ½ teaspoon coriander
- ¾ teaspoon oregano
- 1 teaspoon salt
- 1 teaspoon chopped parsley
- 1½ cups uncooked rice

Sauté onions, bell pepper and squash in 4 tablespoons butter until tender. Add corn, seasonings and parsley; set aside.

Cook rice according to package instructions. Place cooked rice in mixing bowl; add ½ cup melted butter and toss lightly. Add vegetable mixture; toss. Place in greased 3-quart deep casserole and bake at 350° for 20 minutes or until thoroughly heated.

Yield: Serves 10-12.

EASY RICE

- 1 cup uncooked long-grain rice
- 1 cup sharp Cheddar cheese, cubed
- ½ cup pimiento stuffed olives and juice
- 1 cup tomatoes with juice
- 1 medium onion, chopped
- 3 tablespoons butter, melted
- 1 cup water
- Salt and pepper
- 3 tablespoons Burgundy wine

Mix all ingredients (it will be soupy). Pour into greased 1½-quart casserole. Cover and bake at 350° for 1 hour.

Yield: Serves 4-6.

RAPIDES RICE

- ¾ cup chopped onion
- 6 tablespoons butter
- 1 (10¾-ounce) can chicken broth
- 1 tablespoon grated orange rind
- ¾ cup orange juice
- 1 cup water
- ¾ teaspoon poultry seasoning
- ½ teaspoon salt
- ½ teaspoon pepper
- 1½ cups uncooked rice
- ½ cup ripe olives, drained and chopped
- 1 cup sliced celery

Sauté onion lightly in butter; add broth, orange rind, juice, water and seasonings and bring to a boil. Stir in rice and olives, return to boil, lower heat, cover tightly and cook 10 minutes. Add celery and continue cooking about 10 minutes more or until rice is tender and water is absorbed. Fluff with a fork.

Yield: Serves 6-8.

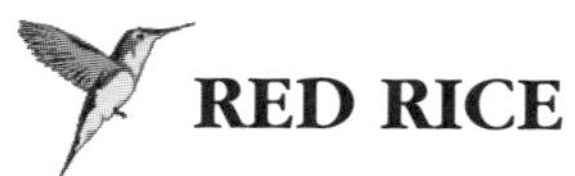

RED RICE

- 4 slices bacon
- ½ cup chopped bell pepper
- 1 medium onion, chopped
- 1 (14.5-ounce) can tomatoes, diced
- 1 cup long-grain uncooked rice
- Salt and pepper to taste
- ½ teaspoon sugar

Cook bacon in large skillet over medium heat until crisp; remove, drain and crumble. Sauté bell pepper in bacon drippings until almost tender; add onions and cook until limp. Add tomatoes, rice, salt, pepper and sugar. Cover and cook over low heat 25 minutes. Check rice; cook longer if necessary. Top each serving with crumbled bacon.

Yield: Serves 6.

RISOTTO

- **1 tablespoon butter**
- **2 tablespoons minced onion**
- **1 cup uncooked Arborio rice**
- **Salt and pepper**
- **2 cups chicken broth**
- **3 tablespoons grated Parmesan or Gruyère cheese**

Sauté onion in butter until tender. Add rice; stir with fork until butter is absorbed. Add 1 cup chicken broth; bring to boil stirring constantly. Add remaining cup chicken broth and cook over low heat 10-15 minutes or until rice has absorbed liquid. Season with salt and pepper to taste; add cheese, stir gently with fork. Serve immediately.

Yield: Serves 4.

One cup raw rice yields 3 cups cooked.

WONDERFUL RICE

- **1½ cups uncooked rice**
- **½ cup butter**
- **1 (10¾-ounce) can onion soup**
- **½ (10½-ounce) can beef bouillon**
- **½ bouillon can water**
- **½ bouillon can dry vermouth**
- **1 (6-ounce) can water chestnuts, sliced**
- **1 (4-ounce) can sliced mushrooms**
- **3 tablespoons parsley**
- **Salt and pepper to taste**

Sauté rice in butter until golden; add remaining ingredients, mixing well. Pour into a deep 1½-quart casserole. Cover and bake at 325° for 1 hour; remove cover and cook 30 minutes.

Yield: Serves 8.

WILD RICE WITH MUSHROOMS AND ALMONDS

- **½ cup butter**
- **1 cup wild rice (or wild and white rice)**
- **½ cup slivered almonds**
- **2 tablespoons chopped chives**
- **½ pound fresh mushrooms, sliced**
- **3 cups chicken broth**
- **Salt to taste**

Melt butter in heavy frying pan. Stir in rice, almonds, chives and mushrooms. Sauté on low heat about 30 minutes, stirring frequently. Add chicken broth and salt if needed. Pour into an ungreased 1½-quart casserole; cover tightly. Bake at 325° for 1 hour.

Yield: Serves 4.

Cooked rice freezes well.

RICE DRESSING

Serve as a side dish with lamb or turkey, or stuffing for turkey.

- **1 cup vegetable oil**
- **1⅓ cups chopped green onion with tops**
- **1 cup chopped parsley**
- **½ pound ground lamb or ground turkey**
- **4 cups uncooked rice**
- **1 tablespoon salt**
- **4 teaspoons sugar**
- **7 cups chicken broth**
- **1 tablespoon cinnamon**
- **1 cup blanched slivered almonds**

Sauté onion in oil until tender; add parsley. Stir in lamb and cook until well done. Add rice, seasonings and broth. Simmer until all liquid is absorbed, about 25-30 minutes. Add almonds.

Yield: Serves 6-8.

MOTHER-IN-LAW RICE AND OYSTER DRESSING

- 8 ounces chicken livers
- 3 tablespoons vegetable oil
- 1 large onion, chopped
- 6 green onions, chopped
- 4 stalks celery, sliced
- 2 cups uncooked rice, cooked until just tender
- 2 large eggs, slightly beaten
- 1 pint small oysters, drained; reserve juice
- 1 teaspoon sage
- ⅓ cup chopped parsley
- 2 teaspoons salt
- ½ teaspoon cayenne pepper
- ¼ cup butter

Coarsely chop livers; sauté in vegetable oil until no longer pink; set aside. Add onions and celery and sauté in oil until tender.

Combine cooked rice, liver, onion mixture, eggs, oysters and remaining ingredients (except butter).

Heat butter, fry rice mixture; cook until eggs thicken and oysters curl. (Reserved oyster juice may be added at this point.) Spoon into a greased 3-quart baking dish and bake at 350° for 45-60 minutes or until lightly browned.

Yield: Serves 8-10.

Keep rice white by adding 1 teaspoon lemon or vinegar to cooking water.

NOTES

Breads
© L. SPRAGINS &
P. DAWSON

BREADS

BANANA BREAD SUPREME

Even better the next day.

- **2 cups all-purpose flour**
- **2 teaspoons baking powder**
- **1 teaspoon baking soda**
- **¼ teaspoon salt**
- **½ cup plus 2 tablespoons butter, softened**
- **½ cup chopped walnuts**
- **½ cup firmly packed brown sugar**
- **3 teaspoons vanilla extract, divided**
- **1½ cups sugar**
- **2 eggs, slightly beaten**
- **1 cup very ripe mashed bananas**
- **½ cup sour cream**

Sift flour, baking powder, baking soda and salt together; set aside. Mix 2 tablespoons butter, nuts, brown sugar and 1 teaspoon vanilla extract together; set aside. Cream remaining butter with sugar until light and fluffy. Blend eggs, bananas, sour cream and 2 teaspoons vanilla extract and add to butter, sugar mixture. Stir in flour mixture and mix until just blended. Pack half of nut mixture into bottom of two well-greased 8½ x 4½-inch loaf pans. Pour batter over nut mixture and top batter with remaining nut mixture. Bake at 350° for 50-60 minutes or until wooden pick inserted in middle comes out clean. Do not overbake.

Yield: 2 banana loaves.

SOUR CREAM BISCUITS

- **2 cups self-rising flour**
- **1 cup butter, melted (no substitute)**
- **1 (8-ounce) carton sour cream**

Blend all ingredients together, mixing well. Spoon into tiny lightly greased muffin tins; fill to top and bake at 400° for 12-15 minutes.

Yield: about 3½ dozen.

BEST BANANA BREAD

Extremely moist and easy to prepare.

- 2 **cups sugar**
- 1 **cup vegetable oil**
- 4 **eggs, beaten**
- 1 **pound very ripe bananas, mashed (4 medium to large)**
- 2 **cups all-purpose flour**
- 1½ **teaspoons salt**
- ½ **teaspoon ground cinnamon**
- 1 **tablespoon baking soda**
- 1 **cup buttermilk**
- 1 **cup chopped pecans**

Beat sugar and oil together. Add eggs and bananas; mix well. Sift flour, salt, cinnamon and baking soda together. Add to banana mixture alternately with buttermilk; beginning and ending with flour mixture. Stir in pecans. Pour batter into two greased 8½ x 4½-inch loaf pans. Bake at 300° for 30 minutes then at 350° for 30 minutes longer until a wooden pick inserted in center comes out clean.

Yield: 2 banana loaves.

ANGEL BISCUITS

- 2 **(¼-ounce) packages active yeast**
- ¼ **cup warm water**
- 2 **cups warm buttermilk**
- 5 **cups all-purpose flour**
- ⅓ **cup sugar**
- 1 **tablespoon baking powder**
- 1 **teaspoon baking soda**
- 2 **teaspoons salt**
- 1 **cup solid shortening**
- **Melted butter**

Dissolve yeast in warm water; let stand 5 minutes. Stir in buttermilk; set aside. In large mixing bowl, combine flour, sugar, baking powder, soda and salt. Cut in shortening with fork or pastry blender until mixture resembles coarse meal. Stir in yeast buttermilk mixture; blend well. Turn out onto lightly floured surface; knead lightly 3-4 times. Roll to a ½-inch thickness. Cut with biscuit cutter. Place on greased baking sheet. Cover and let rise in warm place (1½ hours). Bake at 450° for 8-10 minutes. Lightly brush tops with melted butter.

Yield: About 2½ dozen.

MILE-HIGH BISCUITS

- **3 cups all-purpose flour**
- **2 tablespoons sugar**
- **4½ teaspoons baking powder**
- **¾ teaspoon cream of tartar**
- **¾ teaspoon salt**
- **¾ cup vegetable shortening**
- **1 egg, beaten**
- **¾ cup whole milk**

In a mixing bowl, sift flour, sugar, baking powder, cream of tartar and salt together. Cut in shortening until mixture resembles coarse meal. In another bowl, combine egg and milk and beat lightly with a fork. Add to flour mixture all at once, stirring enough to make a soft dough. Turn out onto a floured board and knead 15 times. Roll out to 1-inch thickness. Cut into 2-inch rounds and place on ungreased baking sheet 1 inch apart. Bake in a preheated 450° oven for 12-15 minutes, or until golden.

Yield: 16 biscuits.

PETITE BLUEBERRY MUFFINS

- **1 cup fresh blueberries**
- **1¾ cups self-rising flour, divided**
- **½ cup vegetable shortening**
- **1 cup sugar**
- **⅔ cup milk**
- **3 tablespoons boiling water**
- **3 eggs, beaten**
- **1 teaspoon vanilla extract**
- **½ teaspoon almond extract**

Dredge blueberries in ¼ cup flour; set aside. Cream shortening and sugar in mixing bowl. Add remaining flour, milk and boiling water; beat 2 minutes with electric mixer. Add eggs and flavorings; beat 2 minutes more. Gently fold in dredged blueberries. Place miniature paper cups in miniature muffin tins; fill two-thirds full. Bake at 375° for 20-25 minutes. Serve warm.

Yield: About 7 dozen.

CREAM CHEESE BRAIDS

An excellent Christmas gift bread. Wonderful aroma while baking and delicious for holiday breakfasts or brunches.

- **1 cup sour cream**
- **½ cup sugar**
- **1 teaspoon salt**
- **½ cup butter, melted**
- **2 (¼-ounce) dry yeast packets**
- **½ cup warm water**
- **2 eggs, beaten**
- **4 cups all-purpose flour**
- **2 (8-ounce) packages cream cheese, softened**
- **¾ cup sugar**
- **1 egg, beaten**
- **⅛ teaspoon salt**
- **2 teaspoons vanilla extract**

In saucepan, heat sour cream, sugar, salt and butter. Cool to lukewarm. Sprinkle yeast over warm water stirring until yeast dissolves. Combine sour cream mixture with yeast in a mixing bowl. Blend in eggs and flour; mixing well. Cover tightly; refrigerate overnight.

For the filling, combine cream cheese and sugar; add egg, salt and vanilla, mixing well. Set aside.

Divide dough into 4 equal parts. Roll out each part on a well-floured board into a 12 x 8-inch rectangle. Spread quarter of cream cheese filling on each rectangle. Roll up jelly-roll fashion, beginning at long sides. Pinch edges together; fold ends under slightly. Place roll seam down on greased baking sheets. Slit each roll at 2-inch intervals about two-thirds of way through dough to resemble a braid. Cover and let rise in a warm place until doubled in bulk (about 1 hour). Bake at 375° for 12-15 minutes. Drizzle with Glaze while warm.

Yield: 4 loaves.

Glaze

- **2 cups powdered sugar, sifted**
- **4 tablespoons milk**
- **2 teaspoons vanilla extract**

Combine all ingredients, mix well. Drizzle over warm braids.

Cornbread has always been an important part of Southern cooking, but when you ask the best cooks how to make it, you set off a big controversy. Some only use yellow cornmeal and some only white. Some only use buttermilk or eggs, others may add sugar and flour. Some swear by a preheated cast-iron skillet for baking. So, regardless of which type you grew up with or how you bake it, try some of the following favorites and enjoy!

COTTAGE CHEESE CORNBREAD

- **4 tablespoons butter, divided**
- **1 small onion, finely chopped**
- **¾ cup corn kernels**
- **1½ cups small-curd cottage cheese**
- **2 eggs, beaten**
- **1¾ cups buttermilk**
- **½ teaspoon baking soda**
- **2 (7½-ounce) boxes corn muffin mix**

Sauté onion in 2 tablespoons of the butter until slightly limp; add corn. Set aside to cool.

Blend cottage cheese with eggs, buttermilk and baking soda. Add corn muffin mixes; beat by hand, stirring in onion and corn until blended.

Place remaining butter in 13 x 9-inch baking pan; set pan in 400° oven until butter melts. Tilt pan so butter coats bottom and part way up the sides. Pour in corn muffin mixture and return baking pan to oven for 30 minutes. Do not overbake; center should barely be set. Serve hot.

Yield: Serves 10-12.

BROCCOLI CORNBREAD

Even George Bush would love it!

- **1 (10-ounce) box frozen chopped broccoli, thawed**
- **1 (8½-ounce) box cornbread mix**
- **4 eggs, lightly beaten**
- **¾ cup small-curd cottage cheese**
- **½ cup butter, melted**
- **⅓ cup chopped onion**

Drain thawed broccoli well, pressing between layers of paper towels; set aside.

Combine cornbread mix and next 4 ingredients; mix well. Stir in broccoli, blending well. Pour into an 8 x 8-inch greased baking pan. Bake at 350° for 45 minutes or until golden brown. Let cool just slightly; cut into squares.

Yield: Serves 6-8.

CRUSTY CORNBREAD

Using a greased and oven-heated cast-iron skillet for baking causes a delicate crust to appear on the bottom and sides of the bread.

- **1 cup cornmeal**
- **½ cup all-purpose flour**
- **1 tablespoon baking powder**
- **½ teaspoon baking soda**
- **½ teaspoon salt**
- **1 egg, beaten**
- **1 cup buttermilk**
- **¼ cup bacon drippings**

Combine dry ingredients; mix well. Add egg and buttermilk; stir until smooth.

Place bacon drippings in a 9-inch cast-iron skillet; heat in oven at 425° for 3-5 minutes until very hot. Remove skillet from oven and pour almost all drippings into batter; mix well. Quickly pour batter into hot skillet. Bake at 425° for 20-25 minutes or until golden brown.

Yield: Serves 8.

CUSTARD CORNBREAD

- 1 cup white or yellow cornmeal
- 1 cup all-purpose flour
- 1 teaspoon baking powder
- ½ teaspoon baking soda
- ½ teaspoon salt
- ½ teaspoon sugar
- 2 large eggs, beaten
- 2 cups milk
- 3 tablespoons butter, melted
- 1½ tablespoons white vinegar
- 1 cup heavy cream
- ¼ teaspoon salt

Combine first 6 ingredients in mixing bowl; make a well in center. Combine eggs, milk, butter and vinegar and beat together until well mixed. Add gradually to dry ingredients, stirring to mix well. Grease a 9-inch iron skillet or pan; place in a 350° oven for 10 minutes until hot. Remove from oven and pour batter into hot pan. Mix heavy cream and ¼ teaspoon salt and pour into center of batter. Do Not Stir. Bake at 350° for 1 hour or until golden brown. Serve hot.

Yield: Serves 8-10.

JALAPEÑO CORNBREAD

- 3 cups cornbread mix
- 2½ cups milk
- ½ cup oil or bacon drippings
- 3 eggs, beaten
- 3 tablespoons sugar
- ¼ teaspoon salt
- 1 large onion, chopped
- 1 (8¾-ounce) can creamed corn
- 3 ounces minced jalapeño peppers
- 1½ cups (6-ounces) grated sharp Cheddar cheese

Combine all ingredients. Pour into a greased 13 x 9-inch pan. Bake at 375° for 30-35 minutes or until brown.

Yield: Serves 12-15.

Variation: Add 6 slices bacon, cooked and crumbled, to batter before baking.

CORNBREAD STICKS

- 1¼ cups cornmeal
- ¾ cup all-purpose flour
- 1 tablespoon plus 1 teaspoon baking powder
- 2 teaspoons sugar
- 1 teaspoon salt
- 2 eggs, slightly beaten
- 1 cup milk
- ¼ cup oil or bacon drippings

Combine cornmeal, flour, baking powder, sugar and salt; mix well. Combine remaining ingredients, mixing well and add to dry ingredients, stirring until smooth.

Place a well-greased cast-iron corn stick pan in a 425° oven for 3 minutes or until hot. Remove pan from oven; spoon in batter filling two-thirds full. Bake for 12 minutes or until lightly brown.

Yield: 2 dozen corn sticks.

ZESTY SPOON BREAD

- 1 cup yellow cornmeal (plain)
- 1 teaspoon salt
- ½ teaspoon baking soda
- ¾ cup milk
- ⅓ cup vegetable oil
- 2 eggs, beaten
- 1 (17-ounce) can cream-style corn
- 1 (4-ounce) can chopped mild green chilies
- 1½ cups (6-ounces) grated Monterey Jack cheese

Mix cornmeal, salt and baking soda. Stir in milk and oil and mix well. Add eggs and corn; mix well. Spoon half of mixture into a well-greased 9 x 9-inch baking pan. Sprinkle half of the chilies on top, then half of the cheese. Repeat layers, ending with cheese. Bake uncovered at 350° for 45 minutes or until wooden pick inserted in center comes out clean.

Yield: Serves 6-8.

SOUTHERN CORNBREAD

- **2 cups cornmeal**
- **1 teaspoon baking soda**
- **1 teaspoon salt**
- **2 eggs, beaten**
- **2 cups buttermilk**
- **¼ cup bacon drippings**

Combine cornmeal, soda and salt; stir in eggs and buttermilk. Heat bacon drippings in an 8-inch cast-iron skillet until very hot (3-5 minutes). Add hot drippings to batter, mixing well. Quickly pour batter into hot skillet. Bake at 450° about 25 minutes or until golden brown.

Yield: Serves 8-10.

Variation: Add 1 cup cracklings to batter before baking for Crackling Cornbread.

CRANBERRY BREAD

A Christmas morning treat.

- **2 cups all-purpose flour**
- **1 cup sugar**
- **1½ teaspoons baking powder**
- **⅛ teaspoon salt**
- **½ teaspoon baking soda**
- **¼ cup butter**
- **¾ cup orange juice**
- **1 egg, beaten**
- **1 cup fresh cranberries, coarsely chopped**
- **1 cup golden raisins**
- **1 cup chopped pecans**

Combine first 5 ingredients in a mixing bowl; cut in butter until mixture resembles coarse meal. Combine orange juice and egg and stir into dry ingredients. Add cranberries, raisins and nuts. Mix together.

Pour batter into a greased and floured 9 x 5-inch loaf pan. Bake at 350° for 1 hour 5 minutes. Cool 10 minutes before removing from pan.

Yield: 1 loaf.

DATE NUT BREAD

- 1 teaspoon baking soda
- 1 cup boiling water
- 1 (8-ounce) package chopped dates
- ¼ cup butter, softened
- ¾ cup sugar
- 1 egg
- 1¼ cups all-purpose flour
- ¼ teaspoon baking powder
- ¼ teaspoon salt
- 2 cups chopped pecans

Dissolve baking soda in boiling water; stir in dates; set aside.

Cream butter with electric mixer; gradually add sugar, beating well. Add egg and mix well.

Combine flour, baking powder and salt; add to creamed mixture. Add date mixture, blend well. Stir in pecans.

Pour batter into greased and floured 8½ x 4½-inch loaf pan. Bake at 350° for 55-60 minutes or until wood pick inserted in center comes out clean.

Yield: 1 loaf.

KILLER BREAD

- 1 cup mayonnaise
- 1 cup freshly grated Parmesan cheese
- 1½ teaspoons minced garlic
- 1 round (1-pound) sourdough bread
- ½ cup butter, softened
- 2 tablespoons finely minced fresh basil (or dried)

Mix mayonnaise, Parmesan cheese and garlic; blend well. Slice bread in half horizontally and place both halves, cut side up, on baking sheet. Spread with mayonnaise, Parmesan mixture; broil until top is puffed and golden brown. Sprinkle with minced basil. Cut into wedges. Serve warm.

Yield: Serves 12.

Embassy Suites Hotels

DATE NUT LOAF

A real date and nut treat with just enough batter to hold them together.

- **2 pounds dates**
- **4 cups pecan halves**
- **1 cup sugar**
- **1 cup all-purpose flour**
- **3 teaspoons baking powder**
- **1/8 teaspoon salt**
- **4 eggs, separated**

Separate dates and cut each in half. In a large mixing bowl, mix dates and nuts together.

Combine dry ingredients and sprinkle over nuts and dates; mix together.

Beat egg whites until stiff. Beat egg yolks and fold into egg whites. Stir egg mixture into nuts and dates moistening well. Pack mixture into two 8½ x 4½-inch loaf pans lined with wax paper. Bake at 275° for 1 hour 10 minutes. Cool. Remove from pans; peel away wax paper. Slice while slightly warm and serve with whipped topping.

Yield: 2 loaves.

QUICK CHEESE MUFFINS

- **1¼ cups biscuit mix**
- **¾ cup grated Cheddar cheese**
- **¼ cup minced onion**
- **1 tablespoon butter**
- **1 egg, beaten**
- **½ cup milk**
- **4 teaspoons sesame seeds, toasted**
- **2 tablespoons butter, melted**

Sauté onions in 1 tablespoon butter until transparent. Mix biscuit mix and cheese together. Combine egg, milk and onion. Add to biscuit cheese mixture beating well for 30 seconds. Fill well-greased muffin tins two-thirds full. Sprinkle tops with sesame seeds and drizzle with melted butter. Bake at 400° for 12-15 minutes.

Yield: 12 muffins.

KAHLUA BREAD

- 1 cup chopped dates
- ½ cup Kahlua (or other coffee liqueur)
- ½ cup warm water
- 1 teaspoon grated orange rind
- ⅔ cup firmly packed brown sugar
- 2 tablespoons butter, softened
- 1 egg, beaten
- 2 cups all-purpose flour
- 1 teaspoon salt
- 1 teaspoon baking soda
- ⅔ cup chopped pecans

Combine dates, Kahlua, water and orange rind; set aside.

Cream sugar and butter until light and fluffy; add egg, mixing well. Sift flour, salt and baking soda together; add to creamed mixture alternately with date mixture. Stir in pecans. Pour into a greased, floured 9 x 5-inch loaf pan. Bake at 350° for 1 hour or until just done. Cool. Remove from pan.

Yield: 1 loaf.

SOUR CREAM PEACH MUFFINS

- 1 cup chopped peaches
- 1 cup sour cream
- 1 egg, beaten
- ¼ cup butter, melted
- 2 cups all-purpose flour
- 1 tablespoon baking powder
- ¼ teaspoon baking soda
- ¼ teaspoon salt
- ½ cup sugar

Combine peaches, sour cream and egg; stir in butter, blending well; set aside.

In a mixing bowl, mix flour, baking powder, baking soda, salt and sugar. Pour sour cream peach mixture over flour mixture, stirring only to blend. Mixture will be thick. Divide batter among 12 well-greased muffin tin cups, filling two-thirds full. Bake at 375° for 35 minutes or until golden and tops spring back when gently touched. Cool 10 minutes; remove from tins. Serve warm.

Yield: 12 muffins.

LAVOSH

- **4 cups all-purpose flour**
- **1 tablespoon sugar**
- **2 teaspoons salt**
- **1/8 teaspoon cayenne pepper**
- **6 tablespoons butter, softened**
- **1 (1/4-ounce) package active dry yeast**
- **1 cup warm water**

In a large mixing bowl, add the flour, sugar, salt, cayenne, butter and yeast. Blend together. Add water; with dough hooks or by hand, mix until all is incorporated. Place the dough on a floured sheet pan or bowl. Cover and let rest in refrigerator 3 hours. Dough needs to be firm and cold to roll.

Divide dough into 8 pieces for easy rolling. Sprinkle with topping of choice. Roll on a floured surface until paper thin. Place on dry sheet pan, dust off excess flour. Cut into desired serving size. Bake at 375° (do not preheat) for 8-10 minutes until crisp and golden brown. Watch closely. Serve warm.

Yield: Serves 16.

Toppings: Poppy seeds, sesame seeds, caraway seeds, Italian herb mix, Parmesan cheese, onion or garlic powder or curry powder.

The Grove Park Inn
Asheville, North Carolina

An ice cream scoop makes filling muffin tins easier.

LEMON BREAD

- ½ cup butter, softened
- 1 cup sugar
- 2 eggs
- 1½ cups all-purpose flour
- 1½ teaspoons baking powder
- ¼ teaspoon salt
- ½ cup milk
- Grated rind of 1 lemon
- ½ cup chopped nuts
- Glaze

Combine butter and sugar, creaming until light and fluffy. Add eggs, one at a time, beating after each addition.

Combine flour, baking powder and salt. Add to creamed mixture alternately with milk, mixing well after each addition. Stir in lemon rind; add nuts.

Pour batter into a well-greased 9 x 5-inch loaf pan. Bake at 350° for 50-60 minutes until just done. Pour glaze over hot bread. Cool bread in pan 10 minutes. Remove from pan.

Yield: 1 loaf.

Glaze:

- ¾ cup sifted powdered sugar
- ¼ cup lemon juice

Combine sugar and lemon juice, mixing well. Pour over hot bread.

Dust raisins, chocolate chips, candied fruit and nuts with portion of recipe flour to prevent sinking.

BANANA SPLIT MUFFINS

- 2 cups biscuit mix
- ¼ cup sugar
- 2 egg yolks, beaten
- ⅔ cup milk
- 2 tablespoons butter, melted
- ½ small banana
- 12 maraschino cherries, halved
- 12 pecan halves
- 2 egg whites
- ⅓ cup sugar
- ⅔ cup flaked coconut

Combine biscuit mix and sugar; set aside. Mix egg yolks, milk and butter; add all at once to biscuit mix. Stir just to moisten well. Spoon 1½ tablespoons batter into heavily greased muffin tins. Cut banana into 12 cubes. Place a banana cube, a cherry half and a pecan on top of batter and cover with 1 tablespoon more batter.

Beat egg whites until foamy; gradually add sugar 1 tablespoon at a time beating constantly until stiff peaks form. Fold in coconut. Place 1½ tablespoons meringue on top of each muffin. Top with remaining cherries. Bake at 400° for 18-20 minutes.

Yield: 12 muffins.

FRESH HERB POPOVERS

- 1 cup all-purpose flour
- ¼ teaspoon salt
- 2 large eggs
- 1 cup milk
- ½ teaspoon fresh thyme, finely chopped
- 1 tablespoon unsalted butter, melted
- 2 tablespoons unsalted butter

Combine flour, salt, eggs, milk, thyme and melted butter. Beat with a wooden spoon until mixture is consistency of heavy cream. Divide the remaining 2 tablespoons butter into 6 pieces and place 1 piece in each cup of a popover pan. Place pan in 450° oven for 1 minute until butter is bubbly. Fill each cup half full of batter. Bake for 20 minutes; reduce heat to 350° and continue baking 15-20 minutes. Serve immediately.

Yield: 6 popovers.

SURPRISE MUFFINS

The marshmallows disappear during baking leaving a gooey cinnamon roll muffin.

- **1 (8-ounce) can refrigerated crescent rolls**
- **¼ cup sugar**
- **1 tablespoon ground cinnamon**
- **8 large marshmallows**
- **¼ cup finely chopped pecans**
- **¼ cup butter, melted**

Separate crescent rolls into 8 triangles. Combine sugar and cinnamon. Dip each marshmallow into melted butter, roll in sugar cinnamon mixture; place on a triangle. Pinch dough around marshmallows, sealing all edges. Dip tops of dough into butter and sugar cinnamon mixture.

Place sugar side up in well greased muffin tins. Sprinkle with pecans. Bake at 375° for 13-15 minutes until lightly browned. Serve warm.

Yield: 8 muffins.

GIANT POPOVERS

- **6 tablespoons butter, melted**
- **6 eggs**
- **2 cups whole milk**
- **2 cups all-purpose flour**
- **1 teaspoon salt**

In a large mixing bowl, beat eggs until frothy; beat in milk and butter until blended. Beat in flour and salt. Pour batter into 8 deep (7-ounce) well-greased custard cups; fill three-quarters full. Place cups on flat baking sheet. Bake at 375° for 1 hour; make small slits in top of each to let out steam. Bake 10 minutes longer.

Immediately remove popovers from cups. Serve piping hot.

Yield: 8 giant popovers.

ORANGE MUFFINS

- **1 cup butter, softened**
- **1 cup sugar**
- **2 eggs**
- **1 teaspoon baking soda**
- **¾ cup buttermilk**
- **3 cups all-purpose flour**
- **Grated rind of 1 orange**
- **¼ cup orange juice**
- **1 teaspoon lemon extract**
- **1 cup currants**
- **¾ cup orange juice**
- **1½ cups sugar**

Cream butter and sugar until light and fluffy. Add eggs one at a time, beating well after each addition.

Combine soda and buttermilk, stirring well; add to creamed mixture alternately with flour. Stir in orange rind, orange juice, lemon extract and currants; mix well. Place individual miniature paper cups in miniature muffin tins; fill three-quarters full. Bake at 400° for 10-12 minutes or until lightly browned. Remove from tins; dip tops in Orange Sauce or spoon over tops.

Yield: About 7½ dozen.

Orange Sauce

- **¾ cup orange juice**
- **1½ cups sugar**
- **Grated rind of 1 orange**

Combine orange juice, sugar and rind in a small saucepan; bring to boil, stirring until sugar dissolves.

Yield: 1 cup.

OATMEAL BREAD

- **2 (¼-ounce) packages active dry yeast**
- **1 cup very warm water**
- **2 teaspoons sugar**
- **⅓ cup butter, softened**
- **1 cup boiling water**
- **1 cup regular oats**
- **½ cup molasses**
- **2 teaspoons salt**
- **4½ cups all-purpose flour, divided**
- **1 egg**

Dissolve yeast in very warm water; add sugar and let stand 10 minutes. Stir well.

In a large mixing bowl, add butter and boiling water; stir until butter is dissolved. Stir in oats, molasses and salt; blend well and cool to lukewarm. Add dissolved yeast mixture, mixing in well. Reserve ½ cup flour. Sift remaining flour into oat mixture, mix well. Add egg and beat well. Turn dough out on board dusted with reserved ½ cup of the flour; knead about 10 minutes. Put dough into large greased bowl; turn upside down to grease top. Chill about 2-3 hours. Remove second half of dough; place in 2 well-greased 9 x 5-inch loaf pans and let rise in warm place until doubled in bulk (about 2 hours).

Bake at 350° for 40 minutes or until brown and done (bread should sound hollow when tapped). Do not overbake.

Yield: 2 loaves.

Warm syrups before serving with waffles.

PHYLLO TULIP CUPS

Use tulip cups for dessert filling, chicken or tuna salad, mushrooms or your choice. Very versatile.

4 sheets phyllo dough
¼ cup butter, melted

Work with one sheet of phyllo at a time. Keep remainder wrapped in plastic wrap and a damp towel at all times.

Brush one sheet of phyllo with butter. Layer another sheet on top and butter lightly. Repeat using all 4 sheets.

Cut phyllo sheets into 4-inch squares (9 squares). Press each square into a buttered 2½-inch muffin tin, pressing the bottom flat and folding excess dough to create a petal effect on the sides.

Bake in bottom third of 375° oven for 12 minutes until golden brown.

Yield: 9 tulip cups.

EASY HERBED ROLLS

¼ cup butter, melted
1½ teaspoons dried parsley flakes
½ teaspoon dill seeds
¼ teaspoon dried onion flakes
1 (8-count) can refrigerated buttermilk biscuits

Pour melted butter into a 9-inch round baking pan. Sprinkle parsley flakes, dill seed and onion flakes evenly over the butter. Cut biscuits into fourths; roll each one in the herbed butter as you place them in the pan. Bake at 425° for 10-12 minutes. Let sit for 5 minutes before serving.

Yield: Serves 4-6.

EASY BREAD STICKS

- **5 hot dog buns**
- **1 cup butter, melted**
- **¼ teaspoon dried basil**
- **¼ teaspoon dried parsley**
- **¼ teaspoon dried thyme**
- **¼ teaspoon dried rosemary**
- **1 teaspoon garlic powder**
- **Parmesan cheese**

Cut each hot dog bun in half. Cut each half down the middle making 4 bread sticks per hot dog bun. Mix butter with next 5 ingredients; stirring well. Generously cover bread sticks with butter mixture. Sprinkle each bread stick lightly with Parmesan cheese. Place on baking sheet and bake at 300° until golden brown and crisp (crisp and firm but not too dark).

Yield: 20 bread sticks.

TOMATO BREAD

- **1¾ cups all-purpose flour**
- **2 teaspoons baking powder**
- **½ teaspoon baking soda**
- **1 teaspoon cinnamon**
- **½ teaspoon nutmeg**
- **¼ teaspoon salt**
- **1 egg, beaten**
- **1 (8-ounce) can tomato sauce**
- **¾ cup firmly packed brown sugar**
- **½ cup vegetable oil**
- **½ cup chopped walnuts**
- **Powdered sugar, sifted**

Combine dry ingredients; set aside. In a large mixing bowl, mix egg, tomato sauce, brown sugar and oil. Stir in dry ingredients lightly; add nuts.

Pour batter into a well-greased 9 x 5-inch loaf pan. Bake at 350° for 40-45 minutes until pick inserted in center comes out clean. If loaf browns too quickly, cover pan with foil last 15-20 minutes. Cool in pan 5 minutes. Remove, let cool; sprinkle with powdered sugar.

Yield: 1 loaf.

FRENCH TOAST GRAND MARNIER

- 6 slices Texas toast bread
- 4 eggs, beaten
- 1 cup milk
- 2 tablespoons Grand Marnier liqueur
- 1 tablespoon sugar
- ½ teaspoon vanilla extract
- ¼ teaspoon salt
- ¼ teaspoon freshly grated orange rind
- Vegetable oil
- 3 tablespoons butter, melted
- Powdered sugar, sifted

Combine beaten eggs and milk, mixing well. Add Grand Marnier, sugar, vanilla, salt and orange rind; mix well. Dip bread slices into liquid mixture until well saturated. Place in a flat baking dish or pan; pour remaining liquid over bread slices. Cover and refrigerate overnight.

Heat oil in skillet and brown bread slices until golden on both sides. Brush with melted butter, sprinkle with powdered sugar and serve.

Yield: Serves 3-6.

ZUCCHINI BREAD

The use of cinnamon is a matter of taste; adjust the recipe to suit yours.

- **2 cups flour**
- **2 cups sugar**
- **½ teaspoon salt**
- **1½ teaspoons baking powder**
- **3 level tablespoons cinnamon**
- **3 eggs**
- **1 cup vegetable oil**
- **3 teaspoons vanilla**
- **2 cups grated, unpeeled zucchini**

Combine first 5 ingredients in a large mixing bowl; make a well in center of mixture. Set aside. Beat eggs slightly; add oil, vanilla and zucchini. Add to dry ingredients, mixing well. Pour into two greased and floured 9 x 5-inch loaf pans. Bake at 350° for 1 hour or until wooden pick inserted in center comes out clean. Cool in pans.

Yield: 2 loaves.

Cool breads completely before freezing.

QUICK MONKEY BREAD

- ½ cup chopped pecans
- ½ cup sugar
- 1 teaspoon cinnamon
- 3 (10-ounce) cans refrigerated buttermilk biscuits
- 1 cup firmly packed brown sugar
- ½ cup butter, melted

Sprinkle pecans evenly in bottom of well-greased 10-inch bundt pan; set aside.

Combine sugar and cinnamon. Cut biscuits into fourths; roll each piece in cinnamon-sugar mixture and layer in pan.

Combine brown sugar and butter; pour over dough. Bake at 350° for 30-40 minutes. Cool bread 10 minutes in pan; invert onto serving platter.

Yield: 1 coffee cake.

ALMOND PUFF

Wonderful coffee cake for special occasions; worth the extra effort.

- **2 cups all-purpose flour, divided**
- **½ cup butter, softened**
- **1 cup plus 2 tablespoons water, divided**
- **½ cup butter, melted**
- **2½ teaspoons almond extract, divided**
- **3 eggs, beaten**
- **1½ cups sifted powdered sugar**
- **2 tablespoons butter, softened**
- **1½ tablespoons warm water**
- **¼ cup sliced almonds**

Place 1 cup flour in mixing bowl; cut in ½ cup butter with fork or pastry blender until mixture resembles coarse meal. Sprinkle 2 tablespoons water over surface; stir with fork until moistened. Shape dough into ball; divide in half. Pat each half into a 12 x 3-inch strip on an ungreased baking sheet leaving 3 inches between strips.

Combine 1 cup water and melted butter in saucepan; bring to boil. Add 1 teaspoon almond extract and remaining flour all at once, stirring over low heat until mixture leaves sides of pan and forms a ball. Cool slightly.

Add eggs; beat until smooth. Spread batter evenly over pastry strips. Bake at 350° for 1 hour.

Combine powdered sugar, the 2 tablespoons butter, the remaining almond extract and warm water in a mixing bowl, beating well. Spread over tops of puffs; sprinkle with almonds. Slice and serve warm.

Yield: Serves 12.

BLUEBERRY COFFEE CAKE

- **1 cup all-purpose flour**
- **1½ teaspoons baking powder**
- **½ teaspoon salt**
- **⅓ cup butter, softened**
- **⅓ cup sugar**
- **1 egg**
- **½ cup milk**
- **1 cup fresh blueberries**
- **¼ cup sugar**
- **⅓ cup firmly packed brown sugar**
- **¼ cup all-purpose flour**
- **½ teaspoon cinnamon**
- **⅛ teaspoon salt**
- **2 tablespoons butter**
- **2 tablespoons all-purpose flour**

Combine flour, baking powder and salt; set aside. Cream butter and sugar until fluffy; add egg, mixing well. Add dry ingredients to creamed mixture alternately with milk, beginning and ending with dry ingredients.

Combine ¼ cup sugar, ⅓ cup brown sugar, flour, cinnamon and salt. Cut in butter until mixture is crumbly like coarse meal.

Pour batter into a greased and floured 8 x 8-inch baking pan. Dredge blueberries in 2 tablespoons flour; scatter over top and sprinkle with crumbly sugar mixture. Bake at 375° for 40 minutes. Serve warm.

Yield: Serves 6.

SOUR CREAM COFFEE CAKE

A treasure to have on hand for the many times we have houseguests here in the mountains.

- ¾ cup butter, softened
- 1½ cups sugar
- 3 eggs
- 2 teaspoons vanilla extract
- 3 cups all-purpose flour
- 1½ teaspoons baking powder
- 1½ teaspoons baking soda
- ½ teaspoon salt
- 2 cups sour cream
- ¾ cup firmly packed light brown sugar
- 2 teaspoons cinnamon
- 1 cup coarsely chopped walnuts
- 1½ cups powdered sugar
- 2 tablespoons milk
- 1 teaspoon vanilla extract

Cream butter and sugar until light and fluffy; add eggs, one at time, beating well after each addition. Stir in vanilla.

Combine flour, baking powder, baking soda and salt; add to creamed mixture alternately with sour cream, mixing well.

Combine brown sugar, cinnamon and walnuts, mixing well. Spoon one-third of batter into a greased and floured 10-inch tube pan; sprinkle with one-third of nut mixture. Repeat twice. Bake at 350° for 1 hour or until just done. Let stand 5 minutes.

Combine 1½ cups powdered sugar, milk and vanilla; mix well. Remove cake; place on serving plate and drizzle with glaze.

Yield: One 10-inch coffee cake.

Sauces,
Condiments

SAUCES

CONDIMENTS

BARBEQUE SAUCE

- 1 cup catsup
- 1/4 cup lemon juice
- 2 tablespoons brown sugar
- 1 tablespoon soy sauce
- 1 tablespoon prepared horseradish mustard
- 1 tablespoon grated onion
- 1½ teaspoons salt
- ½ teaspoon ground pepper
- ¼ teaspoon oregano
- ¼ teaspoon Tabasco
- ¼ teaspoon cayenne pepper
- 1 clove garlic, mashed
- ½ cup cider vinegar

Combine all ingredients in pan and simmer at least 10 minutes. Use immediately or cool. Store in refrigerator.

Yield: About 2 cups.

BARBEQUE SAUCE PAPRIKA

- 1 cup catsup
- ½ cup vinegar
- ½ cup butter
- ¼ cup paprika
- 2 lemons, juiced
- ¼ cup firmly packed brown sugar
- 4 teaspoons prepared horseradish
- 1 tablespoon black pepper
- 2 teaspoons prepared mustard
- 1 teaspoon Worcestershire sauce
- 1 clove garlic, minced
- ¼ teaspoon Tabasco

Combine all ingredients in a large saucepan; mix well. Bring to a boil; reduce heat and simmer 10-15 minutes, stirring occasionally.

Yield: 2 cups.

BOURBON BARBEQUE SAUCE

- **1 cup catsup**
- **⅓ cup bourbon**
- **¼ cup vinegar**
- **¼ cup molasses**
- **2 cloves garlic, crushed**
- **1 tablespoon Worcestershire sauce**
- **1 tablespoon lemon juice**
- **2 teaspoons soy sauce**
- **½ teaspoon dry mustard**
- **½ teaspoon pepper**

Combine all ingredients, mixing well. Good with pork or beef.

Yield: 2 cups.

BUTTER BARBEQUE SAUCE

- **½ cup butter**
- **3 cups catsup**
- **½ cup cider vinegar**
- **½ cup firmly packed dark brown sugar**
- **¼ cup Worcestershire sauce**
- **4 tablespoons lemon juice**
- **½ teaspoon salt**
- **1 tablespoon Tabasco**

Combine all ingredients in saucepan; simmer until butter melts and flavors blend.

Yield: 3½ cups.

CASHEW SAUCE

- **½ cup butter**
- **¼ cup fresh lemon juice**
- **½ teaspoon marjoram**
- **¾ cup coarsely chopped salted cashew nuts**

Melt butter in saucepan; add lemon juice, marjoram and cashews. Simmer over low heat 5 minutes.

Yield: 1½ cups.

BÉARNAISE SAUCE

- 3 tablespoons white wine vinegar
- 2 teaspoons minced shallots
- 1½ teaspoons chopped fresh tarragon
- 3 egg yolks
- ⅛ teaspoon salt
- ⅛ teaspoon red pepper
- 2 tablespoons lemon juice
- ½ cup butter

Combine vinegar and shallots in a small saucepan; bring to a boil over medium heat. Reduce heat, simmer until half of the liquid evaporates. Strain; reserve liquid. Cool slightly, stir in tarragon; set aside.

Beat egg yolks, salt and red pepper in top of double boiler; gradually add lemon juice, stirring constantly. Add one third of the butter to egg mixture; cook over hot water stirring until butter melts.

Add another third of the butter, stirring constantly. As sauce thickens, stir in remaining butter; cook until thickened. Add vinegar mixture to sauce, stirring well. Serve immediately.

Yield: ¾ cup.

BORDELAISE SAUCE

Excellent served with beef tenderloin.

- 2 carrots, chopped
- 2 stalks celery, chopped
- ¼ cup chopped shallots
- ½ teaspoon thyme
- ½ teaspoon salt
- ¼ teaspoon pepper
- 2 cups red wine
- 1 cup beef broth
- 2 tablespoons butter, melted
- 1 tablespoon all-purpose flour

Combine carrots with next 6 ingredients in saucepan. Bring to boil. Cook uncovered over low heat 10 minutes. Add broth and cook 10 minutes. Blend butter and flour; add to a little of the sauce in a cup; mix until smooth and stir into sauce. Simmer sauce until thickened.

Yield: 3 cups.

CHEESE SAUCE

- 2 tablespoons butter
- 2 tablespoons all-purpose flour
- 1 cup milk
- ¼ teaspoon salt
- ½ cup shredded sharp Cheddar cheese

Melt butter in heavy saucepan over low heat; add flour and cook 1 minute, stirring constantly. Gradually add milk; cook over medium heat, stirring constantly until thickened and bubbly. Add salt and cheese; stir until cheese melts.

Yield: 1¼ cups.

GREATEST SAUCE IN LIFE

Unbelievable! Put it on meatballs, crab cakes, chicken, rice or bathe in it as a cure for all ailments!

- 1 (10-ounce) jar all-fruit apricot (or red currant)
- 1 (6-ounce) jar yellow prepared mustard
- Worcestershire sauce to taste

Combine in saucepan and heat. Refrigerate leftovers.

Yield: About 1½ cups.

HOMEMADE MUSTARD

Very hot.

- 2 (2-ounce) cans dry mustard
- 1 cup cider vinegar
- 2 eggs
- ½ cup sugar

Soak mustard overnight in vinegar. Blend well with eggs and sugar. Cook in double boiler over hot water until thickened. Jar and refrigerate.

Yield: About 2 cups.

ZESTY ORANGE SAUCE

Excellent served with chicken, lamb, fish or steak.

1 orange
1 cup very dry sherry
Dash of cayenne pepper
1 tablespoon lemon juice
½ cup currant jelly

Cut orange in half; juice both halves. Cut rind of one half into thin strips. Combine orange strips and sherry in saucepan; simmer uncovered until liquid is reduced to ½ cup. Remove and discard rind. Add orange juice, cayenne pepper, lemon juice and jelly. Simmer until jelly has melted.

Yield: 1¼ cups.

PESTO SAUCE

Sauce is enough for 2 pounds of pasta. When ready to use, add a little heavy cream to moisten pasta then toss with sauce.

2 cups fresh basil leaves, washed, dried, packed
4 large cloves garlic, chopped
1 cup walnuts
1 cup virgin olive oil
1 cup freshly grated Parmesan cheese
¼ cup freshly grated Romano cheese
1 teaspoon salt
½ teaspoon freshly ground pepper

Combine basil, garlic and walnuts in food processor with steel blade; process. Leave motor running; add olive oil in small stream. Shut off motor; add cheeses, salt and pepper. Process to blend. Use immediately or place in a container. Pack sauce down; cover with a layer of olive oil to seal out air. Refrigerate up to 6 months.

Yield: 2 cups.

JALAPEÑO TARTAR SAUCE

Wonderful with crab cakes.

- **1 cup mayonnaise**
- **1 small jalapeño pepper, seeded, finely chopped**
- **3 tablespoons finely chopped cucumber**
- **2 tablespoons finely chopped onion**
- **1 tablespoon lemon juice**
- **¼ teaspoon Worcestershire sauce**

Combine all ingredients; cover and chill.

Yield: 1½ cups.

WHITE SAUCE MIX

- **2⅔ cups powdered milk**
- **1 cup butter**
- **1½ cups all-purpose flour**
- **3 teaspoons milk**

Blend ingredients with a pastry blender until they become the consistency of sand. Keep in a jar in the refrigerator. To make 1 cup of white sauce, add ½ cup mix to 1 cup water. Blend together well; simmer until thickness desired.

Yield: 5 cups.

NEW ORLEANS RÉMOULADE SAUCE

A must for boiled shrimp or shrimp cocktail.

- **1 jar Mister Mustard**
- **¼ cup vinegar**
- **2 tablespoons paprika**
- **¼ cup horseradish**
- **Salt and pepper**
- **½ cup olive oil**
- **1 bunch green onions, minced**
- **2 tablespoons parsley flakes**

Combine vinegar, mustard, paprika, salt, pepper and horseradish. Add olive oil; beat with rotary beater or whisk until well blended. Stir in onions and parsley.

Yield: 1 pint.

BANANA JAM

Nice to share with family and friends at Christmas.

- **3 quarts medium ripe bananas, sliced (12-14)**
- **6 cups sugar**
- **1½ cups orange juice**
- **¾ cup lemon juice**
- **¼ teaspoon banana extract**

Cook all ingredients (except banana extract) in a large heavy pan over moderate heat until sugar is dissolved. Simmer ingredients until thick, about 15-20 minutes. Stir in banana extract. Pour into hot sterilized jars and seal with paraffin.

Yield: 4 quarts.

BLACKBERRY JELLY

Use this formula and method for all berries.

- **¼ cup water for each**
- **4 cups berries**

Cook to boiling. Crush to remove seeds. Rub through sieve. Place in cheesecloth over bowl and let drip 2 hours. Press gently to extract juice.

For:

- **3½ cups juice**
- **5 cups sugar**
- **1 lemon, juiced**
- **½ teaspoon butter**
- **1 (1¾-ounce) box fruit pectin**

Pour juice into 6-8 quart pot. Add lemon juice, butter and fruit pectin. Bring mixture to full rolling boil over high heat, stirring constantly. Quickly add sugar and bring to a full rolling boil, stirring constantly. Continue boiling 1 minute, stirring constantly. Remove from heat. Skim off foam with large metal spoon. Pour into sterilized jars to ⅛-inch of the top. Cover with lids; screw on tightly. Invert jars 5 minutes; turn upright. Place jars on rack in large pot and fill with water to cover jars. Boil 10 minutes. Remove and let cool.

Yield: 5½ cups.

BLUEBERRY JAM

- **4½ cups blueberries, crushed**
- **¼ cup lemon juice**
- **1 (1-inch) cinnamon stick**
- **½ teaspoon butter**
- **7 cups sugar**
- **2 pouches liquid fruit pectin**

Combine all ingredients except fruit pectin in a Dutch oven; bring mixture to a boil, stirring constantly until sugar dissolves.

Bring to a full rolling boil (doesn't stop bubbling when stirred), stirring constantly. Add pectin to blueberry mixture. Bring to a full rolling boil and boil exactly 1 minute, stirring constantly.

Remove from heat. Discard cinnamon stick. Skim off foam with metal spoon. Quickly pour into hot sterilized jars; cover with metal lids and screw on bands tightly. Process in boiling water bath for 10 minutes. Let cool.

Yield: 9 half-pints.

CRANBERRY FRUIT CHUTNEY

Mixture lasts for months in refrigerator.

- **12 ounces fresh cranberries**
- **2 apples, pared, cored, cut in chunks**
- **2 pears, pared, cored, cut in chunks**
- **1 cup raisins**
- **⅔ cup sugar**
- **⅓ cup honey**
- **½ cup fresh-squeezed orange juice**
- **1 tablespoon grated orange rind (colored part only)**
- **1¼ teaspoons cinnamon**
- **⅓ cup cranberry liqueur**

Put all ingredients except liqueur in a saucepan. Bring to a boil and reduce heat to a slow simmer. Cook uncovered for 30-45 minutes or until the mixture thickens slightly. Stir occasionally. Add the liqueur, stir until blended. Refrigerate for at least 3 hours. Serve chilled.

Yield: Serves 12.

GRANNY'S PEACH CHUTNEY

This is especially good over cream cheese as an appetizer with crackers. Just like Major Grey's, only better!

- **1 pound lemons, chopped and seeded (leave rind on)**
- **1 pound onions, chopped**
- **2 pounds bell pepper**
- **5 pounds sugar**
- **1 quart white vinegar**
- **1 pound cucumbers, peeled and cubed**
- **10+ peaches, peeled and chopped**
- **1 cup almonds, slivered and blanched**
- **3 tablespoons allspice**
- **3 tablespoons ground ginger**
- **1½ tablespoons turmeric**
- **3 tablespoons curry powder**
- **1 (1-pint) jar green tomato relish**
- **1 pound crystallized ginger, cut into long strips**
- **1 pound raisins**

Grind lemons, onions and half of bell pepper. Cut rest of bell pepper into long strips. Bring sugar and vinegar to a boil and add all ingredients except tomato relish, ginger and raisins. Cook until thick, about 2½ hours. Stir often so it doesn't stick to the bottom of the pan. Add tomato relish, ginger and raisins. Put in hot sterilized pint-size Mason jars, screw on lids lightly. When completely cool, tighten lids.

Yield: 6-8 pints.

STRAWBERRY PRESERVES

A welcome back to the mountains in the spring...big baskets overflowing with juicy sweet local strawberries.

- **1 full quart firm, ripe strawberries**
- **2½ cups sugar, divided**

Cap and rinse strawberries; place in a large colander. Pour boiling water over berries; let drain 1 minute.

Combine berries and 1 cup sugar in a heavy large saucepan. Bring to a boil; boil 7 minutes, stirring frequently. Stir in remaining 1½ cups sugar; boil an additional 7 minutes, stirring frequently.

Pour mixture into a shallow 13 x 9-inch pan; skim off foam with metal spoon. Let stand uncovered in a cool place 12 hours; shake pan occasionally (do not stir) so that berries absorb syrup and remain plump and whole.

Skim off foam with metal spoon; pour preserves into sterilized jelly jars. Cover with ⅛-inch layer of paraffin. Cover with lids.

Yield: About 2½ cups.

GARLIC PICKLES

- **1 gallon sour pickles**
- **12 cloves garlic, peeled**
- **½ box whole peppercorns**
- **½ box whole mustard seed**
- **5 pounds white sugar**

Drain juice from pickles and discard. Cut pickles in ½-inch rounds and place in large crock or bowl. Add garlic, peppercorns and mustard seed. Pour sugar over all. Let stand 24 hours, stirring occasionally. When sugar is dissolved, pour mixture back into gallon jar or into smaller jars. Refrigerate.

Yield: 1 gallon.

Variation: Substitute 1 gallon large dill pickles cut lengthwise into ¼-inch strips (in place of sour pickles); follow all other directions.

TABASCO JELLY

Great with turkey, roast beef or game or as an appetizer served over cream cheese.

1 cup water
⅓ cup lemon juice
2 teaspoons Tabasco or more to taste
3 cups sugar
6 tablespoons liquid fruit pectin
2 drops red food coloring

In a saucepan combine water, lemon juice, Tabasco and sugar. Bring to boil, stirring constantly. Add fruit pectin and food coloring. Stir until mixture comes to a full rolling boil. Boil 30 seconds more. Skim off foam. Pour into hot, sterilized jars. Seal with paraffin.

Yield: 4 cups.

CINNAMON APPLES

6 medium Jonathan or Winesap apples
1 cup sugar
½ cup "red hots" (cinnamon candies)
6 whole cloves
1½ cups water
Red food coloring

Core and pare apples. Combine sugar, red hots, cloves and water; boil 5 minutes. Add food coloring to desired shade of red; add apples and simmer slowly until almost tender. Turn apples in syrup for even color.

Remove apples and place in a deep dish; cover with syrup. Marinate until apples absorb deeper color. Garnish with mayonnaise.

Variations:

- Stuff a combination of walnuts and raisins in center of apple.
- Stuff a combination of cream cheese and pecans in center of apple.

CHEESE APPLE CASSEROLE

- ½ cup butter
- 1 cup sugar
- ½ pound processed cheese loaf, diced
- ¾ cup all-purpose flour
- 3 (1.5-pound) cans sliced apples, drained

Combine butter, sugar, cheese and flour; mix thoroughly.

Pour apples into a greased shallow 2-quart baking pan; spread cheese mixture evenly over top. Bake at 350° for 30-40 minutes until cheese melts and mixture is thoroughly heated.

Yield: Serves 6.

CURRIED FRUIT

- 1 (1-pound 4-ounce) can pineapple chunks
- 1 (1-pound 4-ounce) can sliced peaches
- 1 (1-pound 4-ounce) can apricot halves, sliced
- 1 (1-pound 4-ounce) can purple plums
- ½ cup butter
- 1 cup firmly packed brown sugar
- 3 teaspoons curry powder

Drain all fruit and arrange attractively in a 13 x 9-inch glass dish. In a saucepan, melt butter, add sugar and cook over low heat until sugar melts and ingredients are well blended. Pour over fruit. Bake at 350° for 45 minutes or until bubbly and heated through.

Yield: Serves 8-12.

TOMATO JAM

Dip tomatoes into boiling water and easily remove skin.

- **4 cups peeled and diced tomatoes**
- **2½ cups sugar**
- **2 (3-ounce) packages red raspberry gelatin**

Combine tomatoes and sugar. Bring to boil and cook right at boiling for 30 minutes. Remove from heat; add gelatin and stir to dissolve. Pour into hot sterilized jars.

Yield: 3 pints.

MUSTARD FRUIT COMPOTE

- **1 (8-ounce) can pineapple chunks, undrained**
- **2 bananas, sliced**
- **1 (16-ounce) can peach slices, drained**
- **1 (16-ounce) can pear slices, drained**
- **1 (10-ounce) jar maraschino cherries, drained**
- **½ cup firmly packed brown sugar**
- **¼ cup butter**
- **1½ tablespoons prepared mustard**

Drain pineapple, reserve juice. Toss bananas in pineapple juice; drain. Combine pineapple, bananas and next 3 ingredients in a 1½-quart baking dish.

Combine remaining ingredients in a small saucepan. Cook over medium heat, stirring constantly until smooth and bubbly; pour over fruit. Bake uncovered at 325° for 20-30 minutes or until thoroughly heated.

Yield: Serves 8.

PICKLED PEACH HALVES

Peach halves may be served topped with cranberry sauce or topped with mincemeat for a holiday meal.

- **1 (1 pound 13-ounce) can peach halves in heavy syrup**
- **¼ cup cider vinegar**
- **½ cup sugar**
- **¼ teaspoon ground allspice**
- **½ teaspoon whole cloves**
- **½ stick cinnamon**

In a saucepan, combine heavy syrup from canned peaches with vinegar, sugar and spices. Boil 5 minutes. Add peaches; simmer 5 minutes. Chill peaches in syrup overnight. To serve, drain peaches reserving syrup. Serve as a side dish. Serve topped with some of syrup.

Yield: Serves 4.

Add a small pat of butter when cooking fruit for jellies and you will have less foam to skim off the top.

Desserts

DESSERTS

SAUCES

CAKES

PIES

COOKIES

WHITE CHOCOLATE CRÈME BRÛLÉE

- **5 egg yolks**
- **½ cup sugar, divided**
- **2 cups whipping cream**
- **3 ounces imported white chocolate, finely chopped**
- **½ teaspoon vanilla extract**
- **4 tablespoons brown sugar**

Whisk egg yolks with ¼ cup sugar. Bring whipping cream and remaining ¼ cup of sugar to simmer in heavy saucepan. Reduce heat to low. Gradually add chocolate to cream mixture; whisk until smooth. Gradually whisk hot chocolate mixture into yolk mixture. Stir in vanilla. Mix well.

Pour custard into 4 (10-ounce) custard cups. Place cups in large baking pan. Add enough hot water to pan to come halfway up sides of cups. Bake at 300° for 1 hour or until custards are set in center. Cool and refrigerate.

Preheat broiler. Sprinkle 1 tablespoon brown sugar over each custard. Broil until sugar carmelizes, watching carefully (about 2 minutes). Cover and refrigerate overnight.

Yield: Serves 4.

Do not substitute margarine for butter in any recipe.

CHOCOLATE MOUSSE ROLL

- **¼ cup plus 2 tablespoons all-purpose flour**
- **¾ teaspoon baking powder**
- **¼ teaspoon salt**
- **¼ cup plus 2 tablespoons cocoa**
- **4 large eggs, separated**
- **1 teaspoon vanilla extract**
- **¾ cup sugar**
- **4 tablespoons powdered sugar**
- **Chocolate Mousse**
- **Crème Anglaise**
- **Grated chocolate**

Sift first 4 ingredients together. Combine egg yolks and vanilla; beat well; set aside.

Have egg whites at room temperature; beat on high speed of electric beaters until frothy. Add sugar 1 tablespoon at a time until stiff peaks form. Fold into yolk mixture; add dry ingredients, mixing well. Grease a 15 x 10-inch jelly-roll pan, line with wax paper; grease and flour the wax paper. Spread batter evenly into pan. Bake at 400° for 8 minutes.

Sift powdered sugar in a 15 x 10-inch rectangle on a kitchen towel. Loosen cake; turn out onto sugared towel and peel off wax paper. Starting at narrow end, roll up cake and towel. Place seam side down; cool.

Unroll, remove towel. Spread chocolate mousse on cake leaving a 1-inch margin around edges; re-roll cake. Place on serving plate. Slice and serve topped with Crème Anglaise and grated chocolate.

Yield: Serves 8-10.

Chocolate Mousse

- **6 ounces semi-sweet chocolate morsels**
- **1 tablespoon sugar**
- **3 eggs, separated**
- **2 teaspoons vanilla extract**
- **¼ teaspoon cream of tartar**
- **¼ cup sugar**

Combine chocolate morsels and sugar in top of double boiler over high heat until melted and blended.

Combine egg yolks and vanilla; stir into chocolate mixture; cook 6 minutes, stirring constantly. Cool. Have egg whites at room temperature; beat with cream of tartar until foamy. Add sugar gradually until stiff peaks form; fold into chocolate mixture. Chill 1 hour.

Yield: 2⅔ cups.

(Chocolate Mousse Roll continued)

Crème Anglaise

1	**vanilla bean**	**4**	**egg yolks**
1⅓	**cups whipping cream**	**½**	**cup sugar**
⅔	**cup milk**	**½**	**cup Irish cream liqueur**

Split vanilla bean lengthwise; combine with whipping cream and milk in heavy saucepan. Cook over medium heat almost to boiling point. Combine egg yolks and sugar mixing well; gradually add to hot milk, stirring constantly. Cook over low heat 6 minutes or until thickened. Discard vanilla bean. Stir in liqueur. Cover and chill.

Yield: 2⅔ cups.

Never hull a strawberry until after they have been washed.

DEATH BY CHOCOLATE

- **1 (1 pound 6.5-ounce) box family size brownie mix**
- **1 cup Kahlua liqueur**
- **2 (2.8-ounce) boxes instant chocolate mousse mix**
- **8 chocolate covered toffee candy bars, crushed**
- **12 ounces frozen whipped topping**

Prepare brownie mix according to package directions. Pour Kahlua over hot brownies from oven. Cool.

Prepare chocolate mousse according to package directions; refrigerate. When ready to assemble, layer half crumbled soaked brownies in a 3-quart round serving or trifle bowl, then half chocolate mousse, then half crushed toffee candy bars and half whipped topping. Repeat. Chill.

Yield: Serves 10.

POTS DE CRÈME FOR TWO

Recipe can be doubled.

½ package Baker's German's sweet chocolate
2 tablespoons egg substitute
2 teaspoons sugar
¼ cup whipping cream
¼ teaspoon vanilla extract
Whipped cream (optional)

Place chocolate in top of double boiler; bring water to boil. Reduce heat; cook until chocolate melts. Combine next 3 ingredients; gradually stir into melted chocolate. Cook in double boiler over low heat, stirring constantly 5 minutes until thickened. Remove from heat; stir in vanilla. Spoon mixture into two wine glasses. Cover and chill 3 hours. Garnish with whipped cream.

Yield: Serves 2.

To prevent seepage, cover the outside of a springform pan with foil.

GRANDMA'S HOT APPLE CRISP

8-10 large McIntosh apples
⅓ cup flour
⅓ cup brown sugar
⅓ cup white sugar
¼ cup butter
Water

Peel, core and thinly slice apples. Arrange apples in a buttered 13 x 9-inch baking pan. Combine flour, brown sugar and white sugar together; sprinkle over apples. Add enough water to cover bottom of dish. Dot top with bits of the butter, covering well. Bake at 350° for 1 hour. Serve warm.

Yield: Serves 6-8.

MOUNTAIN APPLES IN A DISH

Follow directions carefully and you will be rewarded with a truly delicious apple dessert.

- **6 medium apples**
- **½ lemon, ground (no seeds)**
- **¼ cup sugar**
- **8 slices white bread**
- **1 cup butter**
- **1 (2-pound) package light brown sugar**

Peel, quarter and core apples. Cook in saucepan with lemon and ¼ cup sugar to boiling point. Remove from heat, cover and let stand 1 hour. Pour off any excess liquid and place apples in a 2½-quart oblong baking dish.

While apples are cooking, trim crusts off bread. Cut each bread slice into 4 squares. Melt butter, put half into a small bowl. Put 2 cups of the brown sugar in a pie pan.

Dip each bread square in butter then pat brown sugar on both sides. Stand the first square up against the rim of the casserole. Dip and sugar the second square overlapping two-thirds of the first square. Continue with bread squares overlapping each other until apples are covered (should be at least 3 long rows or more). Make sure and overlap each square. Do not put bread squares flat on apples. Bake at 275° for 1 hour. Don't change temperature or time. Serve warm.

Yield: Serves 6.

Place a miniature marshmallow in bottom of ice cream cone to prevent leaking.

APPLE WALNUT COBBLER

- 4 cups thinly sliced, peeled tart apples
- 1½ cups sugar, divided
- ½ teaspoon cinnamon
- ¼ teaspoon salt
- ¾ cup coarsely chopped walnuts, divided
- 1 cup all-purpose flour
- 1 teaspoon baking powder
- ¼ teaspoon salt
- 1 egg, beaten
- ½ cup evaporated milk
- ⅓ cup butter, melted
- Frozen whipped topping or vanilla ice cream

Arrange thinly sliced apples in a 9-inch baking pan. Combine ½ cup sugar, cinnamon, salt and ½ cup of walnuts; sprinkle evenly over apples.

Combine flour, baking powder and salt. Beat egg, milk and butter together; add to flour mixture. Mix until smooth. Pour over apple mixture in pan. Top with remaining nuts.

Bake at 325° for 40-50 minutes or until top is golden brown. Serve topped with whipped topping or ice cream.

Yield: Serves 4-6.

Blend: To stir 2 or more ingredients together until well mixed.

BLUEBERRY STREUSEL COBBLER

- **2 cups fresh blueberries**
- **1 (14-ounce) can sweetened condensed milk**
- **2 teaspoons grated lemon rind**
- **¾ cup plus 2 tablespoons cold butter**
- **2 cups biscuit baking mix**
- **½ cup firmly packed brown sugar**
- **½ cup chopped pecans**
- **½ cup sugar**
- **1 tablespoon cornstarch**
- **½ teaspoon cinnamon**
- **¼ teaspoon nutmeg**
- **½ cup water**
- **2 cups blueberries**

Combine blueberries, condensed milk and lemon rind; set aside.

Cut ¾ cup butter into 1½ cups biscuit mix until crumbly. Add blueberry mixture. Spread into a well-greased 9-inch square baking pan. Combine remaining ½ cup biscuit mix and brown sugar. Cut in remaining 2 tablespoons butter until crumbly; add pecans. Sprinkle over top of cobbler and bake at 325° for 1 hour or until golden brown.

Combine ½ cup sugar with cornstarch, cinnamon, nutmeg and water. Cook over medium heat until thickened. Stir in blueberries and cook until heated through. Pour over baked cobbler. Top with vanilla ice cream.

Yield: Serves 8.

Flan: In Spain, a custard; in France, a filled pastry.

PEACH-BERRY COBBLER

- **¼ cup sugar**
- **¼ cup firmly packed brown sugar**
- **1 tablespoon cornstarch**
- **½ cup water**
- **1 tablespoon lemon juice**
- **2 cups sliced peaches**
- **2 cups fresh blueberries**
- **1 cup all-purpose flour**
- **½ cup sugar**
- **1½ teaspoons baking powder**
- **½ teaspoon salt**
- **½ cup milk**
- **¼ cup butter, softened**
- **2 tablespoons sugar**
- **¼ teaspoon nutmeg**

Combine sugars and cornstarch; add water, mixing well. Cook in saucepan, stirring constantly over medium heat until thick. Blend in lemon juice, peaches and blueberries. Pour into a 2-quart baking dish.

Blend flour, sugar, baking powder and salt; add milk and softened butter beating until smooth. Spoon mixture over fruit. Mix sugar and nutmeg; sprinkle on top. Bake at 375° for 40-45 minutes. Serve warm topped with whipped topping or ice cream.

Yield: Serves 6-8.

EASY PEACH COBBLER

- **3 cups sliced peaches**
- **1 cup sugar**
- **½ cup butter**
- **¾ cup all-purpose flour**
- **1 teaspoon baking powder**
- **¼ teaspoon salt**
- **1 cup sugar**
- **¾ cup milk**

Combine peaches and sugar; set aside. Heat oven to 350°. Place butter in 1½-quart baking dish and heat in oven until butter melts.

Mix flour, baking powder, salt and sugar. Stir in milk and beat well. Pour batter over butter in baking dish; do not stir. Place peaches evenly over batter; do not stir. Bake at 350° for 50-60 minutes or until golden brown. Serve warm.

Yield: Serves 4-6.

CARAMEL CUP CUSTARD

A very light flan dessert.

- **2 cups sugar**
- **6 egg yolks**
- **⅛ teaspoon salt**
- **4 cups half-and-half, scalded**
- **2 teaspoons vanilla extract**

Place 1½ cups sugar in flat baking dish; bake at 350° for 30 minutes or until sugar has melted and turned caramel color. Immediately pour equal amounts caramel into 10 (6-ounce) custard cups that have been sprayed lightly with cooking spray; set aside.

Whisk egg yolks with remaining sugar; add salt. Slowly pour scalded cream into egg mixture whisking constantly; add vanilla. Pour mixture into prepared custard cups; place in large shallow baking pan. Pour warm water into pan so that custard cups are sitting in water 1 inch deep. Bake in bottom third of oven at 325° for 40-45 minutes or until silver knife inserted in center of custard comes out clean. Do not overcook. Invert onto dessert plates; serve warm or cold.

Yield: Serves 10.

BLUEBERRY DESSERT

- **4 cups fresh blueberries**
- **3 cups sour cream**
- **2 teaspoons vanilla**
- **1 cup brown sugar**

Combine blueberries, sour cream and vanilla. Chill several hours. Pour mixture evenly into 8 individual baking serving dishes. Spoon 2 tablespoons brown sugar on top of each dish. Place under broiler heat in oven until sugar melts and runs down in berries. Serve immediately.

Yield: Serves 8.

CREAM CHEESE FLAN

Reliable and easy.

- **1 cup sugar**
- **½ cup water**
- **6 eggs, beaten**
- **1 teaspoon vanilla extract**
- **1¾ cups evaporated milk**
- **1 (14-ounce) can sweetened condensed milk**
- **1 (8-ounce) package cream cheese, softened**

Combine sugar and water over low heat until sugar dissolves. Boil until syrup is golden brown (about 8 minutes). Pour into 8 (6-ounce) custard cups swirling to coat bottoms. Cool.

Blend eggs, vanilla, evaporated milk, condensed milk with cream cheese in blender or food processor until smooth. Do not overprocess. Pour into custard cups. Place cups in large flat baking pan. Add hot water to pan so that cups are sitting in ½ inch water. Bake at 300° for 40-50 minutes or until knife inserted in center comes out clean. Cool. Invert and serve.

Yield: Serves 8.

BRANDIED GRAPES

Wonderfully light and a perfect ending to a filling meal.

- **1½ pounds red or green seedless grapes**
- **1 cup brandy**
- **1 cup honey**
- **1½ teaspoons lemon juice**
- **3 tablespoons powdered sugar**
- **1 cup sour cream**

Wash, stem and dry grapes. Place in a deep bowl. Mix brandy, honey, lemon juice and sugar; pour over grapes. Chill, stirring occasionally, for 5 hours. Spoon grapes with some juice, into small dessert bowls or stemmed glasses. Serve with a dollop of sour cream on top.

Yield: Serves 8.

HEAVENLY CUSTARD

Old-fashioned rich, smooth custard. Always serve warm.

- **6 tablespoons butter (no substitute)**
- **1½ cups sugar**
- **1 tablespoon all-purpose flour**
- **4 eggs**
- **2 teaspoons vanilla extract**
- **2 cups whole milk**

In a mixing bowl, cream butter and sugar; add flour. Mixing by hand, add eggs one at time, beating only until just blended. Gradually add milk then vanilla. Pour into an ungreased round 2-quart baking dish. Place baking dish into a much larger pan. Add hot water to pan so that custard baking dish is sitting in 1-inch of water. Bake at 450° for 15 minutes then 300° for 40 minutes or until set (or a wooden pick inserted in middle comes out clean).

Yield: Serves 6-8.

DAYSPRING DESSERT

All ice cream sandwiches are not the same size. Just cut them to fill required dish size.

- **7 (5 x 2-inch) ice cream sandwiches**
- **1 cup Amaretto liqueur**
- **8 ounces frozen whipped topping**

Line a 13 x 9-inch dish with ice cream sandwiches. Pour Amaretto over sandwiches; let stand a few minutes then top with whipped topping. Freeze. Cut into squares.

Yield: Serves 16.

Variation: Add a layer of fudge sauce next to Amaretto layer before topping with whipped topping.

FRUIT PIZZA

Recipe makes two pizza crusts. Use one and freeze the other.

- **1 cup butter, softened**
- **2 eggs**
- **1½ cups sugar**
- **½ teaspoon vanilla extract**
- **1 tablespoon almond extract**
- **3 cups flour**
- **1 teaspoon baking powder**
- **1 teaspoon baking soda**
- **1 (8-ounce) package cream cheese, softened**
- **Bananas**
- **Grapes**
- **Plums**
- **Raspberries**
- **Peaches**
- **Blueberries**
- **Kiwi**
- **Pears**
- **1 cup apricot preserves**

Cream butter and sugar; add eggs, blending well. Add extracts; blend in flour, baking powder and baking soda. Divide dough into two equal pieces. Pat one half dough in pizza pan ¼-inch thick. (Reserve other half or freeze.) Bake at 350° for 10-14 minutes. Cool. Spread softened cream cheese over crust. Slice preferred fruit and place over cream cheese in decorative circles. Heat apricot preserves and spread over fruit. Serve at dinner table slicing as pizza. Very pretty and good.

Yield: 1 fruit pizza.

CHOCOLATE ICE CREAM BARS

Keep them on hand in the freezer…if they last!

- **42 chocolate sandwich cookies, crushed**
- **½ cup butter, melted**
- **½ gallon vanilla ice cream**
- **1½ cups Spanish peanuts or toasted almonds**
- **½ cup sugar**
- **1½ cups evaporated milk**
- **⅓ cup butter**
- **⅔ cup semi-sweet chocolate chips**

Combine crushed cookies with ½ cup butter. Pat into a 13 x 9-inch glass dish. Let ice cream soften and spread over crumbs; sprinkle top with half of nuts. Freeze.

In a saucepan, bring sugar, evaporated milk, butter and chocolate chips to a boil. Cook over medium heat until thickened. Cool. Spread over ice cream; sprinkle with remaining nuts. Freeze.

Remove from freezer 5-10 minutes before serving. Cut into 2½-inch bars. Keeps frozen several weeks.

Yield: Serves 16.

GRAPEFRUIT SHERBET

Perfect on a summer day or as a sorbet course.

- **1 cup sugar**
- **½ cup water**
- **2 cups fresh grapefruit juice**
- **1½ tablespoons fresh lemon juice**

Combine sugar and water in saucepan; bring to boil. Shake pan gently until sugar is dissolved. Cool completely. Stir in grapefruit and lemon juice. Pour into ice cream freezer and freeze according to manufacturer's instructions. May also be frozen in the freezer in a plastic container.

Yield: Serves 6.

DIANA TORTE

- **28 macaroons, crushed, divided**
- **1 quart chocolate ice cream, softened**
- **4 tablespoons chocolate sauce**
- **1 quart coffee ice cream, softened**
- **14 pieces English toffee, crushed**

Oil a 9-inch springform pan. Place half of the crushed macaroons on bottom. Spread softened chocolate ice cream on top. Spread 2 tablespoons chocolate sauce over ice cream. Spread remaining crushed macaroons over chocolate sauce. Top with softened coffee ice cream. Spread remaining chocolate sauce over ice cream and top with crushed toffee.

Place torte in freezer 4-5 hours. Release from springform pan; place on round serving platter and let stand at room temperature 30 minutes. Slice and serve. Pass a bowl of Fudge Sauce with torte servings.

Yield: Serves 8-12.

Fudge Sauce

- **4 squares semi-sweet chocolate**
- **1 cup brown sugar**
- **½ teaspoon vanilla extract**
- **⅔ cup cream**
- **Pinch of salt**

Place all ingredients in saucepan over low heat. Stir until chocolate melts and sauce thickens.

Yield: 1 cup.

Reduce oven temperature slightly when baking in a glass dish.

PEACH ICE CREAM

- 6 cups mashed ripe peeled peaches
- 2½ cups sugar
- 2 tablespoons all-purpose flour
- ½ teaspoon salt
- 3 eggs, beaten
- 1 quart whole milk
- 1 (14-ounce) can sweetened condensed milk
- 1 cup whipping cream
- 1 tablespoon vanilla extract

Combine peaches and 1 cup sugar; set aside.

Mix remaining sugar, flour and salt; add eggs, beating well. Gradually add milk and condensed milk until blended. Cook over low heat, stirring constantly until mixture thickens (at least 15 minutes). Cool thoroughly. Stir in cream, vanilla and peaches.

Pour into freezer container of 1-gallon electric freezer. Freeze according to manufacturer's directions. Let ripen 1 hour.

Yield: About 1 gallon.

PEACHES GALLIANO

- 1 quart French vanilla ice cream, softened
- 1 cup whipping cream, whipped
- ½ cup Galliano liqueur
- 3 large fresh peaches, peeled and sliced

Combine whipped cream with Galliano; blend into softened ice cream. Freeze until firm. To serve, place sliced peaches evenly in 6 large wine glasses or serving bowls, top with ice cream. Can be garnished with chocolate curls, whipped topping or chopped toasted almonds. Serve with a simple cookie.

Yield: Serves 6.

EASY VANILLA ICE CREAM

Let your imagination flow and create a favorite flavor ice cream of your own using this basic recipe.

- **2 (14-ounce) cans sweetened condensed milk**
- **1 quart half-and-half**
- **1 tablespoon plus 1 teaspoon vanilla extract**

Combine condensed milk and half-and-half, beating with electric beaters on high speed for 3 minutes. Mix in vanilla. Pour into container of a 1-gallon electric freezer. Freeze according to manufacturer's instructions. Ripen 1 hour.

Yield: 2½ quarts.

Variations:

- Mocha: Stir 1 cup strong coffee and 1 (5.5-ounce) can chocolate syrup into ice cream mixture before freezing.
- Butter Pecan: Add 1 tablespoon butter flavoring and 2 cups coarsely chopped toasted pecans to ice cream mixture before freezing.
- Cookies and Cream: Crush 15 cream-filled chocolate sandwich cookies into small pieces; stir into ice cream mixture before freezing.

Caramelize: Cook white sugar in a skillet over medium heat stirring until sugar becomes a golden syrup.

RUTH AND PAPPY'S VANILLA ICE CREAM

A cherished addition to picnics at Wildcat Cliffs Country Club for over 25 years. So many wonderful memories are contained in this recipe. Thanks, Pappy!

- **2 quarts whole milk**
- **3 cups sugar**
- **2 heaping tablespoons all-purpose flour**
- **2 teaspoons salt**
- **8 egg yolks, beaten**
- **1 quart half-and-half**
- **2 cups whipping cream**
- **2 tablespoons vanilla extract**

Scald milk in top of double boiler. Combine sugar, flour and salt. Add small amount hot milk to sugar mixture, stirring to make a smooth paste. Stir into milk in double boiler stirring constantly until blended and thickened.

Stir small amount hot milk mixture into beaten egg yolks. Stir eggs into hot milk mixture in double boiler, stirring constantly until yolks are cooked, about 2-3 minutes. Let cool.

When ready to freeze, add half-and-half, whipping cream and vanilla to cooled custard. Pour into container of a 1-gallon electric freezer. Freeze according to manufacturer's directions.

Yield: 1 gallon.

SHERRY SAUCE

- **¾ cup sugar**
- **1 tablespoon cornstarch**
- **⅔ cup water**
- **⅓ cup sherry**
- **1 teaspoon vanilla extract**
- **1 tablespoon butter**

Combine first 4 ingredients in a small saucepan; bring to boil over medium heat. Cook 1 minute, stirring constantly. Remove from heat; add vanilla and butter. Stir until butter melts.

Yield: 1½ cups.

LEMON LUSH

- ½ cup butter
- 1 cup all-purpose flour
- ½ cup chopped pecans
- 1 (8-ounce) package cream cheese, softened
- 1½ cups sifted powdered sugar
- 1½ cups frozen whipped topping
- 2 (3.4-ounce) boxes instant lemon pudding mix
- 3 cups cold milk
- 1 cup frozen whipped topping
- Additional chopped pecans

Cut butter into flour until mixture resembles coarse meal; stir in ½ cup pecans. Press mixture into bottom of 13 x 9-inch baking dish. Bake at 350° for 15-20 minutes until golden brown. Cool.

Combine cream cheese and powdered sugar; beat at medium speed of electric mixer until fluffy. Fold 1½ cups whipped topping into cream cheese mixture. Spread over crust; chill.

Beat pudding mix and cold milk on low speed of electric mixer for 2 minutes; spread over cream cheese layer. Refrigerate several hours. Cut into squares. Top each serving with whipped topping; sprinkle with pecans, if desired.

Yield: Serves 15.

LEMON CURD

- 2 cups sugar
- 1 cup butter
- ¼ cup grated lemon rind
- ⅔ cup fresh lemon juice
- 4 large eggs, lightly beaten

Combine first four ingredients in top of a double boiler; bring water to boil. Reduce heat to low; cook until butter melts. Stir one-quarter of the eggs into hot mixture stirring constantly; add remaining eggs. Cook stirring constantly over medium heat until mixture thickens (about 15 minutes). Remove from heat. Cool. Cover and refrigerate up to 2 weeks.

Yield: 3¼ cups.

MERINGUE TORTE

Easy to handle when baked in a tube pan with a removable bottom.

- **6 egg whites**
- **¼ teaspoon salt**
- **½ teaspoon cream of tartar**
- **1½ cups sugar**
- **1 teaspoon vanilla extract**
- **¼ cup light rum, optional**
- **1 cup whipping cream, whipped**
- **Fresh fruits**

Let egg whites stand at room temperature for 1 hour. Lightly butter bottom, <u>not</u> <u>sides</u>, of a 9-inch tube pan. Preheat oven to 450°.

Beat egg whites with salt and cream of tartar until frothy. While beating, add sugar slowly 2 tablespoons at a time; add vanilla and beat until stiff and shiny. Pour into tube pan and place on middle rack in preheated oven. TURN OFF OVEN. Let stand in oven overnight. DO NOT PEEK.

Loosen edges of torte and turn out on serving plate. Sprinkle surface with rum. Refrigerate 4 hours. Frost sides and top with whipped cream. Serve with fresh fruit.

Yield: Serves 10.

GRAND MARNIER SAUCE

Especially good on strawberries and good in coffee, also!

- **1 cup whipping cream**
- **½ cup sugar**
- **3 teaspoons lemon juice**
- **6 tablespoons Grand Marnier**
- **1 teaspoon grated orange peel**

Whip cream until soft peaks form. Fold in sugar and remaining ingredients. Spoon over fresh fruit.

Yield: 1½ cups.

CRANBERRY-PECAN BREAD PUDDING

Updated version of an old favorite comfort food.

Caramel Sauce

- **1 cup whipping cream**
- **1 cup firmly packed brown sugar**
- **5 tablespoons unsalted butter**
- **3 tablespoons bourbon**

Bring whipping cream and sugar to a boil, whisking constantly. Boil until mixture thickens, stirring often, about 5 minutes. Add butter; bring to boil, whisking constantly. Whisk in bourbon. Cool to lukewarm. Can be prepared 1 day ahead. Cover and refrigerate. Reheat before using.

Pudding

- **2 tablespoons plus ½ cup sugar**
- **1¼ teaspoons cinnamon**
- **½ pound egg bread, cut into 1-inch cubes**
- **¼ cup unsalted butter, melted**
- **¾ cup whipping cream**
- **¾ cup half-and-half**
- **3 large eggs**
- **2 large egg yolks**
- **2 teaspoons vanilla extract**
- **¾ cup dried cranberries, dried cherries or raisins**
- **½ cup chopped pecans, toasted**
- **4 ounces white chocolate, broken into ½-inch pieces**
- **¼ cup powdered sugar**
- **¼ teaspoon cinnamon**
- **Vanilla ice cream**

Combine 2 tablespoons sugar and ¼ teaspoon cinnamon. Butter 8 (⅔-cup) soufflé dishes. Coat each lightly with cinnamon sugar; reserve remaining cinnamon sugar. Place bread cubes on heavy baking sheet. Pour melted butter over bread and toss to coat. Bake at 350° until lightly toasted, about 10 minutes. Cool.

Whisk cream, half-and-half, whole eggs, egg yolks, vanilla, ½ cup Caramel Sauce, ½ cup sugar and ¾ teaspoon cinnamon in large bowl; mix well. Stir in cranberries and pecans. Add bread; toss to coat. Let stand until bread has partially soaked up custard but is not mushy, pressing down on bread, about 3 minutes. Divide bread among

(Cranberry-Pecan Bread Pudding continued)

prepared soufflé dishes, mounding in center. Tuck in chocolate pieces. Pour any remaining custard over puddings.

Place soufflé dishes on baking sheet. Sprinkle remaining cinnamon sugar on top and bake at 350° until brown on top and just set, about 40 minutes. Cool 10 minutes.

Mix powdered sugar and ¼ teaspoon cinnamon; sift mixture around edges of dessert plates. Run small knife around edges of soufflé dishes to loosen pudding. Invert each pudding onto small plate; turn right side up and place on dessert plates. Spoon warm sauce around pudding. Top with ice cream.

Yield: Serves 8.

CHAMPAGNE PINEAPPLE GRANITA

- **½ cup sugar**
- **½ cup water**
- **3 cups (½-inch) chunks fresh pineapple**
- **4 cups passion-fruit nectar or juice**
- **¾ cup chilled champagne**

Simmer sugar and water until sugar is dissolved; cool.

Puree pineapple with ¼ cup plus 2 tablespoons syrup in food processor. Stir in nectar and champagne.

Transfer pineapple to shallow metal baking pan and freeze, stirring and crushing lumps with a fork every hour until mixture is firm but not frozen hard (about 3-4 hours). Can be made 2 days ahead and frozen, covered.

Just before serving, scrape granita with fork to loosen ice crystals.

Yield: 8 cups.

BREAD PUDDING

A light pudding, special enough for company.

- **4 eggs, beaten**
- **1 cup sugar**
- **2 cups whole milk**
- **¼ teaspoon salt**
- **10 slices white bread, crusts removed**
- **1 tablespoon vanilla extract**

Beat eggs and sugar by hand until blended. Mix milk, salt and bread together until bread is soaked; stir in sugar mixture. Stir and mix well; add vanilla. Pour into a greased 1½-quart casserole. Place casserole in larger shallow pan; pour warm water in pan so that casserole is sitting in 2 inches of water. Bake at 350° for 45-50 minutes or until knife inserted in center comes out clean. Remove from oven and immediately spread top of pudding with Hard Sauce. Let pudding stand 10 minutes; serve warm with Vanilla Sauce.

Yield: Serves 6.

Hard Sauce

- **1½ cups sifted powdered sugar**
- **⅓ cup butter, softened**
- **3 tablespoons sweet sherry**

Beat sugar and butter with electric beaters on medium until creamy; add sherry. Let stand at room temperature until ready to use.

Vanilla Sauce

- **½ cup sugar**
- **3 tablespoons light brown sugar**
- **2 tablespoons all-purpose flour**
- **1 egg**
- **2 tablespoons butter, melted**
- **1¼ cups whipping cream**
- **1 tablespoon vanilla extract**

Combine sugars with flour, mix in egg, butter and whipping cream. Whisk ingredients in heavy saucepan; cook over medium heat, whisking constantly 10-12 minutes until thickened. Remove from heat; stir in vanilla. Serve warm.

Yield: 1¾ cups.

MICROWAVE BREAD PUDDING

- 6 thick slices day-old bread, toasted
- 2 cups milk
- ½ cup raisins
- ¼ cup chopped pecans
- 1 tablespoon butter
- 2 large eggs
- 1 cup sugar
- 1 teaspoon vanilla extract
- ½ teaspoon cinnamon
- ½ teaspoon salt

Remove crusts and cut bread into 1-inch pieces; place in 8-9-cup bowl. Microwave milk, raisins, pecans and butter in a large bowl on high for 3½ minutes. Beat eggs, add sugar, vanilla, cinnamon and salt; stir in hot milk mixture. Pour over bread; let marinate 10 minutes. Microwave entire mixture uncovered on medium for 4 minutes. Turn bowl one-half turn. Microwave on high 6-8 minutes or until set. Serve with Rum-Butter Sauce.

Yield: Serves 6.

Rum-Butter Sauce

- 2 cups powdered sugar
- ¼ cup cornstarch
- ¼ cup water
- ½ cup butter
- ¼ teaspoon salt
- 2 tablespoons rum

Combine sugar and cornstarch in a small mixing bowl, stir in water.

Melt butter in small saucepan; stir in cornstarch mixture and salt. Bring to a boil stirring constantly. Simmer 3 minutes. Stir in rum.

Yield: ¾ cup.

PEACH-PRALINE SAUCE

- 1 cup peeled fresh peach slices
- ⅓ cup praline-flavored liqueur
- ¼ cup firmly packed brown sugar
- 2 tablespoons butter
- ½ cup chopped pecans

Combine peach slices, liqueur, sugar and butter in saucepan; bring to boil, stirring constantly. Reduce heat; cook 1 minute; set aside to cool slightly. Spoon sauce over ice cream; top with pecans.

Yield: 1¼ cups.

RICE PUDDING

Rice should not be al dente in pudding. The rice should be just discernible within the cream mixture.

- **1 cup long-grain rice**
- **1 teaspoon salt**
- **2 cups water**
- **⅓ cup sugar**
- **3 cups milk**
- **3 egg yolks**
- **1 cup half-and-half**
- **2 teaspoons vanilla extract**
- **½ cup golden raisins, plumped in ½ cup sweet white wine, drained**
- **Freshly grated nutmeg**

Combine rice, salt and water in saucepan; simmer 3 minutes. Drain off excess water, add sugar and milk and simmer over low heat stirring occasionally. Cook uncovered until milk is absorbed and rice is creamy (about 30 minutes). Cool.

Whisk yolks with half-and-half; add vanilla. Combine yolk mixture with cooled rice, mixing well. Stir in raisins. Pour into buttered 2-quart glass baking dish, sprinkle with nutmeg. Bake uncovered at 325° for 35-40 minutes until set around edges but creamy in center. Serve with some of edges and some of center.

Yield: Serves 6.

CARAMEL SAUCE

- **1½ cups firmly packed brown sugar**
- **⅔ cup light corn syrup**
- **¼ cup butter**
- **¼ teaspoon salt**
- **1 (5.3-ounce) can evaporated milk**

Combine brown sugar, corn syrup and butter; cook over medium heat to soft ball stage (234°-240°) stirring constantly, stir in salt and milk.

Yield: 2¼ cups.

Variation: Add 1 cup toasted flaked coconut and 2 tablespoons dark rum.

CARAMEL CRUNCH SAUCE

- **¼ cup butter**
- **⅓ cup chopped or sliced almonds**
- **⅓ cup light corn syrup**
- **⅓ cup firmly packed brown sugar**
- **1 tablespoon water**
- **⅓ cup crispy rice cereal, coarsely crushed**
- **½ teaspoon vanilla extract**

In medium skillet, melt butter. Add almonds, stirring until browned. Add corn syrup, brown sugar and water. Stir until bubbly and brown sugar is dissolved (about 4 minutes). Stir in crispy rice cereal. Serve warm over ice cream.

Yield: 1 cup.

WORLD'S BEST CHOCOLATE FUDGE SAUCE

May be kept in refrigerator several weeks.

- **7 (1-ounce) squares unsweetened baking chocolate**
- **1 tablespoon butter**
- **Pinch of salt**
- **1¾ cups sugar**
- **1 (12-ounce) can evaporated milk**
- **1 teaspoon vanilla**

In double boiler over hot water, melt chocolate, butter, salt and sugar. Add milk. Cook until thick. Add vanilla. Serve hot.

Yield: 2 cups.

FUDGE SAUCE

- **½ cup butter**
- **4 (1-ounce) squares unsweetened chocolate**
- **3 cups sugar**
- **½ teaspoon salt**
- **1 (12-ounce) can evaporated milk**
- **1 teaspoon vanilla**

Melt butter and chocolate over low heat; stir in remaining ingredients. Cook, stirring constantly until sugar is dissolved and sauce is smooth. Serve warm or cold.

Yield: 4 cups.

MIMOSA SAUCE

Wonderful sauce served over French toast.

- **1 cup orange juice**
- **1 tablespoon cornstarch**
- **½ cup dry champagne or white wine**
- **2 tablespoons honey**
- **1 orange, peeled and sectioned**
- **½ cup strawberries, halved**

Combine orange juice and cornstarch in a medium saucepan; whisk until blended. Stir in champagne. Bring to a boil; reduce heat and cook 1 minute. Stir in honey, orange sections and strawberries.

Yield: 1⅓ cups.

PEANUT BUTTER SAUCE

- **1 cup sugar**
- **1 tablespoon light corn syrup**
- **⅛ teaspoon salt**
- **¾ cup evaporated milk**
- **3 tablespoons peanut butter**
- **1 teaspoon vanilla**

Blend sugar, syrup and salt; gradually add milk and cook over medium heat until thickened. Add peanut butter. Beat well; add vanilla.

Yield: 2 cups.

High altitude adjustments for cake recipes will be found on Page 344.

AMARETTO CAKE

- **1½ cups chopped almonds, toasted, divided**
- **1 (18.5-ounce) box yellow cake mix**
- **1 (3½-ounce) box vanilla instant pudding mix**
- **4 eggs, beaten**
- **½ cup vegetable oil**
- **½ cup water**
- **½ cup amaretto liqueur**
- **1 teaspoon almond extract**

Sprinkle 1 cup almonds into bottom of a well-greased and floured 10-inch tube pan. Combine cake mix, pudding mix, eggs, oil, water, amaretto and almond extract. Beat on low speed until dry ingredients are blended; beat 4 minutes. Stir in remaining almonds. Pour batter into prepared pan. Bake at 325° for 1 hour or until pick inserted in middle comes out clean. Cool cake in pan 10 minutes. Pour glaze over hot cake. Let cool.

Yield: One 10-inch cake.

Glaze

- **½ cup sugar**
- **¼ cup water**
- **2 tablespoons butter**
- **¼ cup amaretto liqueur**
- **½ teaspoon almond extract**
- **½ teaspoon butter flavoring**

Combine sugar, water and butter, bring to boil. Cook until sugar dissolves. Cool. Pour in amaretto and flavorings. Pour over cake.

ANGEL FOOD BIRTHDAY CAKE

You don't have to bake a cake to serve a very special one.

- **½ cup butter**
- **1¼ cups sifted powdered sugar**
- **¼ cup dark rum**
- **2 cups whipping cream, whipped**
- **1 teaspoon vanilla extract**
- **1 tablespoon powdered sugar**
- **1 large bakery angel food cake**
- **¾ cup ground almonds**
- **½ cup macaroon crumbs**
- **1 cup toasted sliced almonds**

Cream butter, powdered sugar and rum; set aside. Combine whipped cream, vanilla and powdered sugar; set aside.

Slice cake into 3 layers horizontally. Place bottom layer on serving plate; spread top with half of the butter cream and ¼ cup of the whipped cream. Sprinkle with half of the ground almonds then half of the macaroon crumbs. Place second layer on top and repeat with remaining butter cream, ¼ cup of whipped cream, remaining ground almonds and macaroon crumbs.

Place last layer on top and ice cake with remaining whipped cream. Sprinkle cake with toasted almonds. Chill for 3-6 hours.

Yield: 1 cake.

Preheat ovens for 15-20 minutes for cakes.

BANANA CAKE

- **1 cup butter, softened**
- **3 cups sugar**
- **2 cups mashed bananas**
- **4 eggs, beaten**
- **4 cups all-purpose flour**
- **2 teaspoons baking soda**
- **1 cup buttermilk**
- **1 teaspoon vanilla extract**
- **2 tablespoons bourbon**
- **1 cup chopped pecans**

Cream butter and sugar until light and fluffy. Add bananas; mix until smooth. Stir in beaten eggs.

Combine flour and baking soda; add to banana mixture alternately with buttermilk, mixing well. Stir in vanilla, bourbon and nuts.

Pour batter into 3 greased and floured 9-inch cake pans. Bake at 350° for 35-40 minutes; remove from pans and cool completely. Frost with Banana-Nut Frosting between layers and top of cake.

Yield: One 9-inch cake.

Banana-Nut Frosting

- **½ cup mashed bananas**
- **1 teaspoon lemon juice**
- **⅓ cup butter**
- **1 (16-ounce) package plus 3 cups powdered sugar**
- **3 tablespoons milk**
- **1 cup flaked coconut**
- **⅔ cup finely chopped pecans**

Combine bananas and lemon juice; set aside.

Cream butter; add sugar, bananas and milk, beating until fluffy (add more milk if necessary for proper consistency). Stir in coconut and pecans.

BLACK WALNUT CAKE

- ½ cup butter
- ½ cup vegetable shortening
- 2 cups sugar
- 5 eggs, separated
- 1 cup buttermilk
- 1 teaspoon baking soda
- 2 cups all-purpose flour
- 1 teaspoon vanilla extract
- 1 cup chopped black walnuts
- 3 ounces flaked coconut
- ½ teaspoon cream of tartar
- Chopped black walnuts

Cream butter and shortening; gradually add sugar, beating well at medium speed of electric mixer. Add egg yolks one at a time, beating well after each addition.

Combine buttermilk and baking soda; stir until baking soda dissolves.

Add flour to creamed mixture alternately with buttermilk mixture, beginning and ending with flour. Mix after each addition. Stir in vanilla. Add 1 cup walnuts and coconut, stirring well. Beat egg whites until stiff; fold into batter.

Pour batter into 3 greased and floured 9-inch round cake pans. Bake at 350° for 22-25 minutes. Cool in pans 10 minutes; remove and cool completely. Spread Cream Cheese Frosting between layers, on sides and top of cake; press additional walnuts onto sides of cake.

Yield: One 3-layer cake.

Cream Cheese Frosting

- ¾ cup butter
- 1 (8-ounce) package cream cheese, softened
- 6¾ cups sifted powdered sugar
- 1½ teaspoons vanilla extract

Cream butter and cream cheese; gradually add powdered sugar, beating until light and fluffy. Stir in vanilla.

BUTTER PECAN CAKE

Toasting the pecans in butter brings out the full flavor of the nuts, making this cake a special one—one of the best!

- **4 tablespoons butter**
- **1½ cups chopped pecans**
- **⅔ cup butter**
- **1⅓ cups sugar**
- **2 eggs**
- **2 cups all-purpose flour**
- **1½ teaspoons baking powder**
- **¼ teaspoon salt**
- **⅔ cup milk**
- **1½ teaspoons vanilla extract**

- **3 tablespoons butter, softened**
- **3 cups sifted powdered sugar**
- **3 tablespoons milk plus 1 teaspoon**
- **¾ teaspoon vanilla extract**
- **Reserved ½ cup pecans**

Melt 4 tablespoons butter; stir in pecans until toasted; set aside.

Cream softened ⅔ cup butter and sugar, beating until light and fluffy. Add eggs one at a time beating after each addition. Combine flour, baking powder and salt, add to creamed mixture alternately with milk, beginning and ending with flour mixture. Stir in vanilla and 1 cup pecans, reserving remaining pecans for frosting.

Pour batter into two greased and floured 9-inch cake pans. Bake at 350° for 30 minutes or until cake is lightly browned and pulls away from the sides of the pan and springs back at a touch. Cool in pan 10 minutes. Remove and cool completely.

Cream 3 tablespoons butter; add powdered sugar, milk and vanilla. Beat until light and fluffy. Stir in reserved pecans. Spread frosting between layers, on sides and top of cake.

Yield: One 2-layer cake.

CARAMEL CAKE

- **1 (8-ounce) carton sour cream**
- **¼ cup milk**
- **1 cup butter, softened**
- **2 cups sugar**
- **4 eggs**
- **2¾ cups all-purpose flour**
- **2 teaspoons baking powder**
- **½ teaspoon salt**
- **1 teaspoon vanilla extract**

Combine sour cream and milk. Cream butter and sugar on medium speed of electric mixer. Add eggs one at a time, beating after each addition.

Combine flour, baking powder and salt; add to creamed mixture alternately with sour cream mixture, beginning and ending with flour mixture. Mix well. Stir in vanilla.

Pour batter into 2 greased and floured 9-inch round cake pans. Bake at 350° for 30-35 minutes or until wooden pick inserted in center comes out clean. Cool in pans 10 minutes; remove and cool completely. Spread frosting between layers, on sides and top.

Yield: One 2-layer cake.

Caramel Frosting

- **3 cups sugar, divided**
- **1 tablespoon all-purpose flour**
- **1 cup milk**
- **¾ cup butter**
- **1 teaspoon vanilla extract**

Sprinkle ½ cup sugar in a heavy skillet over medium heat, stirring constantly, until sugar melts (sugar will clump) and turns light golden brown. Remove from heat.

Combine remaining 2½ cups sugar and flour in a large saucepan stirring well; add milk and bring to a boil stirring constantly.

Gradually pour one-quarter of hot mixture into caramelized sugar, stirring constantly; add remaining hot mixture (mixture will lump, but keep stirring until smooth). Turn into saucepan and cook over medium heat until candy thermometer reaches 238°. Add butter, blend well. Remove from heat, cool without stirring (about 1 hour). Add vanilla and beat about 20 minutes until of spreading consistency.

BEST CHEESECAKE

- **2 cups graham cracker crumbs**
- **½ cup sugar**
- **½ cup butter, melted**
- **2 (8-ounce) packages cream cheese, softened**
- **¼ teaspoon salt**
- **5 eggs, separated**
- **1 teaspoon vanilla extract**
- **2 tablespoons lemon juice**
- **1 cup sour cream**
- **1 cup sugar**

Combine first 3 ingredients; blend well (reserve ½ cup). Press into bottom and sides of a 9-inch springform pan. Bake at 325° for 5 minutes; set aside.

Beat cream cheese, salt, egg yolks, vanilla, lemon juice, sour cream and sugar with electric mixer until well blended. Beat egg whites until soft peaks form; fold into creamed mixture. Pour into crust and bake at 350° for 1 hour until center is firm and set; cool. Spread Topping over cheesecake, sprinkle with reserved ½ cup crumbs. Bake at 350° for 5-8 minutes. Refrigerate 3 hours before serving.

Yield: One 9-inch cheesecake.

Topping:

- **1 cup sour cream**
- **1 tablespoon sugar**
- **1 teaspoon vanilla**

Blend all ingredients; spread over cheesecake.

Stagger cake pans in oven so they do not touch.

CHOCOLATE PEANUT BUTTER CHEESECAKE

- **1½ cups graham cracker crumbs**
- **¼ cup sugar**
- **6 tablespoons butter, melted**
- **2 (8-ounce) packages cream cheese, softened**
- **1½ cups sugar**
- **6 ounces creamy peanut butter**
- **5 eggs, separated**
- **½ cup sour cream**
- **2 teaspoons lemon juice**
- **1 cup chocolate chips, coarsely grated**

Combine first 3 ingredients; mix well. Press into bottom and sides of a 9-inch springform pan. Bake at 350° for 5 minutes; cool.

Cream the cream cheese, sugar and peanut butter; add egg yolks, beating well. Stir in sour cream, lemon juice and chocolate chips.

Beat egg whites until soft peaks form, fold into creamed mixture. Pour into prepared pan; bake 50-60 minutes or until center is firm and set. Let cool 15 minutes; spread Topping over cheesecake. Bake at 350° for 10 minutes. Refrigerate 3 hours.

Yield: One 9-inch cheesecake.

Topping

- **1 cup sour cream**
- **6 (1-ounce) squares semi-sweet chocolate, melted**
- **½ cup sugar**

Blend all ingredients; spread over top of cheesecake.

CHOCOLATE TORTE

A pretty cake. Fresh fruit mixed with the whipped cream layer would enhance the presentation.

2/3 cup butter
4 (1-ounce) squares unsweetened chocolate
1 3/4 cups all-purpose flour
1 3/4 cups sugar
1/4 teaspoon baking powder
1 1/4 teaspoons baking soda
1 teaspoon salt
1 1/4 cups water
1 teaspoon vanilla
3 eggs, beaten
2 (4-ounce) bars Baker's German's Sweet Chocolate
3/4 cup butter, softened
1/2 cup chopped toasted almonds
2 cups whipping cream, whipped
1 teaspoon sugar
1 teaspoon vanilla extract

Melt butter and chocolate; let cool. Combine flour with sugar, baking powder, soda and salt. Beat in chocolate mixture, water, vanilla and eggs on medium speed for 2 minutes.

Grease and flour four 9-inch cake pans. Spoon one-quarter batter into each pan. Bake at 350° for 15-18 minutes or until cake tests done. Cool in pans 10 minutes; remove and let cool completely.

Melt sweet chocolate and 3/4 cup butter; beat until smooth. Stir in almonds; set aside.

Combine whipped cream, 1 teaspoon sugar and vanilla; set aside.

To assemble cake, place 1 cake layer on serving platter; spread with half of chocolate mixture. Place another layer over top; spread with half of whipped cream. Repeat. Garnish with grated chocolate if desired.

Yield: One 4-layer torte.

TAKE-ME-TO-A-PICNIC CAKE

1 cup water
1 cup butter
½ cup cocoa
2 cups sugar
¾ cup all-purpose flour
1 teaspoon baking soda
½ teaspoon salt
3 eggs
¾ cup sour cream

Combine water, butter and cocoa; bring to boil and boil 1 minute. Set aside.

Mix sugar, flour, baking soda and salt together; add eggs and sour cream, beating until blended. Batter will be thin. Pour into a greased and floured 15 x 10½-inch jelly-roll pan. Bake at 350° for 25-30 minutes or until pick inserted in center comes out clean. Cool cake in pan. Spread Peanut Butter Frosting over cake.

Yield: Serves 12-15.

Peanut Butter Frosting

⅓ cup butter
⅓ cup milk
1 (10-ounce) package peanut butter chips
1 teaspoon vanilla extract
1 cup sifted powdered sugar

Combine butter, milk and peanut butter chips over low heat until chips are melted; stir until mixture is smooth. Remove from heat; stir in vanilla and powdered sugar. Beat until well blended.

Yield: 2 cups.

Frost sides of cake first then top.

SHERRI'S TEXAS CHOCOLATE CAKE

- **2 cups sugar**
- **2 cups all-purpose flour**
- **1 teaspoon baking soda**
- **1 cup butter**
- **4 tablespoons cocoa**
- **1 cup cola-flavored drink**
- **½ cup buttermilk**
- **2 large eggs, beaten**
- **1 teaspoon vanilla extract**
- **2 cups miniature marshmallows**

Combine sugar, flour and baking soda; set aside. Mix butter, cocoa and cola over medium heat, stirring until mixture boils. Remove from heat; cool. Blend with dry ingredients by hand. Do Not Beat. Add buttermilk, eggs, vanilla and marshmallows, blending gently. Pour into a greased 12 x 15-inch jelly-roll pan. Bake at 350° for 20-25 minutes. Spread frosting over hot cake directly from oven. Serve cake at room temperature.

Yield: One 12 x 15-inch cake.

Fudge Frosting

- **4 tablespoons cocoa**
- **½ cup butter**
- **2 ounces cola-flavored drink**
- **1 (16-ounce) box powdered sugar, sifted**
- **1 cup chopped pecans**
- **1 teaspoon vanilla extract**

Combine cocoa, butter and cola over medium heat, bring to a boil. Stir in powdered sugar, pecans and vanilla until blended. Quickly spread over hot cake, adding more cola if necessary to spread easily.

OLD-TIME FUDGE CAKE

- **2/3 cup butter, softened**
- **2½ (1-ounce) squares unsweetened chocolate**
- **1¾ cups sugar**
- **2 eggs**
- **1 teaspoon vanilla**
- **2½ cups sifted cake flour**
- **1¼ teaspoons baking powder**
- **½ teaspoon salt**
- **1¼ cups ice water**

Melt butter and chocolate; cool. Blend sugar, eggs, vanilla; add chocolate mixture and beat until fluffy. Sift flour, baking powder and salt; add to chocolate mixture alternately with ice water ending with flour mixture. Pour batter into 2 greased 9-inch cake pans. Bake at 350° for 30-35 minutes. Cool in pans 10 minutes. Remove and let cool. Frost cake between layers, on sides and top.

Yield: One 2-layer cake.

Penuche Frosting

- **½ cup butter**
- **1 cup firmly packed brown sugar**
- **¼ cup hot milk**
- **3¼ cups sifted powdered sugar**
- **½ teaspoon vanilla extract**

Melt butter and sugar; bring to boil. Add milk and cook until thick; beat until smooth. Stir in powdered sugar and vanilla until of spreading consistency (add more powdered sugar if needed).

Never sift all-purpose flour, but always sift cake flour.

FOREVER SOUTHERN COCONUT CAKE

1 cup butter
2 cups sugar
4 eggs
3 cups sifted cake flour
2½ teaspoons baking powder
½ teaspoon salt
1 cup milk
½ teaspoon almond extract
1 teaspoon vanilla extract
2 cups flaked coconut
1 cup sugar
3 tablespoons cornstarch
¼ teaspoon salt
¾ cup orange juice
¼ cup lemon juice
½ cup water
3 egg yolks, beaten
1 tablespoon grated orange rind
Angel White Frosting

Cream butter and sugar until light and fluffy; add eggs one at a time, beating well after each addition. Combine flour, baking powder and salt; add to creamed mixture alternately with milk, beginning and ending with flour mixture. Stir in flavorings and coconut. Pour batter into 3 greased and floured 9-inch cake pans. Bake at 375° for 20-25 minutes or until a pick inserted in the middle comes out clean. Cool in pans 10 minutes. Remove and cool completely.

Combine sugar, cornstarch and salt in saucepan; add fruit juices and water. Cook over medium heat, stirring constantly until it has thickened. Remove from heat, stir in orange rind. Cool.

Spread orange filling between cake layers. Spread top and sides with Angel White Frosting and coconut.

Yield: One 3-layer cake.

Angel White Frosting

1½ cups sugar
½ teaspoon cream of tartar
⅛ teaspoon salt
½ cup hot water
4 egg whites
½ teaspoon almond extract
½ teaspoon coconut extract
1 cup flaked coconut

Combine sugar, cream of tartar, salt and water in a heavy saucepan. Cook over medium heat, stirring constantly, until clear. Cook without stirring until candy thermometer reaches 240°. Beat egg whites until peaks form. Slowly add syrup and flavorings beating until stiff peaks form and frosting is thick.

LANE CAKE

An impressive cake and one that has become a traditional holiday favorite. Enjoy it throughout the year!

- **1 cup butter, softened**
- **2 cups sugar**
- **1 teaspoon vanilla extract**
- **3¼ cups all-purpose flour**
- **3½ teaspoons baking powder**
- **¾ teaspoon salt**
- **1 cup milk**
- **8 egg whites, room temperature**
- **8 egg yolks**
- **1¾ cups sugar**
- **½ teaspoon salt**
- **¾ cup butter**
- **½ cup bourbon**
- **½ cup chopped candied cherries**
- **1½ cups chopped pecans, seeded raisins, flaked coconut**

Cream butter and sugar beating on medium speed of electric mixer; add vanilla and mix well.

Combine flour, baking powder and salt; add to creamed mixture alternately with milk, beginning and ending with flour, mixing well.

Beat egg whites until stiff peaks form; fold into batter. Grease three 9-inch round cake pans and line with wax paper; grease wax paper. Pour batter into pans; bake at 350° for 18-20 minutes or until pick inserted in center comes out clean. Cool in pans 10 minutes. Remove and cool completely.

Combine egg yolks with next 3 ingredients in top of double boiler; beat to mix well. Cool, stirring constantly, until mixture is slightly thickened (about 20 minutes). Remove from heat; add bourbon and beat at low speed 1 minute. Stir in candied cherries, pecans, raisins and coconut. Spread mixture between cake layers on sides and top of cake.

Yield: One 3-layer cake.

PETITE LEMON MERINGUE CAKE

- ¼ cup butter, softened
- ½ cup sugar
- 2 eggs, separated
- 1 egg
- 1 cup all-purpose flour
- 1 teaspoon baking powder
- ⅓ cup milk
- ½ teaspoon vanilla extract
- 2 eggs, separated
- 1 cup water
- ¾ cup sugar
- ⅓ cup all-purpose flour
- ½ teaspoon grated lemon rind
- ¼ cup lemon juice
- 1 tablespoon butter
- ½ teaspoon cream of tartar
- ½ cup sugar

Cream ¼ cup butter and ½ cup sugar, beat at medium speed of electric mixer. Add 2 egg yolks and 1 egg to creamed mixture; mix well.

Combine 1 cup flour and baking powder; add to creamed mixture alternately with milk beginning and ending with flour. Mix well. Stir in vanilla. Pour batter into a greased and floured 9-inch round cake pan. Bake at 350° for 28-30 minutes until wooden pick inserted in middle comes out clean. Cool in pan 10 minutes. Remove and cool completely.

Combine 2 egg yolks and water; set aside. Combine ¾ cup sugar and ⅓ cup flour; add egg yolk mixture and lemon rind. Cook over medium heat, stirring constantly until mixture thickens; boil 2 minutes. Remove from heat. Stir in lemon juice and 1 tablespoon butter. Cover with wax paper; cool. Place cake layer on cookie sheet. Spoon filling onto cake.

Beat 4 egg whites with cream of tartar on high speed for 1 minute. Gradually add ½ cup sugar, beating until stiff peaks form. Spread over lemon filling. Bake at 350° for 12-15 minutes or until meringue peaks are lightly browned.

Yield: One 9-inch cake.

LIQUEUR CAKE

- 1 (18.5-ounce) box German chocolate cake mix
- 1 tablespoon grated orange rind
- ⅔ cup orange juice
- ½ cup Kahlua liqueur
- ⅓ cup vegetable oil
- 3 eggs, beaten
- ⅔ cup chopped dates
- ½ cup half-and-half
- ½ cup Kahlua liqueur
- 1 egg, beaten
- ¼ cup sugar
- 1 tablespoon all-purpose flour
- ½ cup chopped pecans
- 1 tablespoon grated orange rind

Combine first 6 ingredients; beat on highest speed of electric mixer for 2 minutes. Pour batter into two greased and floured 9-inch cake pans. Bake at 350° for 30-35 minutes or until pick inserted in middle comes out clean. Cool in pans 10 minutes; remove and cool completely.

Combine dates, cream and Kahlua; cook over medium heat until mixture bubbles. Gradually stir in egg, stirring constantly. Combine sugar and flour; stir into date mixture. Cook over medium heat until mixture thickens. Stir in pecans and orange rind.

Spread date filling between cake layers. Frost sides and top of cake with Fudge Frosting (see Page 331) that has been flavored with 1 teaspoon Kahlua.

Yield: One 9-inch cake.

Always bake a cake on a middle shelf in the oven.

BUTTERMILK POUND CAKE

1 cup solid vegetable shortening
3 cups sugar
1½ teaspoons vanilla extract
6 eggs
3 cups all-purpose flour
¼ teaspoon baking soda
½ teaspoon salt
1 cup buttermilk (or sour cream)
Lemon Glaze, optional

Cream shortening and sugar; add vanilla, mixing well. Add eggs one at a time, beating after each addition. Combine flour, baking soda and salt; add to creamed mixture alternately with milk, beginning and ending with flour mixture. Spoon into well-greased 9-inch tube pan. Bake at 325° for 1 hour 15 minutes or until pick inserted in center comes out clean. Cool 10 minutes; remove from pan and spoon on Lemon Glaze.

Yield: One 9-inch cake.

Lemon Glaze

1 cup powdered sugar
¼ cup butter, melted
¼ cup lemon juice

Combine all ingredients in a small bowl, mixing well.

- A 10-inch tube pan holds 16 cups of batter.
- Grease baking pans with solid vegetable shortening.
- Always flour a greased pan. A slippery surface keeps the cake from adhering to the sides of the pan and rising to its full volume.
- Angel Food and Chiffon cakes require ungreased pans for baking.
- In cake recipes, add required eggs one at a time, beating just until the yellow disappears.

SIX-LAYER LEMON CAKE

Bake this cake for someone you love.

- **1 cup plus 2 tablespoons butter, softened**
- **2¼ cups sugar**
- **6 eggs, separated**
- **3¼ cups all-purpose flour**
- **1 tablespoon baking powder**
- **⅛ teaspoon salt**
- **1 cup plus 2 tablespoons milk**
- **¾ teaspoon grated lemon rind**
- **1¾ teaspoons lemon juice**
- **2¼ cups sugar**
- **¼ cup plus 1½ tablespoons all-purpose flour**
- **2 tablespoons grated lemon rind**
- **½ cup lemon juice**
- **1 egg, beaten**
- **2 tablespoons butter**
- **¼ teaspoon vanilla extract**

Cream butter and sugar; add egg yolks one at a time, beating well after each addition.

Combine flour, baking powder and salt; add to creamed mixture alternately with milk, ending with flour mixture. Stir in lemon rind and juice. Beat egg whites until stiff peaks form; fold into batter.

Spoon batter into 3 greased and floured 9-inch round cake pans. Bake at 350° for 25-30 minutes or until pick inserted in center comes out clean. Cool in pans 10 minutes. Remove layers; cool completely.

Combine 2¼ cups sugar with flour, lemon rind, lemon juice and egg, mixing well. Cook over medium heat, stirring constantly until smoothly thickened. Remove from heat; add butter and vanilla, stirring until blended. Cool.

Cut each cake layer in half horizontally. Place a layer, cut side down, on a serving platter. Spread with lemon filling. Repeat with all layers except top.

Frost top and sides of cake with Cream Cheese Frosting.

Yield: One 6-layer cake.

(Six-Layer Lemon Cake continued)

Cream Cheese Frosting

- **½ cup butter, softened**
- **1 (8-ounce) package cream cheese softened**
- **4 cups powdered sugar, sifted**
- **¾ teaspoon vanilla extract**

Cream butter and cream cheese; gradually add sugar beating at high speed of electric mixer until smooth and creamy. Beat in vanilla.

APRICOT BRANDY POUND CAKE

- **3 cups sugar**
- **1 cup butter**
- **6 eggs**
- **3 cups all-purpose flour**
- **¼ teaspoon baking soda**
- **½ teaspoon salt**
- **1 cup sour cream**
- **½ teaspoon rum extract**
- **½ teaspoon lemon extract**
- **¼ teaspoon almond extract**
- **1 teaspoon orange extract**
- **1 teaspoon vanilla extract**
- **½ cup apricot brandy**

Cream sugar and butter; add eggs one at a time, beating well after each addition. Sift flour, baking soda and salt. Combine sour cream, flavorings and brandy; add to creamed mixture alternately with flour, beginning and ending with flour mixture. Mix until just blended.

Pour into a greased and floured 9-inch tube pan. Bake 1 hour 10 minutes or until pick inserted in middle comes out clean. Do not overbake.

Yield: One 9-inch cake.

COCONUT CAKE

- 1 (18.5-ounce) yellow cake mix
- 1½ cups sugar
- 3 (6-ounce) cans flaked coconut
- 2 cups sour cream

Bake cake according to package instructions for a two-layer cake; cool.

Combine sugar, coconut and sour cream. Split cake layers horizontally and frost between each layer, on sides and top with sour cream mixture.

Wrap cake and refrigerate for 3 days. Sprinkle with additional coconut and serve.

Yield: One 4-layer cake.

THE SPICE CAKE

- 1 (18.5-ounce) box spice cake mix
- 1 (3.4-ounce) package butterscotch instant pudding mix
- ¾ cup vegetable oil
- 4 eggs
- 1 cup water
- ½ cup strawberry preserves
- ½ cup raisins
- 1 cup flaked coconut
- 1 cup chopped pecans
- 1 teaspoon vanilla extract
- 2 cups powdered sugar
- 6 tablespoons lemon juice

Combine cake mix and pudding mix; beat in oil, eggs and water with electric beaters until blended. Stir in preserves, raisins, coconut, pecans and vanilla; mix together well. Pour into a well-greased 10-inch tube pan. Bake at 325° for 1 hour or until just done. Let cool 5 minutes.

Combine powdered sugar and lemon juice. Punch holes in top of baked cake with a fork. Spread icing over hot cake and let soak in. Cool cake in pan.

Yield: One 10-inch cake.

COCONUT POUND CAKE

1½ cups butter
3 cups sugar
6 eggs
½ teaspoon coconut extract
½ teaspoon vanilla extract
3 cups all-purpose flour
½ teaspoon baking powder
¼ teaspoon salt
1 (8-ounce) carton sour cream (or 1 cup milk)
1 (7-ounce) package coconut

Cream butter and sugar; add eggs one at a time beating well (do not overbeat). Add flavorings. Combine flour, baking powder and salt; add to creamed mixture alternately with sour cream, ending with dry ingredients. Fold in coconut. Pour into greased and floured 10-inch tube pan. Bake at 325° for 1 hour or until pick inserted in cake comes out clean. Remove from oven, leave in pan. Spoon half of glaze over hot cake, let stand 5 minutes. Stick holes in cake with two-tined fork; spoon remaining glaze over cake. Let cool.

Yield: One 10-inch cake.

Glaze

1 cup sugar
½ cup water
1 teaspoon vanilla
½ cup butter
1 teaspoon coconut extract
1 teaspoon butter flavoring
½ cup flaked coconut

Combine all ingredients (except coconut). Cook over high heat (boil) for 3 minutes. Spoon over cake. Sprinkle with coconut.

LEMON POUND CAKE

Do not overbake. Cake should be just done.

1 cup butter, softened
½ cup vegetable shortening
3 cups sugar
5 eggs
1 (8-ounce) carton sour cream
¼ cup milk
3 cups all-purpose flour
½ teaspoon baking powder
2 teaspoons lemon extract
1 teaspoon vanilla extract

Cream butter and shortening; gradually add sugar, beating well. Add eggs, one at time mixing well after each addition.

Combine sour cream and milk; stir until smooth. Combine flour and baking powder; add to creamed mixture alternately with sour cream mixture. Mix just until blended. Stir in lemon and vanilla extract.

Pour batter into greased and floured 10-inch tube pan. Bake at 325° for 1 hour 15 minutes or until wooden pick inserted in center comes out clean. Cool cake in pan 10-15 minutes. Remove and cool completely.

Yield: One 10-inch cake.

All fats for cakes should be at room temperature; butter should be soft, not melted.

RUM CAKE

- **1 cup chopped nuts**
- **1 (18.5-ounce) box Golden Butter Cake mix**
- **1 (3¾-ounce) package instant vanilla pudding mix**
- **4 eggs, beaten**
- **½ cup light rum**
- **½ cup water**
- **½ cup vegetable oil**

Grease and flour a 10-inch bundt or tube pan; sprinkle nuts over bottom.

Combine cake mix and pudding mix; stir in eggs, rum, water and oil. Beat with electric beaters for 3 minutes. Pour gently into baking pan. Bake at 325° for 50-60 minutes or until cake begins to pull away from sides of the pan or a pick inserted in center comes out clean. Glaze hot cake.

Yield: One 10-inch cake.

Glaze

- **½ cup butter**
- **1 cup sugar**
- **¼ cup rum**
- **¼ cup water**

Combine all ingredients and heat to boiling. Boil for 3 minutes, stirring constantly. Pour hot glaze over baked cake in pan. Leave cake in pan 1 hour (or until cool).

HIGH ALTITUDE ADJUSTMENTS FOR CAKES

Reduce baking powder, baking soda and cream of tartar. Avoid beating eggs too much. Only beat whites until just stiff. Use extra large eggs. Sour cream or buttermilk adds moisture. Use butter or solid shortening. Use cake flour not self-rising flour.

- 1 teaspoon baking powder, baking soda or cream of tartar, decrease by ⅓ teaspoon.
- 1 cup sugar, decrease by 1½ tablespoons
- Increase liquid by 2-3 tablespoons
- Increase cake flour by 1 tablespoon
- Increase baking temperature 15°

ANN'S BLUEBERRY PIE

You'll love it!

- 1 (14-ounce) can sweetened condensed milk
- 2 lemons, juiced
- ½ cup whipping cream, not whipped
- 1 cup chopped pecans
- 2 cups fresh blueberries
- 1 baked 9-inch pie shell
- 1 cup whipping cream, whipped

Combine condensed milk and lemon juice; add ½ cup whipping cream, blending well. Fold in nuts and blueberries. Pour mixture into baked pie crust. Top with whipped cream. Refrigerate 4 hours or more.

Yield: One 9-inch pie.

CHOCOLATE PECAN PIE

Serve warm or at room temperature. Reheat refrigerated leftovers.

- ½ cup butter
- 3 (1-ounce) squares unsweetened chocolate
- 1½ cups sugar
- 3 tablespoons light corn syrup
- ⅛ teaspoon salt
- 4 eggs
- 1 teaspoon vanilla
- 1 ounce bourbon (optional)
- ¾ cup chopped pecans
- 1 unbaked 10-inch pie shell

Melt butter and chocolate; cool. Stir in sugar, corn syrup and salt. Add eggs one at a time, beating only until eggs disappear. Stir in vanilla, bourbon and nuts. Pour into pie crust. Bake at 350° for 35-40 minutes or until set. Serve warm topped with whipped topping, if desired.

Yield: One 10-inch pie.

SOUR CHERRY PIE

- 2 eggs, beaten
- 2 (8-ounce) packages cream cheese, softened
- ½ teaspoon vanilla extract
- ½ cup sugar
- 1 (9-inch) graham cracker crust
- 1 (16-ounce) can pitted tart water-packed red cherries
- Water
- 1 cup sugar
- 2 tablespoons water
- 3 tablespoons cornstarch

Combine eggs, cream cheese, vanilla and sugar beating together until smooth. Pour into graham cracker crust; bake at 375° for 20 minutes. Cool.

Drain cherries, reserving juice. Combine juice and water to make 1 cup; mix with sugar. Cook in saucepan; bring to a boil. Simmer 10 minutes until syrupy. Blend 2 tablespoons water with cornstarch to make a paste; slowly add to syrup. Cook until mixture thickens and becomes clear; add cherries. Cool until thickened. Spread evenly over cheese layer. Chill several hours until set.

Yield: One 9-inch pie.

EASY FUDGE PIES

- 3 cups sugar
- 7 tablespoons cocoa
- 1 teaspoon salt
- ½ cup butter, melted
- 5 large eggs
- 1 (12-ounce) can evaporated milk
- 2 (9-inch) graham cracker crusts

Combine sugar, cocoa and salt, add butter mixing well. Mix in eggs one at a time, beating until well blended. Add milk and beat with electric beaters until blended well. Pour evenly into the two crusts. Place pies on a cookie sheet and bake at 325° for 45 minutes (middles will be slightly shaky). Cool. Serve topped with whipped topping, if desired.

Yield: Two 9-inch pies.

CHOCOLATE PECAN TOFFEE MOUSSE PIES

A delicious and impressive dessert to serve at luncheons or at special dinners. So-o-o good!

- **½ cup butter**
- **½ cup sugar**
- **4 cups pecan pieces, ground**
- **¼ cup water**
- **28 (1-ounce) squares semi-sweet chocolate**
- **¼ cup vegetable oil**
- **4 cups whipping cream, whipped**
- **2 cups unsalted butter**
- **3½ cups sugar**
- **4 cups heavy cream**

Cream butter and sugar over low heat until mixture forms a thick, smooth paste. Remove from heat; add water, stirring constantly, forming a syrup. Pour over pecans, mix thoroughly. Let cool.

Butter and flour two 10-inch pie pans. Press pecan mixture into pans forming a crust. Bake at 325° for 10 minutes or until golden brown. Cool at room temperature.

Melt chocolate in top of double boiler, add oil. Mix until smooth. Let cool. Combine chocolate with whipped cream, beating until well blended. Refrigerate 2 hours. Spoon equally into the two crusts. Refrigerate.

Melt butter, add sugar stirring over medium high heat until a deep caramel color (butter and sugar will separate). Remove from heat and while whisking constantly, slowly add heavy cream. Strain toffee sauce into a 2-quart container. Refrigerate and heat at serving time. Ladle sauce on dessert plate, place pie slice on top or ladle sauce over pie slice.

Yield: Two 10-inch pies.

TROPICAL COCONUT PIE

- **¼ cup butter, melted**
- **7 ounces flaked coconut**
- **1 (8-ounce) can crushed pineapple, undrained**
- **1 envelope unflavored gelatin**
- **¾ cup cream of coconut**
- **¼ cup light rum**
- **2 (3-ounce) packages cream cheese, softened**
- **1 cup whipping cream, whipped**
- **Kiwi fruit, Mandarin orange slices for garnish**

Blend butter and coconut (reserving 2 tablespoons) together in a 9-inch pie pan; press firmly on bottom and up sides forming pie crust. Bake at 350° for 15 minutes until edge is golden. Cool. Place reserved 2 tablespoons coconut in shallow pan and toast in oven until golden brown; set aside.

Drain pineapple, reserving juice. In a small saucepan, sprinkle gelatin over reserved pineapple juice; cook over low heat until gelatin is dissolved. Blend in coconut cream and rum, remove from heat. In a mixing bowl, beat softened cream cheese until fluffy, add gelatin mixture and beat together until smooth. Stir in pineapple, fold in whipped cream. Chill mixture 20 minutes. Pour into coconut crust; garnish with toasted coconut, sliced kiwi and Mandarin orange slices. Chill 3 hours.

Yield: One 9-inch pie.

FRUIT-ON-A-CLOUD PIE

- **3/4 cup sugar**
- **1/2 teaspoon baking powder**
- **1/8 teaspoon salt**
- **3 egg whites**
- **1/2 teaspoon vanilla**
- **19 round buttery crackers, coarsely crushed**
- **1/2 cup chopped pecans**
- **1 cup whipping cream, whipped**
- **1 tablespoon sugar**
- **2 cups sliced fresh fruit of your choice**

Combine sugar, baking powder and salt. Beat egg whites until foamy; gradually add sugar mixture 1 tablespoon at a time beating constantly until stiff and shiny. Fold in vanilla, cracker crumbs and pecans. Pour into greased 9-inch pie pan, spreading evenly over bottom and up sides forming a pie shell. Bake at 325° for 30 minutes. Remove from oven. Cool away from drafts (shell may sag in center).

Combine whipped cream and sugar. Spread in pie shell. Arrange favorite fruit on top of cream. Refrigerate 8 hours. Serve with additional whipped topping seasoned with Grand Marnier (optional).

Yield: One 9-inch pie.

Add 3 tablespoons of "red hots" to peach or apple pie mixture.

JEFF DAVIS PIE

You'll give a real rebel yell after a slice of this traditional Southern pie.

- **½ cup butter**
- **2 cups firmly packed brown sugar**
- **4 egg yolks**
- **2 tablespoons all-purpose flour**
- **⅛ teaspoon salt**
- **1 teaspoon cinnamon**
- **1 teaspoon nutmeg**
- **1 cup half-and-half**
- **½ cup chopped dates**
- **½ cup chopped pecans**
- **½ cup raisins**
- **1 unbaked 9-inch pie shell**
- **4 egg whites**
- **½ cup sugar**

Cream butter and sugar. Beat in egg yolks, one at a time, by hand. Combine flour, salt and spices; stir into batter until smooth. Gradually blend in cream by hand. Fold in dates, pecans and raisins. Pour into pie crust and bake at 325° for 40 minutes or until set.

Beat egg whites on high speed of electric mixer until frothy. Gradually add sugar 1 tablespoon at a time until stiff peaks form. Spread meringue over hot baked pie, mounding in center and sealing edges. Bake at 350° until evenly browned. Cool to room temperature and serve warm.

Yield: One 9-inch pie.

ICE CREAM PIE SUPREME

1 cup graham cracker crumbs
½ cup chopped walnuts
¼ cup butter, melted
1 pint coffee ice cream, softened
1 pint vanilla ice cream, softened
Brown Sugar Sauce

Combine graham cracker crumbs, walnuts and butter; blend well. Press mixture into a buttered 9-inch pie pan. Bake at 375° for 10 minutes; cool.

Spoon coffee ice cream into crust; spread evenly. Freeze until firm. Spread vanilla ice cream over coffee layer; freeze until firm.

Spoon warm sauce over each pie slice.

Yield: One 9-inch pie.

Brown Sugar Sauce

3 tablespoons butter
1 cup firmly packed brown sugar
½ cup half-and-half
1 cup chopped walnuts
1 teaspoon vanilla extract

Melt butter in heavy saucepan over low heat; add brown sugar. Cook 6 minutes, stirring constantly. Gradually add half-and-half; cook 1 minute. Remove from heat; stir in walnuts and vanilla.

Yield: 1½ cups.

CHOCOLATE ICE CREAM PIES

- 4 egg whites
- ½ teaspoon cream of tartar
- 1 cup sugar
- 1 cup finely chopped pecans
- ½ gallon chocolate ice cream, softened
- 1 cup whipping cream, whipped
- ½ teaspoon vanilla
- 1 cup Fudge Sauce (see Page 320)

Let egg whites stand at room temperature 1 hour. Beat whites and cream of tartar until frothy. Add sugar 1 tablespoon at a time until stiff and shiny. Fold in pecans and pour equally into two greased 9-inch pie pans. Bake at 250° for 40 minutes. Let cool.

Divide softened ice cream into meringue shells. Freeze for 1 hour. Mix whipped cream and vanilla; fold in Fudge Sauce and spread on top of pies. Freeze. Sprinkle tops with additional chopped pecans, if desired, before serving.

Yield: Two 9-inch pies.

DREAM DESSERT PIE

- 12 (1.45-ounce) milk chocolate with almonds candy bars
- 38 large marshmallows
- 2 cups whipping cream, whipped
- ½ gallon chocolate swirl ice cream, softened
- 1 baked 9-inch pie shell or graham cracker crust

Break candy bars into pieces and melt with marshmallows over low heat; mix well. Cool. Fold in whipped cream; pour into crust. Cover with softened ice cream, smoothing top. Freeze.

Yield: One 9-inch pie.

PEPPERMINT ICE CREAM PIE

- 4 egg whites
- ½ teaspoon cream of tartar
- 1 cup sugar
- 1 cup whipping cream, whipped
- 1 cup Fudge Sauce (see Page 320)
- ¼ teaspoon peppermint oil
- 2 quarts vanilla ice cream

Beat egg whites with cream of tartar until frothy. Continue beating on high, adding sugar 1 tablespoon at a time until stiff and glossy. Pour into greased 10-inch pie plate building up sides to form shell. Bake at 300° for 50-60 minutes. Cool.

Gradually add Fudge Sauce to whipped cream. Add peppermint oil.

Soften ice cream and spoon into meringue shell. Pour chocolate mousse over top. Cover well and freeze until firm.

Yield: One 10-inch pie.

LEMON CHIFFON PIE

- 1 tablespoon unflavored gelatin
- ¼ cup water
- ½ cup sugar
- ½ cup lemon juice
- ½ teaspoon salt
- 4 egg yolks, beaten
- 4 egg whites
- ½ cup sugar
- 1 cup whipping cream, whipped
- 1 baked 9-inch pie shell

Soften gelatin in water; combine with sugar, lemon juice, salt and egg yolks. Cook over low heat (or in double boiler) until thickened (consistency of custard). Cool.

Beat egg whites until frothy; gradually add sugar 1 tablespoon at a time until stiff peaks form. Fold into cooled custard. Fold whipped cream into custard mixture. Spoon into baked pie shell. Refrigerate. Serve with whipped topping or top with meringue (see Page 362).

Yield: One 9-inch pie.

A LIME AFFAIR TO REMEMBER

A pie that will impress the best…you!

- 2 cups graham cracker crumbs
- ½ cup butter
- 1 egg
- 4 ounces heavy cream
- 8 (1-ounce) squares unsweetened chocolate
- ½ cup key lime juice
- ½ cup sugar
- 2 eggs
- 3 egg yolks
- 1 tablespoon heavy cream
- 2 ounces sliced butter
- 6 (1-ounce) squares white chocolate
- 2 ounces melted butter
- 2 cups whipping cream, whipped
- ½ cup toasted chopped macadamia nuts

Blend cracker crumbs, cold butter and egg; process in food processor to gravel-like consistency. Do not overmix. Press into bottom and up sides of a deep 9-inch greased pie pan. Bake at 350° for 12-15 minutes; set aside.

Bring heavy cream to boil; add chocolate and stir until blended. Pour into warm graham cracker crust and tilt pan from side to side to evenly distribute chocolate over entire crust. Cool.

Combine key lime juice, sugar, eggs, yolks and heavy cream over low heat (or top of double boiler), whisking until thick and smooth, about 15 minutes. Lay sliced butter over mixture, let melt. Mix together and pour into pie shell.

Melt white chocolate over low heat, mix in 2 ounces butter. Cool. Slowly mix chocolate with whipped cream (do not whisk). Spoon mixture into center of filled pie shell. Slowly spread towards sides, leaving mousse mounded in center. Sprinkle with macadamia nuts. Chill 2 hours. Cut with warm, sharp knife.

Yield: One 9-inch pie.

KEY LIME PIE

A baked pie cooked to end worries about the raw yolks found in most Key lime pies.

- **3 large eggs, separated**
- **1 (14-ounce) can sweetened condensed milk**
- **½ cup lime juice**
- **1 tablespoon grated lime rind**
- **1 tablespoon lemon juice**
- **2 tablespoons sugar**
- **1 cup whipping cream, whipped**
- **1 tablespoon powdered sugar**
- **½ teaspoon vanilla extract**
- **1 (9-inch) graham cracker crust**

Combine egg yolks with condensed milk, lime juice, rind and lemon juice; mix until smooth.

Beat egg whites on high speed of electric beaters until foamy; gradually add sugar, beating until stiff peaks form. Fold into condensed milk mixture. Spoon into graham cracker crust. Bake at 350° for 20-25 minutes until set and lightly brown. Chill 6-8 hours.

Combine whipped cream, powdered sugar and vanilla. Spread over top of pie or dollop around the edge.

Yield: One 9-inch pie.

Add ground pecans to pie crust for extra flavor and flakiness.

FLORIDA ORANGE PIE

- 3 egg yolks, beaten
- ½ cup sugar
- 1 cup orange juice, divided
- 1 envelope unflavored gelatin
- 2 tablespoons grated orange rind
- 1 teaspoon grated lemon rind
- 2 cups whipping cream, whipped, divided
- ⅔ cup powdered sugar
- ⅛ teaspoon salt
- ½ cup flaked coconut
- 1 cup diced orange sections, drained
- 1 baked 9-inch pie shell
- 3 tablespoons powdered sugar

Combine egg yolks, sugar and ½ cup orange juice. Cook over low heat 10-12 minutes, stirring constantly. Sprinkle gelatin over remaining ½ cup orange juice; let stand 1 minute. Add to yolk mixture with orange and lemon rind. Chill until consistency of unbeaten egg whites.

Whip ½ cup whipping cream, ⅔ cup sugar and salt until stiff peaks form; fold into gelatin mixture. Add coconut and orange sections. Spoon into pie crust; chill until firm. Whip remaining 1½ cups whipping cream, gradually adding 3 tablespoons powdered sugar. Beat until soft peaks form. Spoon over pie.

Yield: One 9-inch pie.

PEACH MERINGUE GLACÉ

- 6 egg whites
- 1/4 teaspoon salt
- 1 1/2 teaspoons cream of tartar
- 1 1/2 cups sugar
- 1 teaspoon vanilla extract
- 2 tablespoons all-purpose flour
- 1/3 cup sugar
- 1/8 teaspoon salt
- 6 egg yolks, beaten
- 1 1/2 cups milk
- 1/2 teaspoon vanilla extract
- 1/2 teaspoon almond extract
- 3/4 cup whipping cream, whipped
- 1 quart sliced fresh peaches
- 3 tablespoons lemon juice
- 3 tablespoons sugar
- 1/2 cup fresh blueberries

Have egg whites at room temperature; beat with salt and cream of tartar at high speed of electric beaters until frothy. Gradually add sugar 1 tablespoon at a time beating until stiff peaks form; beat in vanilla. Spoon into a greased 10-inch pie pan forming a shell. Mound sides up. Bake at 250° 1¼ hours. Turn off heat and leave in oven 1 hour longer. Cool.

Combine flour, sugar and salt; stir in beaten egg yolks, mixing well. Gradually add milk and cook over low heat until smooth and thickened stirring constantly. Remove from heat, cool. Add flavorings. Fold into whipped cream. Pour into meringue shell; top lightly with wax paper and refrigerate several hours. Mix peaches, lemon juice and sugar. When ready to serve, spread peaches over filling; sprinkle with blueberries.

Yield: One 10-inch pie.

PECAN PIE

- 1 cup sugar
- 1 cup light corn syrup
- ⅓ cup butter
- 4 eggs, beaten
- 1 teaspoon vanilla extract
- ¼ teaspoon salt
- 1½ cups coarsely chopped pecans
- 1 unbaked 9-inch pie shell

Combine first 3 ingredients; cook over low heat stirring constantly until sugar dissolves. Cool. Add eggs, vanilla, salt and pecans, stirring well. Pour filling into pie crust. Bake at 325° for 50-55 minutes.

Yield: One 9-inch pie.

SWEET POTATO PIE

- 2 cups cooked, mashed sweet potatoes
- 1 cup firmly packed brown sugar
- ½ cup butter
- 3 eggs, separated
- 2 tablespoons bourbon (optional)
- ½ teaspoon ground cinnamon
- ½ teaspoon ground nutmeg
- ¼ teaspoon salt
- ½ cup evaporated milk
- ¼ cup sugar
- 1 unbaked 10-inch pie shell
- Whipped topping (optional)

Combine sweet potatoes, brown sugar, butter, egg yolks, bourbon, spices and salt in a large mixing bowl; beat until light and fluffy. Add evaporated milk; mix just until combined.

Beat egg whites until foamy; gradually add sugar beating until stiff. Fold into potato mixture. Pour filling into pie shell. Bake at 400° for 10 minutes; reduce heat to 350° and bake an additional 45-50 minutes or until set. Cool. Top with whipped topping seasoned with 1 tablespoon bourbon, if desired.

Yield: One 10-inch pie.

FROZEN STRAWBERRY PIE

2½ cups lightly toasted coconut
⅓ cup butter, melted
1 (3-ounce) package cream cheese, softened
1 (14-ounce) can sweetened condensed milk
1½ cups mashed fresh or frozen strawberries
3 tablespoons lemon juice
1 cup whipping cream, whipped
Fresh strawberries

Combine coconut with melted butter; mix well. Press into bottom and up sides of 9-inch pie plate, forming a crust. Chill. In a large bowl, beat cream cheese until fluffy; beat in condensed milk. Stir in mashed strawberries and lemon juice. Fold in whipped cream. Pour into coconut crust. Freeze 4 hours until firm. Garnish with fresh strawberries.

Yield: One 9-inch pie.

VINEGAR PIE

Brings back memories of a Southern childhood.

3 eggs, slightly beaten
1½ cups sugar
2 tablespoons flour
2 tablespoons vinegar
1 tablespoon vanilla extract
½ cup butter, melted
1 unbaked 9-inch pie shell

Mix flour with sugar; add eggs beating by hand and only to blend. Stir in butter, vinegar and vanilla, mixing to blend. Pour into uncooked pie shell and bake at 300° for about 1 hour or until pick inserted in center comes out clean.

Yield: One 9-inch pie.

GREEN TOMATO PIE

A family recipe handed down many generations. The handwritten directions said that the taste was a cross between a rhubarb and a gooseberry pie.

- **Pastry for double-crust 10-inch pie**
- **1 cup sugar, divided**
- **5 cups very thinly sliced green tomatoes**
- **1 lemon, peeled, seeded and halved**
- **1 cup sugar**
- **2 heaping tablespoons all-purpose flour**
- **½ teaspoon nutmeg**
- **¼ cup butter**

Roll half of pastry to ⅛-inch thickness; fit into a 10-inch pie pan.

Sprinkle ½ cup sugar over bottom of crust. Add full layer of green tomato slices. Thinly slice a lemon half and place over tomatoes. Mix ¾ cup sugar, flour and nutmeg together; sprinkle half of mixture over lemons. Repeat layers, mounding in center of pie. Dot with butter.

Roll out remaining pastry to ⅛-inch thickness; carefully place over pie, leaving 1 inch rim beyond edge of pan. Seal and flute edges; cut slits in top for steam to escape. Decorate with pastry scraps cut into decorative shapes. Cover pastry edges with foil to prevent excess browning.

Bake at 350° for 45 minutes. Remove foil; bake 10-15 minutes.

Yield: One 10-inch pie.

Variation: Instead of lemon slices, use 3 tablespoons lemon juice.

BASIC VANILLA CREAM PIE

In this recipe, the term "basic" means it is the base for several other pies using the same ingredients. Add extra ingredients for individual flavors.

- **¾ cup sugar**
- **⅓ cup all-purpose flour**
- **¼ teaspoon salt**
- **2 cups milk**
- **3 egg yolks, beaten**
- **2 tablespoons butter**
- **1 teaspoon vanilla extract**
- **1 baked 9-inch pie shell**

Combine sugar, flour, salt; gradually stir in milk. Cook over medium heat until mixture thickens. Stir small amount of hot mixture into egg yolks. Add egg yolks to cooked mixture, stirring constantly 2 minutes. Remove from heat. Add butter and vanilla. Pour into pastry shell. Top hot pie mixture with meringue, spreading to edges or cool and top with whipped topping.

Yield: One 9-inch pie.

Variations:

- Banana Cream Pie: Slice 3 bananas into cooled pastry shell. Pour vanilla filling over bananas.
- Coconut Cream Pie: Add 1 cup flaked coconut to Vanilla Cream Pie filling.
- Chocolate Cream Pie: Increase sugar to 1 cup in basic recipe then add 2 (1-ounce) squares melted unsweetened chocolate to Vanilla Cream recipe.

When making pumpkin pie, place a layer of marshmallows on the bottom. While pie is baking, they will rise to the top and form a topping.

MERINGUES

Always have egg whites at room temperature.

Never-Fail Meringue

- **1 tablespoon cornstarch**
- **2 tablespoons cold water**
- **½ cup boiling water**
- **3 egg whites**
- **6 tablespoons sugar**
- **1 teaspoon vanilla extract**
- **⅛ teaspoon salt**

Blend cornstarch and cold water; add boiling water and cook in saucepan until clear and thickened. Let stand until cold.

Beat egg whites on high speed of electric beaters until frothy. Gradually add sugar, 1 tablespoon at a time, until stiff peaks form. Add salt and vanilla. Gradually beat in cold cornstarch mixture. Spread over hot pie. Bake at 350° until browned. Cuts beautifully.

Yield: Covers one 9-inch pie.

Foolproof Meringue

- **3 egg whites**
- **⅛ teaspoon salt**
- **1 cup marshmallow crème**

Beat egg whites and salt until soft peaks form. Gradually add marshmallow crème a little at a time, beating until stiff peaks form. Spread over hot pie sealing to edge of crust. Bake at 350° 12-15 minutes or until lightly browned.

Yield: Covers one 9-inch pie.

Spread meringue over the pie while it's still hot.

CRUSTS

Buy a store-bought crust? Two good reasons not to:

Graham Cracker Crust

- **2½ cups graham cracker crumbs**
- **2 tablespoons light brown sugar**
- **¼ cup ground pecans**
- **½ cup butter, softened**

Combine graham cracker crumbs, sugar and pecans; stir in butter and mix well. Press firmly and evenly into a 9-inch pie plate. Bake at 350° for 12-15 minutes.

Yield: One 9-inch pie shell.

Pastry Crust

- **4 cups all-purpose flour**
- **1 teaspoon baking powder**
- **1 teaspoon salt**
- **1 tablespoon sugar**
- **1¾ cups solid vegetable shortening**
- **1 egg, beaten**
- **1 tablespoon vinegar**
- **½ cup cold water**

Combine dry ingredients; cut in shortening until mixture resembles coarse meal. Stir in remaining ingredients. Divide dough into 5 equal parts; shape each into a ball and wrap tightly. Chill. May be stored up to 2 weeks refrigerated or frozen.

Yield: Pastry for five 9-inch pie shells.

AMBROSIA COOKIES

- ½ cup butter, softened
- ½ cup solid shortening
- 1 cup firmly packed brown sugar
- 2 eggs
- 1 tablespoon grated orange rind
- 2 cups all-purpose flour
- 1 teaspoon baking powder
- ½ teaspoon salt
- ½ teaspoon baking soda
- 3 tablespoons orange juice
- 1½ cups oatmeal
- 3 cups flaked coconut

Cream butter, shortening and sugar until light and fluffy. Add eggs and orange rind, beating in well. Combine next 4 ingredients; add to creamed mixture alternately with orange juice. Stir in oats and coconut. Chill 1 hour.

Drop dough by heaping teaspoons onto an ungreased cookie sheet. Bake at 375° for 12 minutes.

Yield: About 8 dozen.

BROWN SUGAR BROWNIES

- 7 ounces butter
- 1 pound dark brown sugar
- 2 eggs, beaten
- 1½ cups all-purpose flour
- 2 teaspoons baking powder
- 2 teaspoons vanilla extract
- 1½ cups chopped pecans

Melt butter and brown sugar in top of double boiler. Remove from heat; blend in next 4 ingredients in order listed, stirring until smooth. Add nuts. Pour into a 13 x 9-inch pan which has been lined with lightly-buttered foil. Bake at 350° for 30 minutes or until pick inserted in middle comes out clean. Cool in pan. Remove from pan, peel off foil; cut into squares while still slightly warm.

Yield: 1½ dozen.

BROWNIES SUPREME

- 1 cup butter
- ⅓ cup cocoa
- 4 eggs, beaten
- 2 cups sugar
- 1½ cups all-purpose flour
- ⅛ teaspoon salt
- 1 teaspoon vanilla
- 1½ cups chopped pecans
- 1 (7-ounce) jar marshmallow creme

- ½ cup butter
- ⅓ cup cocoa
- 1 (1-pound) box powdered sugar, sifted
- ⅛ teaspoon salt
- 1 teaspoon vanilla extract
- Milk

Melt butter and cocoa together; set aside. Combine eggs and sugar, mixing well. Stir in flour, salt and vanilla. Add the butter cocoa mixture; mix together well. Fold in nuts. Pour mixture into a greased 13 x 9-inch baking pan. Bake at 350° for 20-25 minutes. Spread marshmallow creme over hot from oven brownies.

Melt ½ cup butter with cocoa; pour over powdered sugar. Add salt and vanilla. Gradually blend in enough milk to make spreadable. Spread over marshmallow topping on brownies. Let cool in pan. Cut into squares.

Yield: About 2 dozen.

BUTTER COOKIES

- **1 cup butter, softened**
- **3/4 cup sugar**
- **1 egg**
- **1 teaspoon vanilla extract**
- **2 1/2 cups all-purpose flour**
- **1 teaspoon baking powder**
- **1/4 teaspoon salt**
- **Buttercream icing**

Cream butter; add sugar, beating until light and fluffy. Add eggs and vanilla, mixing well. Combine flour, baking powder and salt; add to creamed mixture blending well.

Using a cookie press, press dough into desired shapes onto an ungreased cookie sheet. Bake at 350° for 10-12 minutes.

Yield: 6 dozen.

Buttercream Icing

- **3 tablespoons butter**
- **2 1/3 cups sifted powdered sugar**
- **1/8 teaspoon salt**
- **2 tablespoons milk**
- **1/2 teaspoon vanilla extract**

Cream butter; add sugar beating well. Add salt, milk and vanilla; mix well. Decorate cookies with icing.

Yield: 1 cup.

CHEESECAKE DREAMS

- **1 cup all-purpose flour**
- **¼ cup firmly packed light brown sugar**
- **1 cup finely chopped pecans**
- **½ cup butter, melted**
- **2 (8-ounce) packages cream cheese**
- **1 cup sugar**
- **1 teaspoon vanilla extract**
- **3 eggs, beaten**
- **2 cups sour cream**
- **⅓ cup sugar**
- **1 teaspoon vanilla extract**

Combine flour, brown sugar, pecans and butter; mix together well. Press mixture gently into a lightly greased 13 x 9-inch baking pan. Bake at 350° for 12-15 minutes until lightly browned; set aside.

Beat cream cheese, sugar, vanilla and eggs with electric beaters until mixed and blended well. Pour mixture over crust. Bake at 350° for 20 minutes.

Blend sour cream, ⅓ cup sugar and vanilla. Spread over top of baked filling. Return to oven and bake for 5 minutes. Cool and chill several hours. Cut into 2-inch squares; cut each square diagonally in half.

Yield: 32.

CHESS COOKIES

- 1 cup butter, melted
- 1 (16-ounce) box brown sugar
- 1 cup sugar
- 4 eggs, separated
- 2 cups all-purpose flour
- 2 teaspoons baking powder
- ¼ teaspoon salt
- 1 cup chopped pecans
- 1½ teaspoons vanilla extract
- Powdered sugar

Cream butter and brown sugar by hand; blend well. Add egg yolks; beat well. Sift dry ingredients and add to butter sugar mixture. Fold in nuts and vanilla.

Beat egg whites until stiff and fold into batter. Spread batter evenly into a greased 13 x 9-inch baking pan. Bake at 350° for 30-35 minutes. Sprinkle top with powdered sugar. Cool and cut into squares.

GIANT WHITE CHOCOLATE MACADAMIA NUT COOKIES

- 1½ cups butter
- 1¼ cups firmly packed light brown sugar
- 1¼ cups sugar
- 2 teaspoons vanilla extract
- 3 large eggs
- 3½ cups all-purpose flour
- 1 teaspoon salt
- 1½ teaspoons baking soda
- 12 ounces white chocolate, chopped
- 2 cups coarsely chopped macadamia nuts

Cream butter and both sugars. Add 3 eggs one at a time, beating well; add vanilla. Sift flour, salt and baking soda; add to creamed mixture. Stir in white chocolate and nuts. Drop level ¼ cupfuls of batter 3 inches apart on greased cookie sheet. Flatten into ½-inch thick rounds with wet hands. Bake at 350° for 12-15 minutes.

Yield: About 2 dozen.

CHOCOLATE CHIP COOKIES

- **1½ cups regular oatmeal**
- **½ cup all-purpose flour**
- **1 teaspoon baking soda**
- **1 teaspoon baking powder**
- **½ cup butter, softened**
- **⅔ cup firmly packed dark brown sugar**
- **½ cup sugar**
- **1 egg**
- **1 teaspoon vanilla**
- **¾ cup chopped dates**
- **¾ cup chopped pecans**
- **⅔ cup semi-sweet chocolate chips**

Combine first 4 ingredients; set aside. Cream butter and both sugars until light and fluffy. Beat in egg and vanilla. Mix in oatmeal mixture. Fold in remaining ingredients. Drop by tablespoons onto a greased cookie sheet and bake at 375° for 10 minutes or until lightly browned.

Yield: About 2 dozen.

CHOCOLATE PECAN BARS

- **¾ cup butter, softened**
- **½ cup powdered sugar**
- **½ teaspoon salt**
- **2 cups all-purpose flour**
- **4 eggs**
- **1½ cups firmly packed light brown sugar**
- **1½ cups (6 ounces) pecans, coarsely chopped**
- **½ cup light corn syrup**
- **2 (1-ounce) squares unsweetened chocolate, melted**
- **2 teaspoons vanilla extract**
- **½ teaspoon salt**

Cream butter, sugar and salt until smooth. Stir in flour until crumbly. Press into bottom of 15½ x 10½-inch jelly-roll pan. Bake at 350° for 15 minutes.

Beat eggs and sugar together until fluffy. Stir in remaining ingredients. Pour over crust and bake 20 minutes more. Cool. Cut into diamonds or squares.

Yield: About 25.

MOCHA CHOCOLATE COOKIES

- 4 (1-ounce) squares unsweetened chocolate, chopped
- 3 cups semi-sweet chocolate chips, divided
- ½ cup butter
- ½ cup all-purpose flour
- ½ teaspoon baking powder
- ½ teaspoon salt
- 4 large eggs
- 1½ cups sugar
- 1½ tablespoons instant coffee powder
- 2 teaspoons vanilla
- 1 cup coarsely chopped pecans

Melt unsweetened chocolate, 1½ cups chocolate chips and butter, stirring until smooth; set aside.

Sift flour, baking powder and salt. In large bowl, beat eggs with sugar until thick and pale; beat in coffee powder and vanilla. Fold chocolate mixture into egg mixture; fold in flour mixture and remaining 1½ cups chocolate chips. Let mixture stand 10 minutes.

Drop batter by heaping tablespoons 2 inches apart onto baking sheets lined with parchment paper. Bake at 350° for 8-10 minutes in middle of oven until puffed, shiny and cracked on top. Do not overbake. Cool on sheets 5 minutes. Remove; cool completely.

Yield: About 36 cookies.

CHRISTMAS COOKIES

- ½ cup butter, softened
- ¼ cup sugar
- 1 egg, separated
- 1 tablespoon grated orange rind
- 1 tablespoon lemon juice
- 2 teaspoons vanilla extract
- ⅛ teaspoon salt
- 1 cup sifted cake flour
- 1 cup chopped pecans
- 18 candied cherries, halved

Cream butter and sugar until light and fluffy; add egg yolk and beat 1 minute. Add orange rind, lemon juice, vanilla and salt; beat well. Add flour; mix well. Chill dough 2 hours.

Beat egg whites. Shape dough into ¾-inch balls. Dip in egg white; roll in pecans. Place 2 inches apart on greased cookie sheet; slightly flatten. Place cherry half on each cookie. Bake at 325° for 20 minutes.

Yield: 3 dozen.

LEMON COOKIES

- 1 (18.25-ounce) box lemon cake mix
- 2½ cups frozen whipped topping, thawed
- 1 egg, beaten
- Powdered sugar, sifted

Combine cake mix, whipped topping and egg; mix well. Drop by teaspoonfuls onto sifted powdered sugar; shape into balls, coating well. Place on greased cookie sheet; bake at 350° for 12-15 minutes. Coat with powdered sugar again, if desired.

Yield: 4 dozen.

Variation: Omit whipped topping in recipe. Add ½ cup melted butter and 1 cup crispy rice cereal to recipe and follow same directions. Coat warm cookies with powdered sugar.

DREAM BARS

- 1/3 cup butter, softened
- 1/3 cup firmly packed brown sugar
- 1 cup all-purpose flour
- 2 eggs, beaten
- 1 cup firmly packed brown sugar
- 1/4 cup all-purpose flour
- 1/2 teaspoon baking powder
- 1 teaspoon vanilla extract
- 1 (3½-ounce) can flaked coconut
- 1 cup chopped pecans
- 1/2 cup semi-sweet chocolate chips

Cream butter and 1/3 cup brown sugar until light and fluffy; add 1 cup flour, mixing well. Press into bottom of a lightly greased 13 x 9-inch baking pan. Bake at 350° for 12 minutes until lightly browned; set aside.

Combine eggs and 1 cup brown sugar, mix in 1/4 cup flour, baking powder, vanilla and coconut. Stir in pecans and chocolate chips. Spread mixture over hot crust. Bake at 350° for 20-25 minutes or until lightly browned. Cool. Cut into small bars.

Yield: About 2 dozen.

QUICK MACAROONS

Bake these larger and use as a base for ice cream or fruit fillings.

- 4 egg whites
- Pinch of salt
- 3/4 cup sugar
- 1 teaspoon vanilla extract
- 1/2 teaspoon almond extract
- 2 cups shredded coconut

Beat egg whites with salt until foamy. Continue beating on high gradually adding sugar 1 tablespoon at a time until stiff. Fold in vanilla, almond extract and coconut.

Drop batter by teaspoons onto greased baking sheets. Bake at 300° until lightly browned, about 25 minutes. Store in airtight container.

Yield: About 5½ dozen.

FRUITCAKE COOKIES

- **½ pound candied pineapple, chopped**
- **½ pound candied cherries, chopped**
- **1½ cups raisins**
- **4 cups chopped pecans**
- **1½ cups chopped dates**
- **1½ cups all-purpose flour, divided**
- **½ cup butter, softened**
- **½ cup firmly packed brown sugar**
- **2 eggs, beaten**
- **¼ cup strawberry jelly**
- **2 teaspoons baking soda**
- **1½ tablespoons milk**
- **½ teaspoon ground allspice, cinnamon, cloves, nutmeg**

Combine first 5 ingredients; dredge in ¾ cup flour, coating well; set aside.

Cream butter and sugar, beating until light and fluffy. Mix in eggs and jelly; blend well. Dissolve baking soda in milk, add to creamed mixture with remaining ¾ cup flour and spices. Fold fruit and nuts into batter. Drop by rounded teaspoons onto greased cookie sheet. Bake at 350° for 12 minutes or until lightly browned. Cool.

Yield: 12 dozen.

MOCK BABY RUTH BARS

- 4 cups oatmeal
- 1 cup firmly packed light brown sugar
- ¼ cup light corn syrup
- ¼ cup peanut butter
- 1 teaspoon vanilla extract
- ¾ cup butter, softened
- 6 ounces chocolate chips
- 3 ounces butterscotch chips
- ⅔ cup peanut butter

In large mixing bowl, combine oatmeal, sugar, corn syrup, peanut butter, vanilla and butter. Mix well. Spread into a greased 13 x 9-inch baking pan. Bake at 400° for 12 minutes.

Mix chocolate and butterscotch chips with peanut butter and immediately spread over hot baked mixture right from oven. Cool and cut into squares.

Yield: 2 dozen.

SNOW BALLS

A melt-in-your-mouth cookie that has been a Christmas favorite of one family for forty years!

- 1 cup butter, softened
- ½ cup sifted powdered sugar
- 1 teaspoon vanilla extract
- 2¼ cups all-purpose flour
- ⅛ teaspoon salt
- ¾ cup finely chopped pecans
- 8 ounces powdered sugar, sifted

Cream butter, ½ cup powdered sugar and vanilla. Blend in flour and salt, mixing well with electric beaters or food processor. Stir in pecans. Chill.

Shape dough into 1-inch balls; place on an ungreased cookie sheet. Bake at 400° for 10-12 minutes until slightly browned on bottom. Do not brown. Roll hot cookies in powdered sugar. Cool and roll again in powdered sugar until thoroughly coated.

Yield: About 4 dozen.

OATMEAL COOKIES

- 1 cup butter, softened
- 1 cup sugar
- 1 cup firmly packed brown sugar
- 1 egg
- 1 cup vegetable oil
- 1 teaspoon vanilla extract
- 3½ cups all-purpose flour
- 1 teaspoon baking soda
- ½ teaspoon salt
- 1 cup oatmeal
- 1 cup crushed corn flakes
- ½ cup flaked coconut
- ½ cup chopped pecans
- 8 ounces chopped dates

Cream butter and sugars, beating well on medium speed of electric mixer. Add egg, mixing well; stir in oil and vanilla.

Combine flour, baking soda and salt; add to creamed mixture. Stir in oatmeal, corn flakes, coconut, pecans and dates; blend well. Shape dough into 1-inch balls. Place on ungreased cookie sheet; flatten each ball with a fork. Bake at 350° for 12-15 minutes. Cool.

Yield: About 8 dozen.

SOUTHERN PECAN BARS

- 1 (18.5-ounce) box yellow cake mix, divided
- ½ cup butter, melted
- 1 egg
- 3 eggs
- ½ cup firmly packed brown sugar
- 1½ cups light corn syrup
- 1½ teaspoons vanilla extract
- 1¼ cups chopped pecans

Combine 3 cups cake mix, melted butter and 1 egg; mix well. Press mixture into a greased 13 x 9-inch baking pan. Bake at 350° for 20 minutes; set aside.

Beat 3 eggs, brown sugar, corn syrup, vanilla together. Stir in remaining cake mix; blend together. Pour over hot crust; sprinkle with pecans and bake at 350° for 35 minutes. Cool in pan. Cut into bars.

Yield: 48 bars.

MOTHER A'S ICE BOX COOKIES

There are some who will always say ice box and not fridge. However, it shows how long this recipe has been in the family.

- **1 cup butter**
- **2 cups firmly packed light brown sugar**
- **2 eggs**
- **3½ cups all-purpose flour**
- **½ teaspoon salt**
- **1 teaspoon baking soda**
- **1 teaspoon vanilla**
- **1 cup minced pecans**

Cream butter and brown sugar at medium speed of electric mixer until light and fluffy. Add eggs, beating well.

Combine flour, salt and baking soda; add to creamed mixture, beating well. Add vanilla. Fold in nuts. Chill 1 hour. Shape dough into two rolls, wrap in wax paper and chill at least 2 hours.

Unwrap rolls and slice into very thin slices. Place on ungreased cookie sheet and bake at 350° for 7-8 minutes. Watch carefully; they burn easily.

Yield: 4-5 dozen.

Mountain Dining

MOUNTAIN DINING

PUMPKIN ROLL

- 1 cup canned pumpkin
- 3 eggs, beaten
- 1 cup sugar
- ¾ cup all-purpose flour
- 1 teaspoon baking powder
- ½ teaspoon salt
- 1 teaspoon cinnamon
- 1 teaspoon ginger
- ½ teaspoon nutmeg
- 1 (8-ounce) package cream cheese
- 2 tablespoons butter, softened
- ½ cup powdered sugar
- 1 teaspoon vanilla

Combine eggs and sugar; beat until creamy. Add pumpkin; mix well.

Combine flour, baking powder, salt, cinnamon, ginger and nutmeg; fold into pumpkin mixture. Grease a 13 x 9-inch baking pan; line with wax paper. Grease and flour paper. Pour batter into pan; spread evenly. Bake at 375° for 15 minutes or until top of cake springs back when lightly touched.

Sift 2-3 tablespoons powdered sugar on a linen towel. Loosen sides of warm cake and turn out onto sugared towel. Remove wax paper. Starting with long side, roll cake and towel together jelly-roll fashion. Cool.

Combine cream cheese, butter, powdered sugar and vanilla; beat at medium speed of electric mixer until smooth.

Unroll cake; spread with cream cheese mixture to ½-inch of edge. Re-roll cake; chill. Slice and serve.

Yield: Serves 10-12.

Ezekiel's Barn
Cashiers, North Carolina

HOLLY MATHIOWDIS' WHITE LASAGNA

- 1/4 cup butter
- 3 1/2 pounds white meat chicken, cut into strips
- 1 tablespoon minced garlic
- 1 1/2 tablespoons Italian seasoning
- Salt and pepper to taste
- 1/4 cup white wine
- 1 pound white mushrooms, sliced
- Tabasco
- 1 1/4 pounds fresh spinach, cooked, drained
- 1 1/2 pounds ricotta cheese
- 2 eggs
- 1 bunch fresh basil, chopped
- 3/4 cup butter
- 3/4 cup all-purpose flour
- 1 1/2 quarts milk
- 1/4 cup fresh bread crumbs
- 7-8 lasagna noodles
- 1 cup Parmesan cheese

Melt butter in very large skillet; add chicken strips, half of garlic and half of Italian seasoning. Sauté about 5 minutes until chicken is lightly browned. Remove to a bowl with a slotted spoon. Season.

Add wine to skillet, stirring up any cooking bits. Add mushrooms, remaining garlic and Italian seasoning, salt and pepper, Tabasco to taste; boil gently over high heat to reduce liquid by one-third. Combine mushrooms, chicken and cooked spinach. Set aside.

Melt butter; whisk in flour and cook over medium heat until flour turns pale brown, stirring constantly. Pour in milk; stir and continue cooking until thickened. Reserve 2-3 cups sauce for topping; combine remaining sauce with chicken mixture.

Combine ricotta cheese with eggs and basil.

Coat a 10 x 11-inch baking pan with butter. Layer half of lasagna noodles then half of chicken mixture and half of ricotta cheese mixture. Repeat layers; top with reserved white sauce and sprinkle with Parmesan cheese. Bake at 350° for 45 minutes until golden brown. Let stand 10-15 minutes.

Yield: Serves 10-12.

Lakeside Restaurant and Rosewood Market
Highlands, North Carolina

LOG CABIN MUSHROOM BISQUE

- **¼ cup extra-virgin olive oil**
- **1 large onion, diced**
- **2 pounds mushrooms (shiitake, portobello, trumpet, porcini), quartered**
- **Salt and pepper, to taste**
- **1 teaspoon sugar**
- **1 bottle dry white wine**
- **1½ quarts light chicken stock**
- **3 tablespoons arrowroot**
- **3 tablespoons cold water**
- **4 tablespoons mixed: tarragon, thyme, chives, parsley, chervil**
- **4 cups heavy cream**

In a large soup pot or Dutch oven, sauté onions in olive oil until translucent. Add mushrooms, salt, pepper and sugar. Sauté over medium-high heat for 4-5 minutes. Stir in wine and simmer; add chicken stock and simmer 20 minutes. Taste and adjust seasonings to taste.

Dissolve arrowroot in cold water; add to soup with herbs. Simmer 5 minutes; add cream.

Serve with freshly baked bread.

Yield: 2⅓-3 quarts.

Log Cabin Steak House
Highlands, North Carolina

STRAWBERRIES GRAND MARNIER

- **1 quart strawberries, washed and hulled**
- **1 cup sugar**
- **1 cup Grand Marnier**
- **1 cup whipping cream, whipped**
- **½ cup sifted powdered sugar**
- **1 teaspoon vanilla extract**

Mix strawberries, sugar and Grand Marnier; chill overnight.

Blend whipped cream, powdered sugar and vanilla. Serve strawberry mixture in fluted glasses topped with whipped cream. Garnish with a sprig of mint.

Yield: Serves 6-8.

Log Cabin Steak House
Highlands, North Carolina

PINEAPPLE CILANTRO SAUCE

- **1 (16-ounce) can crushed pineapple, undrained**
- **2 cups orange juice**
- **1 bunch cilantro, finely chopped**
- **1 cup white wine**
- **3 tablespoons cornstarch**
- **3 tablespoons water**
- **Sugar to taste**

Combine pineapple, orange juice, cilantro and white wine; bring to boil. Mix cornstarch with water and add to hot mixture and stir until thickened. Sweeten with sugar to taste.

Serve with fresh seafood, poultry or smoked meats.

Yield: About 4½ cups.

Log Cabin Steak House
Highlands, North Carolina

CASHEW HAZELNUT BROWNIE CAKE

Nutella is a hazelnut spread with skim milk and cocoa.

- **2 cups butter**
- **8 ounces cocoa**
- **4 cups sugar**
- **8 eggs**
- **2¾ cups all-purpose flour**
- **8 tablespoons hazelnut syrup or Frangelico liqueur**
- **2 cups chopped cashews**

Frosting

- **1 (13-ounce) jar Nutella**
- **3 tablespoons vegetable shortening**

Melt butter and cocoa over low heat, stirring constantly; stir in sugar, mixing well. Combine with eggs, beating after each addition; add hazelnut syrup. Stir in flour and cashews.

Pour into 3 greased and floured 9-inch round cake pans. Bake at 350° for 35-40 minutes until wooden pick inserted in center comes out clean. Cool in pans 10 minutes; remove and cool completely.

In a double boiler over moderate heat, blend Nutella with shortening until smooth. Cool. Spread between and over cake.

Yield: One 3-layer cake.

Michael's Cafe
Highlands, North Carolina

GRILLED RACK OF LAMB MADEIRA

The Bovril called for in this recipe is concentrated beef-flavored liquid bouillon.

- **6 lamb racks**
- **Salt, pepper and garlic powder**
- **1 cup olive oil**
- **5 shallots, minced**
- **1 medium carrot, diced**
- **1 medium onion, diced**
- **2 cups diced mushrooms**
- **3 celery stalks, diced**
- **1 teaspoon cracked black pepper**
- **½ teaspoon minced garlic**
- **2 bay leaves**
- **2 tablespoons fresh thyme**
- **2 cups Madeira wine**
- **3 cups beef broth**
- **1 tablespoon Bovril**
- **3 tablespoons all-purpose flour**

Trim lamb of excess fat and skin; sprinkle with seasonings. Set aside.

Sauté shallots, carrot, onion, mushrooms and celery in olive oil until tender. Add pepper, garlic, bay leaves and Madeira; simmer until reduced by half. Stir in beef broth and bring to boil; reduce by two-thirds. Season with Bovril. Mix flour and ½ cup of sauce and stir into mixture to thicken. When thickened, strain sauce and reserve.

Grill lamb on preheated grill to doneness desired. Cut into chops and arrange on a plate with sauce on bottom.

Garnish with fresh mint or rosemary, if desired.

Yield: Serves 6.

Dominick Sanchez, Executive Chef
Nick's Calico Cottage
Highlands, North Carolina

NEW ENGLAND CLAM CHOWDER

- 5 ounces bacon, diced
- ½ cup oil
- ½ pound bell pepper, diced
- 1 pound celery, chopped
- 1 (16-ounce) can clams, chopped
- 2 quarts water or clam juice
- 1 quart milk
- 1 pound butter
- 7 ounces all-purpose flour
- 2 pounds potatoes, cubed
- 1 ounce thyme
- ½ ounce garlic salt
- 2 cups heavy cream
- Salt and pepper

In a large pot or Dutch oven, sauté bacon until soft. Add oil, peppers and celery and sauté for 5 minutes. Stir in clams and water; bring to a boil. Lower heat and simmer.

Bring milk to a boil (avoid scalding). Melt butter, add flour and stir constantly 2 minutes. Gradually add milk, stirring constantly until blended. Add thyme and garlic salt; pour into clam mixture.

Boil potatoes until done (not too soft). Add to chowder with heavy cream. Salt and pepper to taste.

Enjoy!!!

Yield: 2 gallons.

Dominick Sanchez, Executive Chef
Nick's Calico Cottage
Highlands, North Carolina

CRÈME BRÛLÉE

- **4 cups heavy cream**
- **2 teaspoons vanilla**
- **9 large egg yolks**
- **1 cup plus 2 tablespoons sugar**
- **⅛ teaspoon salt**
- **¼ cup plus 2 tablespoons firmly packed light brown sugar**

In heavy saucepan, heat cream until hot but not scalded; add vanilla. Using electric mixer, beat egg yolks and sugar until thick and pale. Beat in cream and salt mixing well until combined.

Divide custard among 15 (¾-cup) ramekins. Set ramekins in large baking pan and add enough hot water to the pan to reach halfway up the sides of ramekins. Bake at 325° for 40 minutes or until knife inserted comes out clean. Cool on a rack.

Force the brown sugar through a sieve evenly over the custards. Set custards on a baking sheet, put baking sheet under a preheated broiler 6 inches from heat for 1-2 minutes until sugar is melted and browned. Chill for 1 hour.

Yield: Serves 15.

...On the Verandah Restaurant
Highlands, North Carolina

THAI SALAD

- **1 (14-ounce) can Coco Lopez**
- **1 cup creamy peanut butter**
- **1 cup canola oil**
- **1 teaspoon Thai seasoning**
- **Mandarin orange slices**
- **Pine nuts**

Blend all ingredients well; chill. Serve over mixed greens with Mandarin orange slices and pine nuts to taste.

Yield: About 4 cups.

Log Cabin Steak House
Highlands, North Carolina

SWEDISH MUSHROOM SOUP

- 2 cups chopped onion
- 1/4 cup unsalted butter, divided
- 3/4 pound fresh mushrooms, sliced
- 1/2 cup dry white wine
- 2 tablespoons dried dill
- 1 tablespoon sweet Hungarian paprika
- 1 tablespoon soy sauce
- 3 tablespoons all-purpose flour
- 1 cup milk
- 1 1/2 cups chicken broth
- 1/2 cup sour cream
- Salt and freshly ground pepper

Sauté onion in 2 tablespoons butter until softened; add mushrooms, wine, dill, paprika and soy sauce. Simmer covered 15 minutes, stirring occasionally.

In another saucepan, melt remaining butter over moderate heat, stir in flour and cook, stirring, for 3 minutes. Remove pan from heat; whisk in milk. Return pan to heat and whisk until thickened. Add mushroom mixture, stir in broth. Simmer 15 minutes, stirring occasionally.

Remove pan from heat, stir in sour cream. Season with salt and freshly ground pepper.

Yield: Serves 4-6 (5 cups).

... *On the Verandah Restaurant*
Highlands, North Carolina

GRILLED THAI CHICKEN BREAST

Seafood or most meats may be prepared in this manner.

4 (6 or 8-ounce) boneless, skinless chicken breast halves

Marinade

- **1 cup orange juice**
- **¼ cup soy sauce**
- **¼ cup sesame oil**
- **3 tablespoons minced garlic**
- **3 tablespoons minced ginger root**
- **2 tablespoons lemon grass**

Blend marinade ingredients. Marinate chicken for 2 hours. Bake or grill until done.

Serve with rice and seasoned vegetables.

Variation: Add hot chili sauce or cayenne pepper to marinade for extra heat.

Yield: Serves 4.

Skyline Restaurant
Flat Mountain Road
Highlands, North Carolina

STEAKS WHITE GOOSE CAFE

- **2 (12-ounce) rib-eye steaks**
- **Cajun seasoning**
- **1½ teaspoons olive oil**
- **1 teaspoon chopped fresh rosemary**
- **¼ cup apricot brandy**

Thoroughly rub steaks with Cajun seasoning. Heat cast-iron skillet over high heat; place steaks in skillet and blacken both sides. Lower heat and cook 1 minute per side to desired doneness. Steak should have a slightly crisp black-brown color.

Warm olive oil in a large sauté pan; stir in rosemary. Place steaks in pan; pour brandy in pan and light with a match from edge of pan. Be careful, pan will ignite quickly. While gently shaking pan back and forth, turn steaks. Remove from heat when flame subsides. Do not leave over heat too long or brandy will burn.

Enjoy!

Yield: Serves 2.

The White Goose Cafe
Cashiers, North Carolina

TROUT WINSLOW

Two famous restaurants of the 70's in Cashiers, North Carolina.

Béarnaise Sauce

- **5 cups tarragon vinegar**
- **1½ medium onions, chopped**
- **¼ cup chopped fresh parsley**
- **5 tablespoons coarsely ground pepper**
- **1½ pounds butter**
- **12 egg yolks**
- **6 (8-ounce) boned rainbow trout**
- **Whole wheat flour**
- **Peanut oil**
- **½ cup white wine**
- **1 pound lump crabmeat**
- **½ cup butter, melted**
- **Parsley, paprika, lemon wedges**

Combine vinegar, onions, parsley and pepper in a 3-quart pot. Cook over medium heat until liquid is almost evaporated. Place in food processor and puree. Melt butter in same pot. Add puree. Place egg yolks in top of double boiler, slowly stir in puree mixture, stirring until sauce has thickened. Remove from heat. Oil a 9 x 5-inch baking dish; place in 375° oven to preheat.

Roll trout in flour and cook in skillet coated with oil. Brown trout on one side. Place trout browned side up on preheated baking dish. Bake 8-10 minutes at 375° until trout flakes with a fork. Remove from oven, sprinkle with wine. Sauté crabmeat in butter until heated. Stuff each trout cavity with crabmeat. Cover with Béarnaise Sauce. Garnish with parsley, paprika and lemon.

Yield: Serves 6.

Chef Winslow Jones
Yesterday's and Winslow's Restaurants
Cashiers, North Carolina

BANANA BREAD

- 1 pound butter, softened
- 6 cups sugar
- 8 eggs
- 12 mashed bananas
- 2 cups sifted cake flour
- 6 cups all-purpose flour
- 4 tablespoons baking soda
- 1 teaspoon salt
- 1 cup buttermilk
- 4 cups chopped pecans
- 4 cups raisins

Cream butter and sugar; add eggs one at a time, beating after each addition. Stir in bananas.

Combine flours, baking soda and salt. Add to creamed mixture alternately with buttermilk, beginning and ending with flour mixture. Stir only to blend, do not overmix.

Pour into 6 greased and floured 9 x 5-inch loaf pans. Bake at 350° for 1 hour or until just done and a toothpick inserted in center comes out clean. Cool in pan 10 minutes.

Yield: 6 loaves.

Wolfgang
Wolfgang's on Main
Highlands, North Carolina

MEDALLIONS OF VEAL WOLFGANG

- **12 (3-ounce) medallions of veal**
- **1 cup all-purpose flour**
- **3 eggs**
- **1 teaspoon chopped parsley**
- **4 ounces butter**

Stuffing

- **3 ounces butter**
- **2 ounces bacon**
- **5 ounces finely chopped chicken livers**
- **1 ounce finely chopped shallots**
- **2 cloves garlic, finely chopped**
- **4 ounces finely chopped spinach**
- **4 ounces finely chopped mushrooms**
- **2 tablespoons all-purpose flour**
- **½ cup brandy**
- **½ cup dry white wine**
- **Salt, pepper, nutmeg, thyme and marjoram**
- **2 eggs**
- **½ cup whipping cream**

In a heavy skillet, melt butter; stir until golden brown. Sauté bacon until crisp; add chicken livers, shallots, garlic, spinach and mushrooms and sauté until vegetables are tender and livers done. Sprinkle with flour. Pour brandy and white wine into mixture stirring constantly; add seasonings and eggs. Simmer until thickened. Remove from heat; cool. Fold in whipping cream.

To assemble: Pound veal to ⅛-inch thickness. Fill 6 medallions generously with stuffing, top with other 6 medallions (making sandwiches). Beat eggs and parsley. Coat medallions with flour, dip in egg mixture.

Brown medallions in 4 ounces butter until golden. Place on baking sheet and bake at 375° for 15 minutes; deglaze sheet to use as a light sauce for top of veal.

Serve with rice or buttered penne pasta.

Yield: Serves 6.

Wolfgang
Wolfgang's on Main
Highlands, North Carolina

PHEASANT CALVADOS

- 1 pheasant, wing tips removed
- 3 tablespoons butter
- 1 small shallot, minced
- 1 clove garlic, minced
- 2 ounces sliced mushrooms
- ½ sweet apple, chopped, or 2 teaspoons brown sugar
- 2 ounces apple brandy
- 2 ounces chicken stock base
- 1½ ounces cream
- 3 whole chestnuts

Brown breast sides in hot butter in 1½-quart baking pan. Place in 350° oven for 30-40 minutes or until done. Remove pheasant. Sauté shallot, garlic and mushrooms in drippings; add apple brandy and flame; deglaze pan. Add stock base and cream; reduce. Add chestnuts.

Present by discarding leg tips, place pheasant in individual clay Dutch oven and cover with sauce.

Yield: Serves 1.

Wolfgang
Wolfgang's on Main
Highlands, North Carolina

CRAB CAKES

Use your favorite spices in this recipe (dill, celery seed, etc.).

- **¼ cup butter**
- **1 cup minced Vidalia onion**
- **½ cup minced green and red bell peppers**
- **¼ cup minced fresh parsley**
- **¼ cup finely diced celery and carrot**
- **2-3 tablespoons lemon juice**
- **Old Bay Seasonings**
- **3 pounds lump crabmeat**
- **1 cup mayonnaise**
- **Fresh white bread crumbs**
- **1 cup butter, melted**

Sauté onion, carrot, peppers and celery in ¼ cup butter until tender; combine with all remaining ingredients. Mix in enough bread crumbs to tighten.

Form mixture into cakes; coat each cake in bread crumbs and sauté in butter until golden brown on each side. Serve with your favorite seafood sauce.

Yield: 2 dozen.

Chef Thomas Huddas
Wildcat Cliffs Country Club

FRESH CORN AND BLACK-EYED PEA SALAD

This salad is a natural for outdoor occasions featuring grilled chicken, pork or hamburgers. It even makes a great dip served with corn chips.

- **⅓ cup balsamic vinegar**
- **1 tablespoon hot sweet mustard**
- **¼ cup chopped fresh parsley**
- **½ teaspoon salt**
- **¼ teaspoon freshly ground pepper**
- **½ teaspoon Creole seasoning**
- **¼ cup extra virgin olive oil**
- **1 (10-ounce) package frozen corn, cooked**
- **1 (10-ounce) package black-eyed peas, cooked**
- **1 medium red bell pepper, chopped**
- **1 medium Vidalia onion, chopped**
- **3 stalks celery, chopped**

Blend vinegar, mustard, parsley, salt, pepper and Creole seasoning. Whisk in oil; set aside. Combine corn, peas, bell pepper, onion and celery. Toss dressing with vegetables; refrigerate until ready to serve, not longer than 12 hours.

Yield: Serves 6-8.

Variation: Add 3 medium tomatoes, peeled and diced.

Chef Thomas Huddas
Wildcat Cliffs Country Club

PUMPKIN MUFFINS

- **3 large eggs, beaten**
- **2½ cups sugar**
- **¾ cup vegetable oil**
- **3 cups canned pumpkin**
- **2¾ cups all-purpose flour**
- **1 teaspoon salt**
- **1½ teaspoons baking soda**
- **2 teaspoons cinnamon**
- **1 teaspoon nutmeg**
- **¾ teaspoon cloves**
- **¾ teaspoon allspice**
- **1 cup chopped walnuts**
- **½ cup golden raisins**
- **½ cup sugar**
- **1 tablespoon cinnamon**

Cream eggs and sugar until light and fluffy; beat in oil until blended. Beat in pumpkin until well mixed.

Combine flour, salt, baking soda and spices; add to creamed mixture, a little at a time, on low speed of electric mixer until blended well. Stir in walnuts and raisins. Spoon into well greased muffin tins, filling two-thirds full. Mix sugar and cinnamon and sprinkle lightly on top. Bake at 350° for 25-30 minutes.

Yield: About 2½ dozen.

Mark Sitzer
Sous Chef, Wildcat Cliffs Country Club

Index

WILDCAT SEASONS
P.O. Box 1219
Highlands, NC 28741

Please send ____ copy(ies) @ $ 19.95 each ________
Postage and handling @ $ 5.00 each ________
North Carolina residents add sales tax @ $ 1.40 each ________
Total ________

Name ____

Address ____

City ____________________ State __________ Zip __________

Make checks payable to ***Wildcat Seasons****.*

WILDCAT SEASONS
P.O. Box 1219
Highlands, NC 28741

Please send ____ copy(ies) @ $ 19.95 each ________
Postage and handling @ $ 5.00 each ________
North Carolina residents add sales tax @ $ 1.40 each ________
Total ________

Name ____

Address ____

City ____________________ State __________ Zip __________

Make checks payable to ***Wildcat Seasons****.*

WILDCAT SEASONS
P.O. Box 1219
Highlands, NC 28741

Please send ____ copy(ies) @ $ 19.95 each ________
Postage and handling @ $ 5.00 each ________
North Carolina residents add sales tax @ $ 1.40 each ________
Total ________

Name ____

Address ____

City ____________________ State __________ Zip __________

Make checks payable to ***Wildcat Seasons****.*